INDIAN MODERNITY

INDIAN MODERNITY

CONTRADICITIONS, PARADOXES AND POSSIBILITIES

By

Avijit Pathak

GYAN

Published by

Gyan Publishing House
5, Ansari Road
Daryaganj, New Delhi-110002
Phone: 011-47034999, 9811692060
E-mail: books@gyanbooks.com

Distribution Network
gyanbooks.com
India, USA, Canada, UK, Australia, France

ISBN: 978-81-212-0612-9 (HB)

Reprint in India, 2024
First Published, 2013

Printed at: Gyan Press, Delhi.

Indian Modernity: Contradicitions, Paradoxes and Possibilities
Author: Avijit Pathak

To my mother
— the life-affirming power of maternity

Contents

Preface

My sociology has emerged out of my urge to make sense of my life and understand the socio-cultural context in which I find myself—the context that arouses hope, causes anxiety and, at times, provokes me to alter it. As a result, in the process of writing this book, my different identities—a sociologist, a political being, an observer, a participant, an analyst, a dreamer—have been merged together.

What is the context I am talking about? Essentially, what comes to my mind is *modernity*, its overwhelming presence in our life. Modernity, it is argued repeatedly, is a celebration of *scientific rationality*—something that observes the empirical reality, overcomes all presuppositions and arrives at some kind of *causal explanation* of nature as well as human society. Modernity, we are told, is *technological development*—the instrumental application of science for the perpetual material well-being of the human species. Modernity, it is believed, is a *secular orientation* to life—the ability to experience the world without the guidance of any revealed/divine truth. Modernity, it is hoped, leads to the *democratization* of society. In other words, modernity is often endowed with a positive meaning. It is seen as development, progress, affluence, prosperity—an effective weapon to fight the 'backwardness' of our cultural tradition. Modernity, to put it otherwise, is projected as a future-oriented, optimistic, life-affirming doctrine. It was with this vision of modernity that we, the children of Nehru, grew up in post-independence India.

Although modernity remains a dominant worldview and continues to shape our aspirations, there are moments of *ambiguity*.

The reasons for this ambiguity are diverse and many. For example, modernity is also seen as an invasion, a principle of domination. A relationship is established between modernity and colonialism. It is argued that modernity legitimates Western science and technology. It undermines our collective memories, our cultural traditions and indigenous knowledge systems. As a result, the proponents of modernity are accused of their elitism. This elitism separates reason from tradition. What it forgets is that tradition is not static; there are many possibilities in tradition that can give new meaning to modernity, rescue it from its *Eurocentric* ambition and generate a new alternative.

There is also an acute awareness of the discontents and pathologies of modernity. Its instrumental rationality; its engineering mentality, its excessive materialism—everything has led to a deep-rooted spiritual crisis. It has destroyed the harmonic relationship between the individual and the community, between man and nature, between man and woman. In other words, it is thought, there is a close relationship between modernity and violence.

Another important critique of modernity is coming from *post-modernists*. They challenge what they call the *Enlightenment project of modernity*. Its 'universal' mission, its 'grand' theories, its 'certainty' about the cognitive power of science—everything is suspected. Instead, we are asked to believe that we live in a post-modern world—a world in which not uniformity and homogeneity, but *differences* are respected. A world in which there is no more any 'certainty' about science, about grand/universal theories. A world in which no particular culture/knowledge system has got the right to hegemonize itself. Instead, there is a celebration of all that is local. There are differences and multiple possibilities. With post-modernism cultural specificity assumes added significance. It need not be overcome in order to embrace universal modernity. Although it is debatable whether in a society like ours post-modernity has got any enduring value, the fact remains that, at least in the intellectual domain, it is fast becoming a force to reckon with.

This makes it possible to identify the context in which the book has been written. I live amidst modernity. Yet, I am aware of its discontents. This affects my life, my ways of engagement with the world—state, science, technology, culture, tradition, gender, media and social movements. I, therefore, need to understand this context.

There is another important aspect. We know that this is an age that promises emancipation—emancipation from exploitation and domination. In fact, the agenda of modernity is inseparable from the vision of emancipation—reason emancipating us from superstitions and prejudices, technology from the bondage of nature, and secularity from religious orthodoxies and institutions. Yet, we also experience the betrayal of this promise. At a deeper level, we see the violence in the growing technologization of the life world. We see the objectification of the human spirit. We see the all-pervasive alienation and the resultant 'one-dimensional' existence. But even at a mundane level, we see the growing threat to emancipation. For example, as socialism (a modernist vision deeply devoted to the doctrine of equality) tends to 'disappear' from the world, there is growing disillusionment. One is told that, in the final analysis, it is the victory of the world capitalist system —a system that breeds competition, reduces everything into the rationale of the market and causes economic inequality. In other words, market-forces are becoming overwhelmingly powerful all over the world. As we look at India, we see this trend. The proponents of economic liberalization, consumerism and free market want India to integrate with the world capitalist system. In other words, the egalitarian potential of modernity is denied. In contemporary India (or post-Nehruvian India) modernity often emerges as market capitalism—something that can hardly be regarded as an experience of emancipation for the larger collective.

In fact, the paradoxical consequence of modernity can be seen in the assertion of *Hindutva* in our times. True, it questions secularism, one of the cherished goals of modernity. Yet, the fact is that it is essentially the creation of modern mass politics; it uses traditional symbols for modern purposes, creating an ideology of nationhood. In other words, the growing communalization of society is not necessarily isolated from modernity. The point we are trying to argue is that these two examples—market capitalism and *Hindutva*—reveal that modernity in contemporary India need not necessarily be seen as an emancipatory experience.

While these anti-egalitarian forces are strong, there is also an assertion for justice and equality. Take two examples. First, living in contemporary India is like realizing the power of the Dalit voice (or, to put it broadly, the voice of the oppressed/backward castes). Here is a voice whose potential meaning is justice, equality, human dignity and autonomy. In a way, the Dalit voice is related to the agenda of modernity, its spirit of democratization, its secularity and its egalitarian zeal. It questions the logic of oppression that goes on in the name of 'tradition' or 'religious order'. It can be said that in this subaltern assertion we see the positive gain of modernity: a society democratizing itself and becoming aware of the 'rights' of its citizens.

Second, as feminists and women activists have begun to assert, the *gender question* has acquired added relevance. It has posed a challenge to traditional role-expectations. The spirit of freedom/equality inherent in modernity has given new momentum to the feminist struggle.

Despite these gains of modernity, the crisis is felt no less intensely. The Dalit voice, for example, tends to cause an exclusivist politics; it intensifies one's caste identity in the political arena. In other words, the present assertion of casteism is often a product of modernity. Again, as we see the feminist voice, what is striking is that it questions not just tradition; it also questions modernity, its patriarchal science and violence. Finally, we are realizing that tradition is not something closed and static. Tradition is also a living experience and the life-affirming possibilities in it that can fight the pathologies of modernity.

As a matter of fact, in contemporary India we see the complex interplay of tradition, modernity and emancipation. We see divergent expectations from modernity and we also see its divergent interpretation. We see an urge to transcend the logic of both 'tradition' and 'modernity' and create a new space—a spiritual space—conducive to equality, reciprocity, dialogicity and plurality. This complexity ought to be understood in order to evolve a new art of relatedness and politics.

With this will to understand my times, evolve my politics and share my worldview with my contemporaries, I have written this book. In introduction I have tried to conceptualize modernity, its origin and its salient features. I have also examined how sociology has engaged itself with the agenda of modernity.

Chapter 1 deals with the quality of intellectual tradition in modern India. The purpose is to examine how modern intellectuals born out of India's encounter with colonialism responded to the West, embraced the new age and visualized India's identity in terms of her engagement with tradition and modernity, religion and science. I have also tried to examine how intellectuals find themselves in post-Independence India, how they respond to or experiment with the project of modernity and nation-building or whether they succeed in involving themselves with emancipatory politics. This chapter helps me to know my tradition in which I find myself as a member of the intellectual profession.

This makes it easier to come to Chapter 2, a chapter that deals with modernity and secularism, religiosity and emancipation. Secularism is an important component of the ideal of modernity. Yet, these days we often confront a pertinent question whether secularism as an approach to life understands the contextuality of Indian culture and civilization. Is secularism an elitist doctrine not related to our cultural/religious experiences? Moreover, when communalists are appropriating religion, it is desirable to know whether there are alternate possibilities in religion that can humanize the world. It is impossible to live in modern India without responding to secularism and communalism, modernity and religiosity. This chapter seeks to intervene in this debate.

Chapter 3 has been written with an urge to listen to the feminist voice. There are two reasons. First, the feminist assertion is about emancipation, not just the emancipation of women, but also the emancipation of men from the burden of aggressive masculinity. Moreover, the 'gender sensitivity' gives us fresh insights to look at science and modernity, tradition and religion.

Chapter 4 is about culture. It is in the domain of culture that men and women feel, think, act and evolve their consciousness. It is their culture that relates them to their past, their community and collective heritage. No wonder, one remains extraordinarily sensitive to one's culture. And this sensitivity often leads to anxiety, fear of an 'alien' culture, and threat or damage to one's own culture. As a result, interesting debates are taking place in the arena of culture. What is our culture? Is it dynamic enough to accommodate the spirit of modernity? Or is it under threat because of new forces of globalization, technology and mass media? A look at these debates would help us to examine the dialectic of tradition and modernity. Not solely that, it would also help us to imagine alternate cultural possibilities needed for our collective emancipation.

Chapter 5 takes us to the realm of politics. There are three important political currents—liberalization, *Hindutva* and Dalit assertion. How does one find oneself amidst these conflicting ideologies? It goes without saying that because of the powerful assertion of these ideologies many things are being questioned, reinterpreted and redefined—our cherished ideals of radical politics, emancipation and justice, tradition and community, nation-state and modernity. It is, therefore, important to understand this phenomenon, intervene meaningfully and construct a new agenda.

And, finally, in the conclusion note I have visualized the possibility of a new age: modernity spiritualizing itself!

All these chapters, it is obvious, are centred on a grand theme: understanding the implications of modernity and India's identity. Perhaps this also explains the nature of the book. Technically speaking, this is not an 'empirical' work based on field studies'. Instead, here is an attempt to explore the world of ideas, world views and civilizational issues. As a result, in a work of this kind, sociology does not remain merely an 'empirical science', it embraces philosophy, history, psychology and literature. It does not follow the logic of the 'academic division of labour'. It gets equated with what life is all about: reasoning and feeling, thinking and dreaming. With this aesthetic endeavour the book does not follow any standardized method as prescribed in the texts of research methodology.

I am a teacher and in the process of teaching (which is a dialogic practice) many questions and ideas come to my mind. My research is organically related to teaching. My book is, therefore, inseparable from my classroom experiences. I am grateful to my students and colleagues at the Centre for the Study of Social Systems, JNU. My friends, irrespective of their professions, have given me the confidence to believe that writing is a meaningful act. I remember all of them. With deep gratitude I recall late Dr. Subrata Sengupta who always inspired me, but could not see this book. My family members—my mother, sisters, brothers, nephews, nieces, mother-in-law, wife and daughter—have shaped my thinking. They have made this work possible. I am grateful to them. Finally, if my readers find this work meaningful, I would feel encouraged to write yet another book. Creativity is, after all, the affirmation of hope.

Jawaharlal Nehru University
New Delhi.
26.7.1998

Avijit Pathak

Introduction

Critical Engagement with Modernity

Modernity is becoming a global phenomenon. Despite its visible presence all over the world in the twentieth century, modernity as a distinctive form of civilization originated in the West. It began to emerge in the West from about the fifteenth century. But it was essentially the European Enlightenment in the eighteenth century that gave a specific meaning to it. It was through the philosophic works of Montesquie, Voltaire, Hume, Rousseau, Kant and Adam Smith that the Enlightenment agenda manifested itself. Although there was no such thing as a unifying Enlightenment agenda, there were, however, a set of core characteristics of the new age. It emphasized reason, empiricism, science, progress, secularism and universalism. Immanuel Kant called it the 'light of reason'—a general process of society awakening from the dark slumbers of superstition and ignorance.

In a way, it was this optimism—the possibility of creating a new world through secular reasoning and techno-scientific exploration—that characterized the ethos of modernity. In the nineteenth century modernity became identified with industrialism and the sweeping social, economic and cultural changes associated with it. In the twentieth century many non-western societies began to embrace the ethos of modernity. The growth of modernity is related to the rise of the secular state and polity, the global capitalist system, the advanced form of social and sexual division of labour and the transition from a religious to a secular culture.

Modernity makes us future-oriented. Because, as S.N. Eisenstadt argues, "the sanctity and status quo of the past—or any past—as the major symbolic regulator of social, political and cultural change and innovation, has given way to the acceptance of innovation and orientation to the future as a basic dimension of cultural orientation."[1] Modernity makes one believe that it is possible to change the world. It is through secular reasoning that man can free himself from dogmas and prejudices and create a new world.

Modernity is inseparable from science. It is believed that science is inherently liberating. Moreover, science enables man to tap natural resources for his perpetual material well-being. Modernity is, therefore, the ideology of techno-economic development. Modernity requires a dynamic and expansionist capitalist order, the growth of large-scale administrative and bureaucratic system of social organization, the dominance of secular, materialist, rationalist and individualist cultural values and the formal separation of the private from the public. Modernity attempts at the formation of a rational culture and an efficient economy. Moreover, modernity breeds the ideology of the nation-state; the idea of citizenship or democratic freedom, is its important characteristic.

The promises of modernity are well-known. But then, there are also discontents of modernity. Modernity causes alienation. Its bigness, impersonality and abstraction degrade human uniqueness. Its technical mentality violates nature and destroys the possibility of a symbiotic relationship between the human species and mother earth. Its preoccupation with scientific reasoning represses 'non-rational' faculties of human existence. Its global ambition, it is feared, tends to annihilate all differences and, therefore, makes the world dull, uniform and homogenized. In fact, the prevalent social knowledge is being heavily shaped by the experiences of modernity—its promises as well as its discontents.

Sociology and Modernity

Sociology emerged and grew as an intellectual response to modernity. In fact, early sociologists like Saint Simon and Auguste Comte were trying to make sense of the age of modernity that manifested itself in the French revolution. It was the breakdown of the medieval order; it was the beginning of a new era with its possibilities and anxieties.

The relationship between sociology and modernity can be seen in two ways: First, as modernity privileged science as the most legitimate form of knowledge, sociology was closely related to science. It imagined itself as a 'science of society' striving for 'objective' knowledge. Second, in terms of substantial works, sociology tried to study what constituted modern society: capitalism, industrialism and bureaucracy.

Let us have a close look at the relationship between sociology and science. Saint Simon felt the necessity of a new science of society—social physiology. He proposed a 'religion of Newton' to explain the changing world. Auguste Comte—the founding father of formal sociology—pleaded for positivism. Positivism was based on the grand Enlightenment optimism—unbounded faith in science and its ability to emancipate the human mind from theological and metaphysical stages. 'The fundamental character of the positive philosophy', said the French sociologist, 'is to consider all phenomena as subject to invariable natural laws'. Sociology, according to Comte, should celebrate the 'scientific method' of observation, experimentation, analysis and determinism.

The close affinity between sociology and science was seen even in the classical sociology. Emile Durkheim was indeed true to the French positivist tradition. He was heavily influenced by Bacon and Descartes—two great champions of rational/scientific thinking. He wanted the sociologist to free himself/herself from all 'presuppositions' while studying social facts as 'things'. He naturalized the social reality; it could be seen as an 'objective' reality existing out there. Likewise, Karl Marx was also a great admirer of science. Like Bacon he sought to overcome the 'idols' of the mind—all that could cloud one's vision. He posed the science of historical materialism against ideology as distortion and falsification of the reality. In other words, in the sociological tradition—from Comte to Marx—we saw the celebration of science. In its orientation to knowledge, sociology was indeed a child of the Enlightenment, it was modern. To quote Susan J. Hekman:

> The Enlightenment witnessed a period of spectacular triumphs in the natural sciences. Beginning with Newton

and Galileo, the natural sciences began a conquest of the natural world which was a staggering success. This success did not go unnoticed in the social sciences. Rather, as many commentators have noted, the social sciences were born in the shadow of these triumphs. Furthermore, the methodological lesson that the natural sciences were teaching seemed to be very clear: if the methods of the natural sciences are strictly adhered to then the spectacular success of these sciences could be matched in the social sciences. The social sciences had only to await the arrival of their Newton.[2]

Sociology was also eager to understand the formation of modernity and its institutions. Durkheim tried to comprehend the modern world—the complexity of the division of labour and the process of evolution from 'mechanical' solidarity to 'organic' solidarity leading to an industrial society. Max Weber taught us how to make sense of the modern world—the growing rationalization of every sphere of life and the growth of legal/bureaucratic organizations. For Karl Marx, the major transformative force shaping the modern world was capitalism. With the decline of feudalism, agrarian production based on the local manor was replaced by production for markets of national and international scope, in terms of which not only an infinite variety of material goods but also human labour power became commodified. The emergent social order of modernity, for Marx, was, therefore, capitalistic in both its economic system and its other institutions.

Sociology was also a celebration of modernity. Although, as Anthony Giddens said, modernity is a "double-edged" phenomenon, there was a tendency to emphasize what Giddens would call the "opportunity side" of modernity.[3] For example, although Marx saw class struggle, he imagined the emergence of a more humane social system. Moreover, the Marxian brand of socialism was essentially a product of modernity; the liberating potential of science was never questioned by Marx. Likewise, Durkheim thought that the further expansion of industrialism would establish a harmonious and fulfilling social life, integrated through a combination of division of labour and moral individualism.

It would, however, be wrong to say that sociology was simply a celebration of modernity. Sociology also told us about the discontents of modernity. Comte—the champion of positivism and Enlightenment science—was extremely critical of the consequences of modernity: the excessive individualism he saw in France after the Revolution. Individualism, Comte thought, was a disease of the modern civilization. He was in favour of the 'restoration of moral communities'. Durkheim saw the problem of anomie or normlessness in industrial societies. Marx wrote about alienation—the way capitalism and private property distort human relations, deprive man of his creativity, his joy in his work, and cripple his relationship with nature, women, community and the larger world. And Weber was the most pessimistic among the three founding fathers. Weber saw the process of disenchantment as the crisis of faith and meaning. The 'iron cage' of modernity, for Weber, crushed individual creativity and autonomy.

Robert Nisbet regarded the entire phenomenon as the "paradox" of sociology.[4] Sociology was a creation of modernity; its science was the science of modernity. Yet, it was not indifferent to the discontents of modernity.

In fact, to study contemporary sociology is to study more and more about these discontents. What is striking is that positivism (or 'science' of society) is fast losing the cognitive status it used to enjoy. This means that more and more sociologists are debunking science. In other words, they are questioning the modernist/Enlightenment agenda of knowledge. For instance, from Karl Mannheim's *Sociology of Knowledge* we have learned that sociological knowledge, far from being universal and objective, is contextual and relational. From interpretative sociologists — from Peter Winch to Harold Garfinkel—we have learnt that there are multiple 'forms of living' and there is no universal/objective rationality to explain these forms. Far from 'explaining' social phenomena in terms of the observer's 'context-free' rationality, what is needed is an act of 'understanding'—how people make sense of their world, the meaning they attach to their actions and their shared stock of knowledge. This movement—from explanation to understanding, from universality to specificity, from value-free rationality to contextuality—is indeed a challenge to positivism. It challenges science as the most legitimate form of knowledge.

With this changing character of social knowledge, we also see a sharp critique of the fundamentals of modern civilization. Critical theorists—or Frankfurt School Marxists—contributed quite a lot to the process of debunking modernity. Science does not liberate us. Instead, it becomes 'instrumental', its sole aim is to perpetuate domination over man and nature. Its all-pervasive 'technological rationality' protects rather than conceals the legitimacy of domination. The logic of technological rationality has to be understood. Because the problem is not just the application of technology; technology itself is domination leading to an 'administered society'. In such a society culture becomes an 'industry' that deprives people of their criticality and produces models and stereotypes for blind emulation.

From Adorno to Horkheimer to Marcuse, we see the growing disillusionment with modernity. The convulsions and destruction caused by the First World War, the experience of the National Socialist regime in Germany, the domination and division of the world since 1945 by superpowers increasingly involved in a nuclear arms race—all contributed cumulatively to the sense of cultural loss and decline. In fact, the Frankfurt School was deeply embedded in this tradition of thought, and its growing influence in the 1960s, as Tom Bottomore argued, was undoubtedly connected with the renewal in some sections of the middle class of the revulsion against technological and bureaucratic rationalization.[5]

Peter L. Berger also shows an extraordinary sensitivity while dealing with the discontents of modernity.[6] Modernity is about the 'engineering mentality' — the way it deprives human beings of a 'natural' relationship with the world. The 'abstract' character of public institutions with their implicit 'anonymity' cause 'alienation'. Moreover, the 'pluralistic structures of modern society' have made the life of more and more individuals migratory, ever-changing and mobile; they get uprooted from their original social milieu. This leads to what Berger calls 'homelessness'. This 'homelessness', according to Berger, has found its most devastating expression in the area of religion. The age-old function of religion to provide ultimate certainty amid the exigencies of the human condition has been severely shaken by modernity. Social 'homelessness', as a result, has become 'homelessness' in the cosmos. That's why, in the 'de-modernizing consciousness' modern/urban/technological society is viewed as a 'planetary cancer' eating up the life-giving energies of mother-earth. Berger writes:

> Modernity has indeed been liberating. It has liberated human beings from the narrow controls of family, clan, tribe or small community. It has opened up for the individual previously unheard of options and avenues of mobility. It has provided enormous power, both in the control of nature and in the management of human affairs. However, these liberations have had a high price. Perhaps the easiest way to describe it is to refer to it once more as 'homelessness'. De-modernizing ideas and movements promise liberation from the many discontents of modernity. Again, the most economical way of describing the content of this promised liberation is to call it 'home'. The de-modernizing impulse, whether it looks backwards into the past or forwards into the future, seeks a reversal of the modern trends that have left the individual alienated' and beset with the threats of meaninglessness.[7]

Advent of Postmodernity

We can understand the critique of modernity as reflected in contemporary Western sociology, if we look at the changing socio-cognitive climate — the climate that questions the Enlightenment foundations and premises. To begin with, what is striking is, as Zygmunt Bauman points out, the gradual erosion of the global structure of domination.[8] The domination of the West over the non-West, Bauman thinks, remained self-evident for almost three centuries — for the entire period of modernity. That was, as Bauman would say, a period of 'certainty' in which the West sought to 'enlighten' and 'civilize' the rest of the world. The West was certain about the liberating potential of its secular modernity, its techno-scientific rationality. It is now argued that this period of certainty is over. The violence and brutality implicit in the 'civilizational' project initiated by the modern West and two World Wars revealed this disillusionment and has made it clear that there is no reason to feel certain about the 'superiority' of the Western civilization. Moreover, decolonization movements all over the world have enabled the non-West to resist the monologue of the West.

Another thing has happened, the West itself has undergone a transformation. This is due to the ever-expanding technologies of communication and information. This is indeed an 'era of information and signs'. And this new era has challenged one of the fundamentals of modernity: distinction between high culture and low culture. It would not be wrong to say that, as Bauman argues, throughout the modern era aestheticians were acting like moral teachers: transforming uncertainty into certainty, making decisions, pronouncing authoritative judgments. But now the expanding middle class—a class that is neither ignorant nor educated to the standards boasted by the elite—has begun to threaten the very existence of the 'hierarchy of judgement'. Again, what is worth-recalling is that in the world of 'signs and media spectacles' there is no longer any access to the real world. This is the 'implosion' of all boundaries, regions and distinctions between high culture and low culture, between appearance and reality. It is argued that there is nothing beyond the flow of signs and codes. This is a hyperreal world in which there is no more any grand scale of moral/aesthetic judgment. This is really a relativistic universe. The 'certainty' of modernity ends; interminism begins.

Finally, the collapse of socialism is also a severe blow to the project of modernity. Because in the vision of a socialist society (carefully designed, rationally managed and thoroughly industrialized) lay the nineteenth century 'steam and iron ideal of modern plenty'. Throughout its history socialism was modernity's most rigorous champion. The collapse of socialism, therefore, means the fall of total order. It is the fall of a 'surgical state' designed to subject all local features to one, unifying homogenizing principle of harmony.

All that we have discussed so far tends to suggest that the prevalent socio-intellectual climate is not particularly conducive to the celebration of modernity, its cognitive certainty or the superior status it attaches to the Enlightenment agenda. It is in this period of uncertainty that post-modernists begin to make their presence felt.

To begin with, let us try to understand how postmodernists rethink the status of knowledge in society. In other words, the epistemological questions they raise ought to be understood. A major feature of the Enlightenment agenda is that it regards science as absolutely objective/universal knowledge; science stands in sharp contrast to narratives. Because narratives are merely stories, fables that we invent in order to give meaning and significance to our lives. Narratives do not deliver real knowledge; narratives exist only to provide existential or ideological comfort to us. Narratives, far from being universal, are located in local, personal and social contexts. To strive for true knowledge is to overcome the world of narratives. That was the lesson we learned from all modernist thinkers — from Bacon to Descartes, from Comte to Marx.

But then, as Lyotard, the great exponent of the postmodern condition argues, this binary opposition (science vs. narrative) makes no sense.[9] Because science itself is a narrative of some kind. In fact, science is legitimated by reference to higher level story lines. Lyotard speaks of three metanarratives that legitimize science. First, the creation of wealth; this means that science is valid because it leads to progress and it is essentially a drive for industrial/ commercial growth. Second, the working subject; this means that science serves or ought to serve for the liberation of humanity from exploitation, labour and toil. Imagine Marxism and its love-affair with science. Third, the dialectics of spirit; this means that science is valid because it leads to the emancipation and progress of ideas.

Science, therefore, depends on some sort of metanarrative or other—none of which can be 'objectively' proved or refuted, but each acting as the philosophical rationalization of human ideologies. Moreover, no metanarrative is inherently 'privileged' over any other. As a result, the very claim to 'objectivity' and 'value-neutrality' is suspected. So, argues Lyotard, "abandon metanarratives and embrace the postmodern condition of uncertainty and relativity".

This makes it easier for us to understand why Bauman regards the intellectual as an 'interpreter' in the postmodern condition. This is strikingly different from the role of the intellectual as a 'legislator' in the modern world. As 'legislators', modern intellectuals were certain about the 'superiority' of the Enlightenment agenda. But in the post-modern condition there is no such certainty. As a result, intellectuals can no longer act like 'legislators'. They are just humble 'interpreters' of cultural traditions. Bauman writes:

> With pluralism irreversible, a world scale consensus on world-views and values unlikely, and all extant *Weltanschauungen* firmly grounded in their respective cultural traditions (more correctly, their respective autonomous institutionalizations of power), communication across traditions becomes the major problem of our time. The problem does not seem temporary any more; one cannot hope that it will be solved 'in passing' by a sort of massive conversion guaranteed by the unstoppable march of reason. Rather, the problem is likely to stay with us for a long, long time.... The problem, therefore, calls urgently for specialists in translation between cultural traditions.[10]

To put it simply, postmodernity is a reaction to universal modernity which is generally perceived as positivistic, technocratic and rationalistic. Let us understand post-modernity as a state of mind. It does not substitute one truth for another, one standard of beauty for another, one life-ideal for another. Deconstruction, it may be argued, is one of its concerns. Imagine Derrida. His idea of deconstruction, it seems, challenges the fundamental premises of much of Western philosophy. It calls into question the possibility of defining a ground for absolute knowledge. The deconstructionist does not attempt to find the 'true' meaning of the text or even to identify the author's intention. Instead, it defines interpretation as creating a product that is a literary production in its own right. As a result, different readings are not illegitimate distortions of the text, but merely different species of production. In a way, the 'birth of the reader' causes the 'death of the author'. There is no final truth'; there are multiple possibilities. Indeed, the post-modern mind takes us to a world without any absolute, objective, permanent ideal. We see its difference with the modern mind. The modern mind believes in certainty, orderliness and homogeneity; it tries to eliminate the haphazard and annihilate the spontaneous. It seeks to kill all 'unlicensed differences'. The postmodern mind, however, denies the monologistic temptations of modernity. It embraces differences. It is about chaos and indeterminacy.

Postmodernity can also be understood in terms of political objectives. The politics of modernity is the politics of the state. The goal is to fit everything into the design of a modern state. But the pluralistic ethos of post-modernity speaks of multiple, local, autonomous struggles for liberation. It is against the imperialism of an 'Enlightened minority' that seeks to speak for others — colonized people, blacks, minorities, religious groups, etc. Let us take, for instance, Michel Foucault's critique of a totalizing theory like Marxism.[11] Because of its preoccupation with 'global' issues, argues Foucault, it tends to undermine the significance of local resistances and struggles. Instead of pleading for any 'metatheory' of power, Foucault speaks of how power is exercised: the power of men over women, parents over children, psychiatry over the mentally ill, medicine over population, administration over the ways of people's life. This 'non-class' struggle, argues Foucault, should not be forgotten in the name of globalizing political movements and strategies. That's why, unlike "universal intellectuals" — the "spokesmen of the universal", Foucault talks about " specific intellectuals" — the intellectuals who work within specific sectors at the precise points where their own conditions of life and work situate them into housing, hospital, laboratory, clinic, family and sexual relations.

The fact is that postmodernists reject all metanarratives. All groups have a right to speak for themselves. It privileges heterogeneity and differences. Postmodernity is marked by a view of the world as 'irreducibly pluralistic' split into 'multitude of sovereign units and sites of authority with no horizontal/vertical order.'[12]

It should, however, be remembered that not every critique of modernity can be branded as 'post-modern'. Because one can critique modernity without sharing the relativism/nihilism implicit in post-modernity. This has to be understood. As postmodernists tend to absolutize differences, cross-cultural communication becomes a difficult proposition. This is the beginning of relativism. Post-modernists deprive us of the critical power—the power we need to communicate, persuade, learn and strive for a shared world where consensus is not impossible. Moreover, in the name of tolerating differences, post-modernists may prove to be utterly callous and indifferent to all sorts of exploitation and injustice that go on in the name of cultural specificity. This is the beginning of defeatism or nihilism.

It is true that in the name of 'science','objective truth' and 'justice', modernists have often colonized the world and killed ruthlessly all differences. Yet, protecting these differences does not mean that one should plead for relativism. Perhaps, as it is argued, the challenging task is to keep the emancipatory potential of modernity alive, yet to fight its aberrations, pathologies and Euro-centric colonial ambition. Likewise, the challenge is to live with plurality without being utterly relativistic, and respect differences without absolutizing them.

No wonder, in contemporary Western sociology we also witness a critical orientation to post-modernity. Habermas, for example, is aware of the discontents of modernity, the discontents of scientism or technical consciousness or what he calls the process of 'colonization of the life world'.[13] For Habermas, the life-world—the shared world of communication, mutuality and reciprocity—gets colonized by the system: the rationale of power and money. But, at the same time, Habermas raises his voice against the defeatism/nihilism implicit in the postmodern condition. The reason is that Habermas is not pessimistic about the possibility of modernity. He asserts the importance of communication or communicative rationality. The promise of truly free/undistorted communication is that it is reciprocal, dialogic and reflexive; the goal is understanding and emancipation. But the irony is that the instrumental rationality (here the goal is domination, not understanding) has become all-pervasive; it has colonized almost every sphere of human existence. The need of the hour, argues Habermas, is to fight this colonization, alter the character of the public sphere and make it conducive to dialogue and communication. The need is to rescue communicative rationality. In other words, instead of accepting defeatism or relativism, one should strive for what Habermas regards as the emancipatory project of modernity: communication, reflexivity and freedom.

Anthony Giddens is another important sociologist who has questioned post-modernity. For Giddens, post-modernists have not really understood the meaning of the Enlightenment agenda of modernity. Modernity, they argue, strives for certainty or secure knowledge, and post-modernity unsettles everything. Giddens, however, speaks of the "reflexivity of modernity". "The reflexivity of modern social life", according to Giddens, "consists in the fact that social practices are constantly examined and reformed in the light of incoming information about those very practices, thus constitutively altering their character."[14] This means that the Enlightenment rationality can never become certain about itself. It is inherenity critical and dynamic. "No knowledge under conditions of modernity", argues Giddens, "is knowledge in the 'old' sense, where to know is to be 'certain' ".[15] That's why, Giddens proposes that there is no such thing as post-modernity. Because what postmodernists are talking about—the critique of certainty—is inherent in modernity itself. We are experiencing not postmodernity, but "radicalized modernity": modernity coming to terms with its own reflexivity.

It is at this juncture that we conclude our discussion on the fate of Western modernity. It is a fact that, there are sociologists who are not willing to declare the death of modernity. Yet, the fact remains that the Enlightenment foundations are in crisis. With the critique of science and 'objective' knowledge, we see an 'anti-foundational' trend in sociology. Again, with the changing time, sociology is becoming aware of the discontents of modernity. Instead of celebrating modernity (or the faith in the linearity of progress), sociology is articulating the stories of alienation, homelessness and violence inherent in the logic of modernity itself. Moreover, the grand ambition of modernity—the West's confidence in shaping the entire world—is questioned. Instead, we see a sensitivity to plurality and differences. The fact is that what characterizes contemporary Western sociology is its critical engagement with modernity.

III

Modernity and Indian Social Reality

With this critique of modernity, as we begin to look at Indian social reality, we confront two questions. First, it may be asked whether we can afford the critique of modernity. The reason is that our situation cannot be compared with the West. The West has, after all, experienced hyper-modernity and its pathologies; but we are living in a society in which there are multiple forms of 'pre-modern' oppression, and modernity has not yet exhausted its possibilities. It is argued that we need more science, rationality and technology. A critique of modernity, it is feared, may lead to reactionary conservatism.

Second, it may be asked whether we can at all criticize modernity for its 'alien' character. Because modernity in India, it is often argued, is not the negation of tradition. It does not necessarily mean cultural loss or rootlessness. We may recall, for instance, M.N. Srinivas arguing: "Westernization in one area or level of behaviour does not result in Westernization in another related area or level. The two remain discrete."[16] The bulldozer driver in Rampura, as Srinivas suggests through his celebrated field study, uses Western technology; yet, he may be deeply traditional in his religious belief (he even practises black magic). The manipulation of Western technology does not, therefore, necessarily mean that the manipulators accept a rationalistic and scientific world view. Not solely that. It is possible to use modern technology for traditional purposes. The introduction of printing, for example, has made possible the transmission of not only modern knowledge, but also knowledge of the traditional epics, mythology, the lives of saints, and other religious literature. Or, let us reflect on Milton Singer's work on industrial leaders in Madras.[17] Singer sees how, instead of blindly imitating a Western model of development, they compartmentalize their lives. They follow a 'modern' model in a 'ritually neutralized' work sphere and a 'traditional' one in their domestic and social life. The process of 'technical modernization', argues Singer, does not necessarily destroy the traditional culture. Instead of seeing tradition and modernity as dichotomous, Milton Singer argues: "The traditionalism of Indian civilization lies elsewhere in its capacity to incorporate innovations into an expanding and changing structure of culture and society. The capacity is reflected in a series of adaptive mechanisms and processes for dealing with the novel, the foreign, the strange."[18] Likewise, Rudolph and Rudolph challenge the opposition of modernity and tradition.[19] For example, they argue how Gandhi used traditional symbols for modern mass movements, or how in its transformed stage, caste has helped India's peasant society make a success of representative democracy and fostered the growth of equality by making Indians less separate and more alike. Perhaps in the sociological literature we see an assertion of the "historicity of modernization".[20] As tradition and modernity interact, what happens is a 'selective process of assimilation and syncretism'. A person may adopt the 'instrumental' values of modernity, but, at the same time, may be deeply committed to the 'categorical' values of tradition. In other words, the argument is that modernity in India, because of its creative engagement with tradition, cannot be criticized for its 'alien' character.

This does not mean that modernity is always a happy experience. The fact is that even our brand of modernity can be problematized and re-examined. There are two reasons. First, modernity, despite its 'unique' form in India, cannot be altogether free from the vices one sees in the Western/technologized vision of modernity. Because if we accept the instruments of modernity i.e., big science and technology, we cannot escape what these structures lead to: instrumental rationality, destruction of ecological harmony and repression of local and indigenous knowledge systems. Second, there are limits to cultural adjustment. As modernity becomes overwhelmingly powerful, it may not free itself from its drive towards homogenization; it may threaten our cultural traditions.

In fact, this anxiety is not new. It began with the colonial encounter. India's experience with modernity began with colonialism. With the growth of a universalistic legal system, expansion of education, urbanization and industrialization, increased network of communication and emergence of nationalism, a traditional society began to modernize itself. But then, modernity came to India as colonial modernity with its trauma, anxiety and bitterness. Colonialism, because of its inherent inequality and violence, did severe damage to our self-identity. The West projected itself as a 'superior' civilization. Its 'modernity' could rescue us from our 'inferior' status.

True, modernity was not denied. Yet, modernity was seen as

something 'alien' that might destroy our cultural identity. No wonder, we saw a tension-ridden relationship with modernity. Even when modernity was celebrated, the sanctity of our 'core' culture was not forgotten. It was essentially an ambiguous relationship with modernity: embrace modernity, yet separate yourself from it. As a result, in the process of decolonization we saw a critical enquiry into the nature of modernity. Gandhi, for example, came forward with severe condemnation of modern/Western civilization. His vision of new India cannot be understood through the logic of Enlightenment modernity.

In post-Independence India Jawaharlal Nehru sought to reduce the degree of unhappiness with modernity. Although he was not free from ambiguities, the agenda of nation-building he initiated was essentially modern. It was the vision of a heavily industrialized and technologically developed India: India with solid foundations provided by a 'secular' State, and its intelligentsia—gifted with the 'certainty' of 'scientific temper'—trying to emancipate the Indian mind from cultural superstitions and prejudices.

Yet, India's love-affair with the Nehruvian modernity did not last long. As the crisis of the Nehruvian consensus became more and more evident (the crisis manifested itself in terrible unemployment and poverty, assertion of communal forces, and growth of social movements centered on caste, ethnicity, language and region), we saw the emergence of a new kind of sociological sensitivity, particularly in the writings of Ashis Nandy, Partha Chatterjee, Rajni Kothari and T.N. Madan. Broadly speaking, it questions modernity because of its elitist bias. It criticizes the technologized paradigm of development because of its implicit violence. It is sceptical about secular/scientific rationality because of its incompatibility with our cultural tradition. In a way, it is in tune with what Gandhi wanted : India not corrupted by aggressive technology, not colonized by Western science, but India prospering by decentring herself, India with 'soul-force': ecologically sensitive and spiritually cultivated.

In other words, the emergent consciousness, as we have seen in Western sociological discourses, is critically engaged with modernity. In a way, it reduces the legitimacy of modernity as an emancipatory civilizational project. In contemporary India too (especially after the crisis of the Nehruvian agenda of nation-building) there is a critique of modernity: a critique developed by social scientists who have been influenced by Gandhism, critical theory and even post-modernity.

Here our effort cannot be separated from this intellectual climate. Yet, what should not be forgotten is that things are complex in India. True, the critique of modernity is meaningful. But then, this does not mean the glorification of 'traditionalism'. Because tradition—if not redefined and reformulated—may prove to be oppressive. Moreover, modernity may still have something positive to offer to the oppressed sections of society in their struggle for liberation. In other words, it is this complexity (or different meanings and possibilities of modernity) that manifests itself in this book — the book that deals with the emergent social reality in India.

NOTES

1. S.N. Eisenstadt, *Patterns of Modernity*, Vol. II (London: Frances Printer, 1987), p. 6.
2. Susan J. Hekman, *Hermeneutics and the Sociology of Knowledge* (Cambridge: Polity Press, 1986), p. 5.
3. Anthony Giddens, *The Consequences of Modernity* (Cambridge: Polity Press, 1990), p. 7.
4. Robert Nisbet, *The Sociological Tradition* (London: Heinemann, 1967), p. 17.
5. For further elaboration, see Tom Bottomore, *The Frankfurt School* (Sussex: Ellis Horwood; London: Tavistok Publications, 1984), pp. 27-54.
6. Peter L. Berger; Brigitte Berger and Hansfried Kellner, *The Homeless Mind* (Penguin Books) pp. 163-79.
7. *Ibid.*, p. 175.
8. Zygmunt Bauman, *Legislators and Interpreters: On Modernity, Post-Modernity and Intellectuals* (Cambridge: Polity Press, 1987), Chs. 8-9.
9. J.F. Lyotard, *The Postmodern Condition: A Report on Knowledge* (Manchester: Manchester University Press), pp. 3-11.
   Also see Gregor Mc Lennan, "The Enlightenment Project Revisited" in Stuart Hall, David Held and Tony McGrew (eds)., *Modernity and Its Futures* (Cambridge: Polity Press, 1992), pp. 328-55.

10. Zygmunt Bauman, *Legislators and Interpreters*, p. 143.
11. For further elaboration; see Alan Sheridan, *Michel Foucault: The Will To Truth* (London: Tavistok Publications, 1980), pp. 135-63.
12. For a lucid analysis of postmodernity, see David Harvey, *The Conditions of Postmodernity* (Oxford: Blackwell, 1989), pp. 39-65.
13. For a lucid analysis of Habermas and his reflection on modernity, see Michael Pusey, *Jurgen Habermas* (Chichester: Eills Horwood Ltd.; London and New York: Tavistok Publications, 1987), pp. 105-10.
14. Anthony Giddens, *The Consequences of Modernity*, p. 38.
15. *Ibid.*, p. 40.
16. M.N. Srinivas, *Social Change in Modern India* (New Delhi: Orient Longman, 1972), p. 54.
17. Milton Singer, *When a Great Tradition Modernizes: An Anthropological Approach to Indian Civilization* (Delhi: Vikas Publishing House, 1972).
18. *Ibid.*, p. 385.
19. Lloyd I. Rudolph and Susanne Hoeber Rudolph, *The Modernity of Tradition* (Chicago and London: The University of Chicago Press, 1967).
20. Yogendra Singh, *Modernization of Indian Tradition* (New Delhi: Thomson Press, 1973).

ONE

Intellectual Traditions in Modern India

In this chapter we have tried to understand the development of intellectual traditions in modern India. The reason is that the way intellectuals think and feel, reflect and debate and the culture they evolve help us to understand our destiny or the quality of our collective existence. We have, therefore, concentrated primarily on the debates on tradition, modernity and nation-building in which modern Indian intellectuals—from Rammohun Roy to Nehru, from Gandhians to Marxists—participated. A socio-historical look at these debates would help us to understand the complexity of the relationship between intellectuals and the larger community. It is not possible to speak of every intellectual and his/her contributions. Nevertheless, we have tried to examine a wide spectrum of thought-patterns, trends and worldviews.

I

Intellectuals and their Ideals: A Conceptual Clarification

Broadly speaking, intellectuals are those who contribute directly to the creation, transmission and criticism of ideas. They include writers, artists, scientists, philosophers, religious thinkers, social theorists and political commentators. But this categorization alone is not sufficient. What is equally important to understand is the qualities which, ideally speaking, intellectuals are expected to be gifted with. For us, these ideals, even if not always easy to practise, are relevant. Because without these ideals any critical evaluation of the role of intellectuals is impossible.

Primacy of critical consciousness

One thing that can be said categorically about intellectuals is that they think that they are gifted with *critical consciousness*. It is this critical consciousness which, in fact, distinguishes them and justifies their existence. Because of this critical consciousness they may experience a conflict with the 'taken-for-granted' reality, with the 'iron fact' of common sense and, at times, with the dominant/official truth. For example, Edward Shils would want us to believe that the interior need to penetrate beyond the screen of immediate concrete existence marks the existence of the intellectuals in every society.[1] Perhaps it would not be wrong to say that an intellectual, because of his/her criticality, is a radical of some kind. And even a conservative intellectual cannot escape this spirit, i.e., the spirit of critical enquiry. Because, if one believes Shils, in all societies, even in which the intellectuals are notable for their conservatism, the diverse paths of creativity, as well as inevitable tendency towards negativism, impel a partial rejection of the prevailing system of cultural values.

The point we are trying to state is that one who remains contented with the world as it appears to be, is perhaps not serving the function of an intellectual. An intellectual is restless — perpetually thinking, wondering and reflecting on his/her times. It is impossible to imagine an intellectual without this self-perception.

This distinguishing feature of intellectuals should not mean that everyone else is devoid of critical imagination. In fact, non-intellectuals do not exist. Everyone thinks, wonders and argues. To live in society is to reflect on it. In others words, to live is to think. Let us take an example. It is quite possible to find a bank accountant who thinks and, at times, reads poetry and publishes his letters in newspapers. Likewise, it is possible to find a professor of philosophy who, at times, meets his insurance agent, takes care of his security, goes to the market and buys provisions. While the bank accountant has got his critical/reflexive moments, the professor of philosophy has got his ordinary/mundane moments. Yet, it is not impossible to distinguish the primary function of the professor from that of the bank accountant. The message is that although all men are potential intellectuals, there are people (and the professor is one of them) whose primary function is critical thinking, who live predominantly in the realm of ideas. We call them intellectuals — distinguished by their uncommon reflectiveness about the nature of their universe and the rules which govern their society. In fact, Antonio Gramsci put it sharply: "All men are intellectuals ; . . . but not all men have in society the function of intellectuals."[2]

Faith in dialogue

Is it then possible for intellectuals, despite being acutely aware of their criticality, to share their world with the larger society? The problem arises when intellectuals tend to become extremely proud of their 'faculty of thinking' and fail to relate to ordinary people, their concrete struggles and aspirations. This is the irony of their knowledge; it separates and alienates. Intellectuials want to 'teach' and 'educate'; but never do they want to learn. This exclusivity and the resultant arrogance, needless to add, have done severe damage to the dignity of intellectuals. They are then seen as outsiders with alien habits, beliefs and practices!

Is there any way intellectuals can overcome this elevating distance? To begin with, it has to be realized that populism is no answer. Populism manifests itself in two ways. First, in order to be 'acceptable' to the larger community, intellectuals may begin to accept a very pragmatic version of truth. Truth is what prevails in society. In other words, they may not want to shock or disturb the larger community. Second, as Zygmunt Bauman has shown, post-modernists are fond of arguing that intellectuals can no longer act like "legislators".[3] There is no certainty, no grand truth. There is no coherence; there are only differences. Intellectuals are, therefore, no longer privileged to judge, teach and evaluate; they are just "interpreters"or translators of traditions without any cognitive superiority.

Both these versions of populism, we want to argue, are manifestations of defeatism. Well, it is certainly true that intellectuals ought to understand people and understanding is impossible without respect. It is also correct that truth is problematic and perhaps nobody (intellectuals are not excluded) has got complete monopoly over truth. Nevertheless, it makes no sense if one adopts a defeatist attitude and argues that, amidst uncertainty and plurality, criticality is altogether impossible. In fact, the challenge is to fight this defeatism, retain the critical spirit and evolve a dialogue.

Dialogue is not populism, nor is it defeatism.Dialogue means faith. As Paulo Freire, the radical educationist would argue,"only dialogue, which requires critical thinking is also capable of generating critical thinking. Without dialogue there is no communication, and without communication there can be no true education."[4] It is in this sense that intellectuals ought to be dialogical beings. Dialogue is a process of learning. Intellectuals grow up as they communicate with the larger world. Likewise, this communication makes it possible for those who otherwise do not serve the function of intellectuals to raise their consciousness to a higher plain. Perhaps this ethos of communication can be seen rather sharply in Gramsci's "organic intellectuals"—particularly, the organic intellectuals of the subaltern classes. Because, as Gramsci would say, an organic intellectual is not just a man of letters, instead, he is known particularly for his "active participation in practical life as a constructor, organizer, 'permanent persuader' and not just a simple orator."[5] As a matter of fact, what we are trying to argue is that intellectuals as dialogical beings should not look like colonizers, strangers or outsiders. It is true that critical thinking means dissent. But this dissent is mingled with love—faith in ordinary people.

Freedom of thinking

The critical thinking we are expecting from intellectuals is no ordinary thing. It requires a spirit, a character, a mind. It needs sufficient freedom to overcome the determinants of one's socio-cultural milieu, freedom to learn even from one's opponents and freedom to go beyond purely utilitarian interests like power and money.

It is at this juncture that Karl Mannheim's understanding of "socially unattached" intellectuals becomes relevant.[6] While exploring the conditions conducive to the growth of 'sociology of knowledge' as a discipline, Mannheim also spoke of the 'birth of the new intelligentsia.' To quote Mannheim: ". . . unlike preceding cultures, intellectual activity is not carried on exclusively by a socially rigidly defined class, such as a priesthood, but rather by a social stratum which is to a large degree unattached to any social class and which is recruited from an increasingly inclusive area of social life".[7] This freedom from traditional constraints, according to Mannheim, enables the intellectuals to think freely, overcome the conditionalities of different ideologies and arrive at a "synthesis" or a more adequate definition of social reality. For Mannheim, education plays a very important role in this process. Education subjects the intellectual to the 'influence of opposing tendencies in social reality'[8] and, therefore, there is a wider area of choice and a corresponding need for total orientation and synthesis.

What is, however, important to explore is whether this idealized notion of "socially unattached" or "free" intelligentsia makes sense in our times. To begin with, let us examine how knowledge is really produced. Scientists, for instance, cannot do their work as amateurs or independent and self-supporting individuals. They are today completely dependent for their work on the scientific research laboratory which has grown enormously in size and complexity and to whose discipline they must submit. In other words, research is impossible without institutional/ financial support. As a result of all this, free/critical spirit is often sacrificed and purely instrumental/practical interests — how to get a project, how to get the financial support, how to come closer to power—begin to dominate. This close relationship between knowledge and power means that scientists and technologists are fast becoming new elites pampered by the state or different corporate sectors.

This is true not just for science and technology but, perhaps every sphere of intellectual activity is moving in the same direction. In fact, intellectuals of all varieties are getting incorporated into "organized institutions".[9] When intellectuals are essentially "paid employees", is it possible to feel comfortable with Mannheim's vision? This is indeed a serious problem. Yet, we would insist, there is no reason to overreact. Because it is not altogether impossible to see intellectuals who, despite being employed in universities, research laboratories and newspapers, refuse to bow down. Granted, retaining a free/critical spirit is no easy preposition;

ideals do not generally exist. Yet, what should distinguish intellectuals (we are speaking of our dreams) is that, despite the possibility of failures, they seek to retain and strive for these ideals. It is this perpetual existential tension that makes them potentially disobedient.

Urge to overcome class determinants

There is, however, another serious problem. Intellectuals too have their class identities. Because, like everyone else intellectuals too live in the world and get affected by its mode of production and complex network of social relationships. "Every social group coming into existence . . . in the world of economic production," wrote Antonio Gramsci, "creates together with itself, organically one or more strata of intellectuals who give it homogeneity and awareness of its own function not only in the economic but also in the social and political fields."[10] For Gramsci, the affinity between intellectuals and the classes they belong to is obvious. They create ideas, provide thinking, generate literature in order to legitimate the existence of their classes. As Gramsci said, "the intellectuals are the dominant group's 'deputies', exercising the subaltern functions of social hegemony and political government."[11] That is why, for Gramsci, subaltern classes ought to have their own "organic" intellectuals to fight the ruling class hegemony and create a counter—hegemony. Unlike "traditional" intellectuals who, as Gramsci would say, "put themselves forward as autonomous and independent of the dominant social group"[12], "organic" intellectuals are actually aware of their class affinities and historic responsibilities.

Gramsci's notion of "organic" intellectuals is a refreshing break; it makes us aware of dialogue, communication and radical practice. But, at the same time, we would oppose any deterministic tendency for, class is destiny and one is necessarily bound by it. Intellectuals, precisely because of their free/critical spirit, seek to overcome their class identities. They may not succeed all the time; the tension is, however, kept alive. It is, therefore, not impossible to find many "upper class" intellectuals articulating the voices of the oppressed. History tells us how Marx and Engles transcended the boundaries of their classes. In fact, what characterizes the ethos of intellectual life is this dialectical interpenetration between one's 'historically determined' class and one's critical consciousness. Intellectuals, ideally speaking, are always opening up, trying to emancipate themselves from dogmas.

Reconciling thinking and action as passionate beings

It has often been alleged that intellectuals are merely contemplative beings. They think, they write books and participate in seminars, but seldom do they act! One way of coping with this allegation is to realize that thinking is no less important than action. To imagine otherwise is to see man only as a practical doer, an engineer. But life cannot be reduced into an 'engineering mentality' because man is multidimensional. He is an engineer, a poet, a musician, a philosopher, etc. To argue that his 'engineering identity' is the most dominant one, is to brutalize him. Thinking is meaningful because it helps us to realize that man is a visionary, a dreamer. Poetry and philosophy may not increase the 'growth rate' of the nation. But no one imagines a sane society without its poets, philosophers and all those who live in the world of ideas.

Moreover, it is utterly wrong to believe that thinking is just thinking; it is essentially a great act. It is an intervention. Because what we call the 'real' world is not something static or fixed. Thinking is being engaged in a process of dynamic interaction with this real world. To take an example, a Marxian thinking on capitalism and its discontents is certainly shaping our collective destiny! In other words, what we are trying to argue is that a thinker is not necessarily an actor in the conventional sense of the term. Action is not just what is immediately visible. There is also an invisible act. Thinking is an invisible act.

It is desirable, as Marx or, for that matter, any radical thinker would assert, to strive for the unity of theory and practice.[13] A thinker detached from the world is an abstraction. Thinking is born out of concrete life-experiences. Critical thinking is, therefore, a passionate exercise. No great visionary, be it Marx or Gramsci, Gandhi or Tagore, can be imagined without this passion. It is this passion we believe, which should lead intellectuals to merge with the real battles and struggles of life. And, particularly at peak moments of revolution or national liberation, we witness this merger—intellectuals becoming social activists and social activists becoming intellectuals. We can conclude that intellectuals may not necessarily look like practical doers and activists all the time. But their critical thinking—because it is potent and passionate — is always helping them to relate to the practical world in which all sorts of activities, struggles and rebellions are taking place.

All these are ideals. Those who are known as intellectuals need not necessarily fulfil these ideals. Nevertheless, this desired vision would always help us for rigorous self-introspection.

II

Birth of Modern Intellectuals: Colonialism and the Vision of New India

After this theoretical discussion it becomes easier for us to come back to India and examine the ethos of our intellectual life in the light of the fundamental/desirable qualities we have talked about. This, however, requires an understanding of the concerns which have occupied a central place in the cognitive map of modern intellectuals in India. Broadly speaking, we can speak of two such concerns.

(i) An intense curiosity to understand our tradition, its religiosity, social institutions and cultural practices. Is our tradition an obstacle in the path of modernity—its 'Enlightenment' rationality, its techno-economic institutions or its secular humanism? Or is it possible for our tradition to generate its own resources and create an alternate agenda?

(ii) An urge to make sense of modernity, its global ambitions and projects. Is modernity an elitist project not sensitive to India's subaltern masses, their struggles and aspirations? Or should India as a modern nation-state pursue the same universal objectives—development, production, efficiency, homogeneity and scientific temper?

In fact, it is impossible to find a modern Indian intellectual not concerned with these questions. Intellectuals, needless to add, are divided. There are many (liberals/radicals/Marxists) who should see themselves as agents of the great modernization project.

But, at the same time, it is not difficult to find many who would prefer to remain ambivalent or who are not necessarily contented with modernity. In other words, in these divergent responses we can see the complexity of the relationship between intellectuals and the larger society. For a better appreciation of this relationship we need to examine the origin of their criticality, their social composition, the nature of their involvement/participation in the struggles for social transformation and their ability to relate to ordinary people. But before we come nearer to our times, it is necessary to look at that crucial juncture of our history when modern intellectuals were born in India.

This is like locating the intelligentsia in the context of colonialism and the challenges it posed to the self-perception of our cultural tradition. Colonialism, it has to be realized, is not just about physical power and coercion. It is also about cultural or symbolic power — the way it created the hierarchy of civilizations and privileged the modern West as the superior civilization. Not surprisingly, in the history of colonialism one can see the way it legitimated itself through its 'civilizing mission'. It must enlighten, educate and civilize us! Perhaps in Macaulay's agenda of education this civilizing mission could be seen rather sharply. The assumption was that a package of Christianity, modern science and Western ideas — a gift from the British civilization—would enable Indians to rescue themselves from ignorance. It would not be wrong to say that modern Indian intellectuals were born out of this encounter. The West with its Enlightenment experiences became a reference point, and, as a result, we saw the emergence of a critical enquiry into the nature of our culture, religion and tradition in order to evolve a new identity for India. It was this quest that marked the presence of the intelligentsia in colonial India.

As K.N. Panikkar has written, "the nineteenth century intellectuals were firm believers in the efficacy of enlightenment as a panacea. They traced the source of all ills in Indian society, including religious superstition and social obscurantism, to the general ignorance of the people."[14] In science they saw a great possibility. Rammohun wanted it. Akshay Kumar Dutt rejected the traditional system of education. Vidyasagar ridiculed those who believed that the *shastras* contained all scientific truth.

According to Sayyied Ahmad Khan, the traditional system of Muslim education was a great stumbling block in the way of progress. Even Dayananda and the Arya Samajists, as Panikkar has pointed out, in spite of their obsession with the Vedic knowledge, recognized the importance of science education.

But that was not the only story. Their affinity with science did not prevent them from using cultural or religious resources for their agenda. Rammohun accepted the Vedas as divine revelation. Keshub Chandra Sen introduced *arti, puja* and *sankirtan* in his prayers. Dayanand saw the eternal and universal relevance of the Vedas. In fact, what characterized their thinking was this dynamic interplay of tradition and modernity, religion and science.

Recalling the birth of modern intellectuals in India is like recalling what historians have regarded as the "Bengal renaissance." Raja Rammohun Roy (1772-1833)—the great "renaissance" man—and all those who followed him gave a new momentum to the development of new ideas. In fact, none of them could escape the all-pervasive presence of the West—its reason, science and success in the material sphere. Perhaps it would not be wrong to say that modern Indian intellectuals were born out of this cultural encounter. The result was the growth of a critical consciousness that enabled a section of the intellectuals of the nineteenth century to fight the discontents of their cultural traditions. Many of them redefined/reinterpreted their past. Understanding this new mind-set is important in order to make sense of the intellectual history of modern India. We, therefore, propose to focus our attention on Raja Rammohun Roy who, for many, was a source of inspiration and even those who disliked him could not escape the dynamism he generated.

What was striking about Rammohun was his affirmation of reason, his progressive urge to rescue his countrymen from "imposition and servitude and promote their comforts and happiness."[15] Indeed, he could see the arrival of the new age. Not surprisingly, he pleaded for: mathematics, natural philosophy, chemistry, anatomy and other useful sciences. He sought to fight all that was "stagnant, degraded and corrupt" in his times.[16] His *Tuhfat-ul-Muwahhiddien*—published in 1804 with a Persian text and an Arabic introduction—was a celebration of rationality. For instance, it was a formal attack on any form of idol-worship. We can recall Rammohun arguing that idol-worship is meant only for "persons of mean capacity, persons of feeble intellect and weak and ignorant masses."[17] For Rammohun, a "wise man"—a man with reason—should not tolerate such superstitious practices. For these evil practices he blamed the priesthood, the conspiracy of the Brahmins. To quote him: "Many learned Brahmins are perfectly aware of the absurdity of idolatry . . . But as in the rites, ceremonies and festivals of idolatry, they find the source of their comforts and fortune, they not only never fail to protect idol-worship from all attack, but even advance and encourage it."[18]

Rammohun's rationality, it ought to be realized, was not free from its inherent ambiguity. His faith in the existence of a Supreme Being revealed his religiousity. Never did he forget the emancipatory ideals of religion. "The doctrines of the unity of God are real Hinduism,"[19] said Rammohun. He could, therefore, raise his voice of dissent against "hundreds of useless hardships and privations regarding eating and drinking, purity and impurity, auspiciousness and inauspiciousness" which, as he said, were "causes of injury and detrimental to social life."[20] It was this higher Vedantic teaching that he sought to rescue from the priesthood. With this missionary zeal he published the Bengali translation of the Vedanta and five of the principal Upanishads.

Another manifestation of this zeal could be seen in the activities of Young Bengal. For example, Derozio (1809-31), a godless secularist, thought that for India nothing was more essential than "a dissemination of European thinking and science among her people".[21] Historians tell us how this young professor inspired his students in Hindu College, how he invited them to the new frontiers of knowledge, particularly Western thought and literature. The goal was to fight the burden of the past, the shames of idolatry and priestcraft to overcome all fixations and religious superstitions. Derozio and his students, it appears, were intellectuals with a hammer; they sought to shake the foundations of the taken-for-granted world. Not surprisingly, some of them indulged in forbidden food and drink. As one of them wrote in the college magazine : "If there is anything that we hate from the bottom of our heart, it is Hinduism."[22]

Even this brief familiarity with the discourses of Raja Rammohun Roy and Young Bengal help us to understand the mind of the new intelligentsia. This mind was critical. And this criticality implied openness to Western liberal, rational and scientific thinking and the resultant courage to redefine and reinterpret one's own cultural tradition. Moreover, this criticality was not just academic. It was passionately endowed with a mission of social transformation!

Their thinking and activity were not acceptable to all, particularly the traditionalists. They were often attacked, condemned and criticized by their contemporaries. One knows how Rammohun confronted severe opposition from orthodox pandits like Sankar Sastri, Mrityunjaya Vidyalankar and Subrahmanya Sastri. One also knows how Derozio's disciples and the boys of Hindu College were often called "atheist beasts". Yet, for them, there was a continual effort to come out of their enclaves. Their dialogic spirit was evident in their eagerness to publish their literature in Bengali and thereby popularize their ideas.

It would, however, be wrong if we simplify the development of the intellectual mind and refuse to see its complexities and contradictions. It is true that there are historians and sociologists willing to see the roots of Indian modernization in the intellectual mind of the nineteenth century Bengal. Professor Sushobhan Sarkar saw "Westernism" (with all its "progressive" features like social reform, liberal rationalism and secular humanism) in Rammohun and separated it from conservative "orientalism." But, then, not every historian agrees with this glorification of Rammohun as a great modernizer. Professor Sumit Sarkar, a distinguished historian argues how Rammohun's break with the past was of a "limited and deeply contradictory kind".[23] Sarkar wants us to remember that in social reform the pioneers often failed to live up to the ideals of their youth. The Derozians upon entering middle age increasingly sought social respectability through conformism. And Rammohun as Sarkar asserts, showed his outward conformity to most caste rules, took a Brahmin cook with him to England, wore the sacred thread to the end of his days and, because of his dependence on the Shastras, glorified "ascetic widowhood" in the name of fighting sati!

Apart from these contradictions, Sarkar speaks of the "elitist" character of this intellectual awakening. Brahmoism, according to Sarkar, could never win the hearts of ordinary people. It was 'too intellectual and dry a creed to be ever successful as a popular religion."[24] Moreover, these intellectuals often welcomed "negative, alienating aspects of English education".[25] They even visualized a kind of dependent but still bourgeois development in Bengal in close collaboration with British merchants and entrepreneurs! Therefore, Sumit Sarkar asserts that the 'renaissance' culture which Rammohun inaugurated inevitably remained within a Hindu elitist and colonial framework".[26]

We should, however, argue that all this does not mean the denial of the emancipatory role Rammohun and his disciples played. What is, however, healthy about this debate is that it helps us to examine and reexamine the complexity of the intellectual mind, its different variations and possibilities. We have already implied how their criticality was a product of cultural encounter. It drew its inspiration from the West; yet it was engaged in a dialogue with the indigenous culture; they saw the 'progressive' character of English education, but they were no less eager to promote vernacular languages. They saw the British rule as "divine dispensation", but they were also becoming aware of the exploitative character of the colonial rule. That's why, instead of labelling this intellectual mind, it is better to see the multiple currents flowing inside it.

(i) There was, to begin with, the love affair with Western rationalism. It did debunk many religious and cultural practices. It was also a cause of alienation: intellectuals as rationalists isolating themselves from ordinary believers.

(ii) There was an urge to speak the new language in one's own cultural idiom. For that reason despite Western rationalism, there was an increasing dependence on the Vedas and the Upanishads. The urge was to see rationalism/humanism in one's own religious tradition. At times, it looked like a "synthesis" of the East and the West. And, at times, it looked like an attempt to assert one's cultural identity and cope with the challenge posed by the colonial West.

(iii) There was also an attempt to come closer to people, emerge as communicators and strive collectively for a new practice.

Perhaps a combination of these different possibilities could be found in the intellectual response, particularly in the colonial era. A look at the further development of this process would help us to examine the quality of this dialectical/dialogical relationship between intellectuals and their cultural communities.

The critical mind, in fact, was restless. Its affinity with the West did not mean its indifference to the indigenous cultural tradition. Reform/change was the main agenda and for that cultural resources were no less important. Imagine Iswar Chandra Vidyasagar (1820-91)—the "traditional modernizer". His fight against Kulinism and the ban on widow-remarriage revealed how eager he was to reform his society. Yet, he relied on the Sastras for his radical agenda. Or choose Bankim Chandra Chatterjee (1838-94)—the great intellectual mind of Bengal. It was difficult for him to remain indifferent to the visibility of the West's success. He was disturbed and eager to learn from the success story of the West and regenerate his own country. Bankim glorified the European attitude towards knowledge, its utilitarianism, its affinity with power. "Europeans", wrote Bankim, "are devotees of power."[27] Knowledge, for them, is power and, as Bankim argued, that was the "key to their advancement."[28] And, according to Bankim, Hindus "failed to win on earth" because of their belief that "knowledge is salvation."[29] Not surprisingly, "in culture, education, power, wealth and happiness — in fact, in all respects, the English are superior to the Bengalis."[30] The material culture of the West, according to Bankim, was its superiority. Even when he spoke of the spirituality of Hindu Dharma, he did not forget to reconcile it with the "European industries and sciences". This new "national-cultural" project stimulated Bankim to rediscover Lord Krishna in whom he saw the "consistent and fullest development of all human faculties"[31]—Krishna as a householder, a diplomat, a warrior, a law giver, a saint, a preacher.

Yet, Bankim was not free from ambivalence. As Tapan Raychaudhuri shows, "his constant harping on the multiple imperfections of Indian society did not, however, reduce his sensitivity to Europe's shortcomings."[32] To begin with, Bankim saw the pathology of "European patriotism." For him, "it was a terribly monstrous sin". Not solely that. Despite his love affair with the West, he did not forget to assert that the Hindu concept of Dharma was deeper and wider than the Western notion of religion. Again, despite his positive attitude towards English education, he deplored the emergence of a class of people unable to speak their own language.

In other words, in Bankim one could witness that restless spirit implicit in the intellectual mind — criticality, not conformity; openness, not exclusivism. In this mind one could see the dynamic interplay of two possibilities — a rationalist embracing European sciences and a cultural innovator appropriating and giving a new meaning to religion.

Like Bankim, Vivekananda (1863-1902) too was equally restless, disturbed by the downfall of his country and eager to regenerate his countrymen. "Why is it that we three hundred and thirty millions of people, have been ruled . . . by any and every handful of foreigners . . .?[33] asked Vivekananda. And his reply was quite revealing: "Because they had faith in themselves and we had not."[34] It was this power of faith that Vivekananda wanted his countrymen to learn from the West. "The Englishman believes that he is born the lord of the world. He believes he is great and can do anything in the world; if he wants to go to the sun or the moon, he believes he can; and that makes him great . . . we have less faith—a thousand times less faith."[35]

Yet, what gave Vivekananda a unique place in history was his effort to regenerate Hinduism and give confidence to his countrymen by making them aware of their cultural/spiritual sources. Vivekananda, therefore, did not hesitate to debunk the success story of the West; he saw the denial of spirituality in their success. For example, their "sciences", argued Vivekananda, "can give us only bread and clothes and power over fellowmen."[36] He did not want his countrymen to forget that "the Western man is a body first, and then he has a soul; with us, man is a soul and spirit and he has a body."[37] That is why, Vivekananda's bold assertion: "Our religion is truer than any other religion, because it never conquered and because it never shed blood . . .".[38]

Perhaps this ambiguity towards the West and the growing assertion of India's spirituality reflected an attempt to boost the weakened morale of the vast majority. It was needed to heal the wound colonialism caused to our collective psyche. In this tendency to rely on the "vitality of traditional culture", Professor K.N. Panikkar saw the "cultural defence" rather than cultural revivalism.[39] For instance, a look at Dayananda Saraswati (1824-83)—the founder of the Arya Samaj—shows that he, like Rammohun, Devendranath Tagore and Keshub Chandra Sen—the proponents of the Brahmo Samaj—was no less critical of the prevalent Hindu practices like idolatry and polytheism, child marriage, the taboos on widow remarriage, and foreign travel, Brahmin predominance and the multiplicity of castes based on birth alone. Yet, Dayananda, like many other intellectual minds of his time, did not forget to defend his cultural/religious sources. He asserted the superiority of Hinduism over all other faiths; his "purified Hinduism" was based on "Vedic infallibility".

Even Tilak (1856-1920) who was by no means an obscurantist relied heavily on religious symbols. He reinterpreted the *Bhagavad Gita*, drew inspiration from its celebrated notion of action. He revived the memory of Shivaji's struggle against the Mughal empire for the liberation of Maratha land. And he revived and utilized the Ganpati festival for political propaganda.

The same story repeated itself in Sri Aurobindo (1872-1950) —another great mind of India. His English education, his familiarity with the European literature and culture, his revolutionary political background—nothing could prevent him from seeing the pathologies of modern Western civilization and asserting the richness of India's spirituality.[40] He disliked the ideas of "an average and typical occidental mind on Indian culture". Because such a mind obsessed with the "vitalistic rational" idea could see nothing but despair, passivity and nihilism in Indian culture. Instead, Sri Aurobindo defended Hindu spirituality, refused to equate it with a "tired quietism" or a "conventional monastricism". He argued that this spirituality, far from denying life, accepted the reality of *karma* and *artha* and reconciled these fundamental human interests with *dharma* and *moksa* and thereby imagined the possibility of a complete harmonic existence—something that the West's "vehement secular activism" could never visualize.

A discussion on the role of the intellectuals in the colonial era will remain incomplete unless we locate them in the context of the political struggle for liberation. One thing was becoming clear. With the establishment of universities in the country after 1857, the numerical strength of the students rapidly increased. For example, by the 1880s, the total number of English-educated Indians was approaching 50,000 mark. The number of those studying English went up fairly rapidly from 2,98,000 in 1887 to 5,05,000 in 1907, while the circulation of English language newspapers climbed from 90,000 in 1885 to 2,76,000 in 1905.[41] The aspirations and ambitions of these intellectuals were bound to manifest themselves in politics. Outstanding members of the Indian intelligentsia backed up by a commercial and incipient industrial bourgeoisie founded in 1885, the first national political organization — Indian National Congress. The liberal intelligentsia dominated the Congress from 1885 to 1905. Their English education, their familiarity with the promises of modernity explained their almost unlimited faith in the British democracy. The contact with this modern civilization, they thought, would take India to a new age of freedom and democracy. As Surendranath Banerji said in 1895: "To England we look for inspiration and guidance . . . From England must come the crowning mandate which will enfranchise our people. England is our political guide . . . in the exalted sphere of political activity."[42] This faith in the British rule prevented them from radicalism. Instead, they adopted the method of constitutional agitation.

But as the disillusionment with the British rule began to grow, the liberals lost their importance and militant nationalists like Tilak, Aurobindo and Lajpat Rai emerged as new leaders. Tilak or Aurobindo, unlike the liberals, drew inspiration from India's past. Not solely that. With the emergence of the militants, swaraj or self-governance became the primary agenda. Politics was becoming more and more intense. And finally, with the emergence of Gandhi (1869-1948), politics acquired an altogether different meaning. Gandhi succeeded in mobilizing various sections of the people—workers, peasants, capitalists, students, lawyers and, above all, women—in the nationalist movement. In other words, with Gandhi, politics became a meaningful point of mediation—the intellectuals and the masses were engaging themselves in a communicative act.

Gandhi was indeed a turning-point. Rammohun was showing us the light of reason we needed to embrace the new age. Gandhi was reminding us of the power of morality we needed to fight the lure of modern civilization. In Gandhi one was witnessing the merger of an intellectual and an activist, a seeker of truth and a practical doer. The life he led, the symbols he used, the courage he demonstrated—everything revealed his association with the people, his communicative skill.

It is not impossible to see a similarity between Gandhi and his predecessors. Like them he too was disturbed by the degeneration of his society; like them he too was equally eager to reform/regenerate/radicalize his culture. And like Rammohun, Bankim and Vivekananda, Gandhi too was preoccupied with the religious question, its meaning, its possibilities in the changing world. Moreover, like them Gandhi was commenting on the West —the meaning of India's encounter with the Western civilization. Yet, despite these continuities, Gandhi was an intellectual of a different kind. Unlike his predecessors, his association with politics —the concrete, anti-colonial struggle for national liberation—was more direct, intense and real. He was continually testing his ideas —not excluding spiritual ideas,—in the active realm of politics. Moreover, the meaning he attached to the West was of a different kind.

Rammohun and Bankim, for instance, wanted India to emulate European sciences and industries. But what was striking about Gandhi was his severe condemnation of modern/Western civilization. Far from asking his countrymen to emulate the so-called 'progressive' qualities of modern civilization, he wanted them to see its irreligiosity, barbarism and violence. Indeed, Gandhi could not be understood without this morality. It was this strong moral principle that enabled him to evolve a critique of the entire edifice of bourgeois society, its instrumental science and technology, its education, medicine and craving for luxury. "We notice that the mind is a restless bird; the more it gets the more it wants. The more we indulge our passions, the more unbridled they become.[43] To take an example, for Gandhi, modern medicine—something that every proponent of modernity is proud of—promotes this indulgence. To quote Gandhi : "I overeat, I have indigestion, I go to the doctor, he gives me medicine, I am cured. I overeat again, I take his pills again. Had I not taken the pills in the first instance, I would have suffered the punishment deserved by me and I would not have overeaten again. The doctor intervened and helped me to indulge myself."[44] Perhaps all this led Gandhi to appeal to his countrymen not to be seduced by a "nation of shopkeepers". This critique, its unambiguity, its strong moralistic appeal, needless to add, gave confidence to the colonized people struggling for identity and self-respect. This challenged the right of the West to "educate" the rest of the world.

Yet, it would be wrong to say that Gandhi was just a traditionalist. In fact, his critique of some of the evil practices he saw in his own culture—untouchability, subjugation of women, moral degradation—was no less severe. Gandhi called himself a 'sanatani Hindu'; but he was essentially a rebel Hindu perpetually experimenting with truth and giving a new meaning to Hindu religion. For example, his autobiography suggests how he dissented, disobeyed his caste people who were agitated over his going abroad.[45] This dissent could be seen in his refusal to wear the sacred thread.

> I will not wear the sacred thread for I see no necessity for it, when countless Hindus can go without it and yet remain Hindus. Moreover, the sacred thread should be a symbol of spiritual regeneration, presupposing a deliberate attempt on the part of the wearer at a higher and purer life. I doubt whether in the present state of Hinduism and of India, Hindus can vindicate the right to wear a symbol charged with such a meaning. That right can come only after Hinduism has purged itself of untouchability, has removed all distinctions of superiority and inferiority; and shed a host of other evils and shams that have become rampant in it.[46]

To use Bhikhu Parekh's words, Gandhi valued tradition, but he was not a traditionalist.[47] He used the resources of his tradition and with his intense creativity gave birth to an alternate politico-cultural agenda. For example, for Gandhi, moksa meant not just *ananda*, but also *dukha* or suffering, for to identify oneself with all men was to suffer for and with them and to make their suffering one's own. Likewise, *tapasya* did not simply consist in taking oneself to the forest and sitting down there surrounded by fires. True *tapasya* consisted of suffering in the service of one's fellowmen. That is why, Gandhi was not another orthodox traditionalist. No traditionalist Hindu could say:

> To see the universal and all-pervading spirit of truth face to face, one must be able to love the meanest of creation as oneself. And a man who aspires after that cannot afford to keep out of any field of life. That is why, my devotion to truth has drawn me into the field of politics; and I can say without the slightest hesitation, and yet in all humility, that those who say that religion has nothing to do with politics do not know what religion means.[48]

Indeed, this radicalization of Hinduism gave a new meaning to Gandhi's politico-intellectual endeavour. His critical consciousness manifested itself in his openness. Tradition, for him, was not a closed entity; it was a dynamic possibility. He thought of a living tradition, of critical and unending enquiry. He, therefore, did not hesitate to learn from Islam, Jainism and Christianity and thereby enrich his Hinduism. He was no less open to the saner voices emanating from the West—the voices of Tolstoy, Thoreau and Ruskin. This openness gave him the strength to imagine and strive for a new world (neither 'modern' nor 'traditional') based on soul-force, *ahimsa*, harmonic relationship with life and nature, decentralization/diffusion of power, simplicity and honesty. His "utopia" might not have been appreciated by all. Yet, what was remarkable about his politico-intellectual life was his ability to break the barrier between the elites and the masses, the leaders and the led. Indeed, Gandhi—with his openness and acceptance of his own follies and mistakes and his intense involvement with the destiny of the collective—created an example no radical intellectual could remain indifferent to. One can reduce him into a museum piece. Or one can condemn him. But it is not easy to remain free from him.

For example, this irresistible influence of Gandhi could be seen in S.A. Dange's thinking. It was not possible for Dange, despite his Marxism, to escape Gandhi. The result was the text: *Gandhi vs Lenin* he published in 1921.[49] Like all his predecessors Dange was equally eager to understand the West. A dynamic 'spirit', he thought, characterized and drove modern Europe. But in the absence of corresponding duties and responsibilities, this led to a kind of corrupted individualism. In fact, with its acquisitiveness and corrupted individualism the British corrupted the world. This does not mean that Dange was happy with what he saw in India. In fact, what characterized the typical Indian mind, as he thought, was the notion of predestination. It led to fatalism, passivity and pessimism. Dange wanted a solution. He wanted to learn from the dynamic 'spirit' of the West. At the same time, he wanted to be free from its evils. He sought to Indianize it. This led him to evolve a dialogue with both Lenin and Gandhi.

This critical engagement with the West, for Dange, meant a way of fighting capitalism and its implicit greediness, idleness, cruelty, and luxurious and demoralized life ethos. Gandhism and Bolshevism provided different answers and Dange learned from both. True, Dange didn't agree with the Gandhian critique of industrial civilization. But, at the same time, he could not appreciate the Bolshevik method of coercion and violence. Instead, he saw the potency of the Gandhian method of protest; he learned from its moral or spiritual message. In a way, Gandhi did help Dange to Indianize his Marxism or modernity.

This is merely an example that shows the overwhelming presence of the Gandhian tradition. Even modernists and nationalists could not free themselves from the legacy of Gandhi. Look at the intellectual journey of M.N. Roy: a Marxist and an admirer of Enlightenment rationality. Eventually, Roy—with his radical humanism—came forward with the proposals (like partyless/decentralized/participatory democracy) that brought him nearer to the Gandhian agenda.

It is at this juncture that we can summarize and conclude all that we have discussed so far — particularly, the role of intellectuals and their engagement with the larger society in the colonial era.

(i) The dominant intellectual tradition was extraordinarily preoccupied with social and religious reform, transformation and change. The intellectuals—from Rammohun to Gandhi—were not just contemplative thinkers cut off from the affairs of the real world. They were activists in their own ways. In other words, their critical consciousness was passionate. It was filled with a mission. It sought to create a new India.

(ii) This project (striving for a new identity for India) led them to look at the West. Regarding the perception of the West, they differed amongst themselves. The West, its 'liberal'/'progressive' ideas, science, reason, success in the world influenced many of them. But, at the same time, there were others who refused to get carried away by the West so easily. Regarding the orientation to the West, Bhikhu Parekh sees a spectrum of possibilities—traditionalism, critical traditionalism, critical modernism and modernism.[50] And Ashis Nandy sees the victory of the "psychology of colonialism";[51] many pre-Gandhian protest movements, according to Nandy, were seduced by the West, its categories, its notions of masculinity, history and progress.

(iii) The preoccupation with the West notwithstanding, many of them were eager to rescue the "spirituality" of Indian culture. Even the admirers of European sciences did not want to forget this "strength" of Indian culture. With the result, in the dominant intellectual tradition, "synthesis" became an important issue. The celebration of "spirituality" led the intellectuals to think in terms of Hindu categories/texts—the Vedas, the Upanishads and the *Bhagavad Gita*. These ideals might have alienated the Muslims. Not solely that. Many of them were not free from the perception "Muslim tyranny" or a "medieval dark age".

(iv) The intellectuals came largely from the traditional literary castes because they were more easily inclined to new education. Moreover, their English education or even their discourses on classical Hinduism tended to separate them from the larger folk society. Yet, it would be wrong to say that they were totally cut off from the masses. The fact that they were social reformers was enough to suggest their involvement with the people. They were also becoming aware of the alienating effect of English education; they did try to promote the vernacular languages in order to communicate their ideas. As a matter of fact, many of them were convinced that the vernacular was the only medium through which knowledge could be disseminated to the masses. For example, Rammohun's *Sambad Kaumudi*, Young Bengal's *Gyanaveshan*,

Keshub Sen's *Sulabh Samachar* and Dadabhai Naoroji's *Rast Goftar* were pioneering efforts in that direction. Perhaps the urge was to go beyond the 'Macaulayian system' and communicate with the larger society.

(v) There were intellectuals who were not always acutely aware of the antagonistic relationship between the British colonialism and the Indian society. Instead, at times, they expressed their deep faith in the British rule, in its ability to modernize and industrialize the country. In fact, England was often perceived as a great liberator. With its grand ideals of parliamentary democracy, civil liberties and modern economic development, it was hoped, England would civilize the rest of the world. No wonder, Keshub Chandra Sen once argued: "All the refined and liberal ideals of the West came to India through England"[52] and the British rule was, therefore, welcomed as the chosen instrument—a divine dispensation—to bring about a total change. But in the history of our intellectual traditions we also witness the sharp awareness of the exploitative character of the British rule. Even Tagore who was not always in agreement with Gandhi's vehement critique of modern Western civilization could not escape the experience of disillusionment with the West. What began to shock him, as he wrote in *Crisis in Civilization*, was the "utter and contemptuous indifference of a so-called civilized race to the well-being of scores of Indian people."[53] Tagore went deeper. He saw the spirit of violence in the psychology of the West. "I had at one time believed that the springs of civilization would issue out of the heart of Europe, but today when I am about to quit the world, the hope has gone bankrupt altogether."[54] Moreover, what was important was the presence of egalitarian ideals in the intellectual thought. Bankim's essay on *samyo* (equality), Vivekananda's socialist thoughts and Gandhi's egalitarian projects (or, to borrow Partha Chatterjee's words, Gandhi's ability to incorporate the peasantry—the largest popular element of the nation—in his politico-economic agenda[55]) created a refreshingly new ideal—an ideal to be explored and developed further.

III

Intellectuals and the Project of Modernity in Post-Independence India

With this brief historical background we can now come closer to our times and reflect on the ethos of the intellectual life in post-Independence India. The concerns (interplay of tradition and modernity, religion and science, culture and development) are not dead. And, at the same time, contemporary intellectuals, it seems, are endowed with a new agenda: how to retain freedom, bring order and unity, industrialize and modernize the country and strengthen the power of the nation-state.

In order to understand these concerns it is necessary to look at the mind of Jawaharlal Nehru (1889-1964). He, apart from being the first Prime Minister of Independent India, was an outstanding intellectual. Although his powerful presence was felt even in pre-Independence India, we wish to see him primarily as the leading intellectual mind of our age. Perhaps in his deeds and thoughts we can see the aspirations of a huge section of contemporary intellectuals: how to stabilize, modernize and strengthen the nation-state and take it to the path of development and progress.[56]

It would not be wrong to say that Nehru retained the heritage of Rammohun. Because he too wanted reason and science and relied heavily on the West to create a new agenda for the future. He was an intellectual passionately attached to the project of modernity. He believed that India must modernize herself, overcome her fixation to the past and enter the new era. He was future-oriented and a visionary. He disliked the glorification of the "golden" past. Because such a "foolish and dangerous pastime"[57] would take us nowhere; spiritual greatness could not be founded on starvation and misery. "India", he argued, "must break with much of her past, and not, allow it to dominate the present."[58] Therefore, his vision of modernity was essentially Western with its emphasis on industrialization, secularization and material well-being.

It is, therefore, not impossible to see an asymmetry between the minds of Nehru and Gandhi. Nehru respected Gandhi, relied on Gandhi. It was impossible to imagine Nehru without Gandhi. Yet, Nehru's rational/scientific mind (a mind that learned from Marx, Darwin and Freud) did not always feel comfortable with Gandhi—his critique of modernity, religious language, moral obsession and simplicity. "In spite of the closest association with him (Gandhi) for many years", wrote Nehru in his Autobiography, "I am not clear in my mind about his objective."[59] He did not hesitate to write that he had often felt angry with Gandhi at his "religious and sentimental approach to a political question and his frequent references to God in connection with it."[60] Not solely that. He was absolutely critical of Gandhi's *Hind Swaraj*. For him, it was "wholly at variance with modern ideas and conditions."[61] It was an "utterly wrong and harmful doctrine."[62] In *Hind Swaraj* his modern eyes could see nothing but "the praise of poverty and suffering and the ascetic life."[63] His goal was, therefore, clear: "We cannot stop the river of change or cut ourselves adrift from it, and psychologically we who have eaten of the apple of Eden cannot forget that taste and go back to primitiveness."[64]

This future-orientation or this urge to modernize the country did not mean that Nehru was free from ambiguities. Any careful reader of his Autobiography or *Discovery of India* knows that he, like a critical intellectual, was not willing to lose his openness and his enquiring spirit. He questioned even his cherished modernity and its ability to understand India.

> India was in my blood and there was much in her that instinctively thrilled me. And yet I approached her almost as an alien critic, full of dislike for the present as well as for many of the relics of the past that I saw. To some extent I came to her via the West, and looked at her as a friendly westerner might have done. I was eager and anxious to change her outlook and appearance and give her the garb of modernity. And yet doubts arose within me. Did I know India?...[65]

It was this doubt that led him to "discover" India. In this quest he saw the aliveness of India's tradition. At Sarnath near Benares he 'saw' the Buddha preaching his first sermon! He 'saw' the critical spirit in the Upanishads. He could still 'hear' that inspiring prayer: "Lead me from the unreal to the real, from darkness to light, from death to immortality!" In the *Bhagavad Gita* our lives, than to understand nothing at all."[70] Likewise, for him, secularism was important. Although he was not against spirituality, he was extremely critical of the ideological and institutional function of religion. A modern nation-state willing to undertake a progressive journey ought to be secular!

A "national philosophy" of this kind was needed for India's survival. Moreover, it was implicit in the "logic of history". As Parekh says,

> For Nehru then India both must and should modernise itself: 'must' because this was a historical necessity and the indispensable condition of its survival and economic development, 'should' because modernity represented a higher civilization. Within this historicist worldview, necessity and desirability, history and ethics tended to coincide. Modernization involved not just industrialization but also a secular, rationalist, humanist and scientific worldview and all that it implied.[71]

Nehru initiated a new agenda that indeed fascinated many modern intellectuals. In the Nehruvian vision they found an opportunity to make their presence felt, utilize their knowledge and come closer to the centre of power. It should not be forgotten that he took care of the intelligentsia, created many centres for learning—national science laboratories, institutes of technology, universities and research centres. He gave them the agenda: build up a new nation, modernize/industrialize the country, catch up with the 'developed' West, promote scientific temper! Moreover, for them, it was easier to identify with him—his English education, his strikingly visible modern outlook and his secular humanism. Perhaps, for them, Gandhi (his emphasis on manual labour, village-centred democracy and religiosity) was an obstacle to be overcome. In Nehru they found a new possibility, a breakthrough. We, therefore, seek to propose that in post-independence India no discussion on the role of intellectuals is likely to remain complete unless we realize the Nehruvian vision. Outlined below is a set of salient features that mark this intellectual trend.

(i) Here are the intellectuals who are indeed influenced by Nehru. They accept the inevitability and desirability of universal modernity and its industrial culture, its secular/

scientific ethos. This is not to suggest that all of them, as far as their political affiliations are concerned, belong to the Nehruvian camp. They may belong to divergent political groups. But what unites them is primarily the Nehruvian spirit—the spirit of Enlightenment, rationality and modernity. For example, there are leftists who may have their reservations about the effectiveness of the Nehruvian agenda. Yet, never do they fail to see some 'progressive' features of the Nehruvian project. The reason is that Marxism is also an assertion of Enlightenment/modernist thinking. It privileges reason, accepts science as the legitimate form of knowledge and believes in the linearity of historical progress. Moreover, as it can be argued, Nehru's nationalism was closely related to the Marxian project.[72] Nehru did share the Marxian belief that economic interests determine the behaviour and allegiances of classes; it led him to press the Congress to link the nationalist demand to the most pressing needs of the peasantry and the proletariat. True, it may be argued that Nehru's political ideology was merely a convenient or clever appropriation of Marxian ideas for non-Marxian purposes. It may also be argued that the Nehruvian socialism, because of its incompleteness, was not potent enough to deliver the goods to the people. Yet, what cannot be denied is the Marxian affinity with Nehru. After all, the Marxists as modernizers see in Nehru a turning-point, a departure from the dead weight of the past'. They see themselves primarily as educators whose task is to fight cultural prejudices, promote scientific temper, clarify issues, separate the 'real' problems namely, economic development and national unity from the 'unreal' ones, viz. caste, community and religion.

(ii) All of them do not necessarily belong to economically privileged classes. With the spread of education and the gradual democratization of society, intellectuals are being recruited from almost all classes. Yet, it is not difficult to identify their largely urban or middle class origin. As the sociology of higher education reveals its predominantly Western orientation, it can be said that these intellectuals are more habituated to the discourses emanating from the West.

(iii) Broadly speaking, they belong to India's prestigious centres for learning—colleges, universities, national laboratories and research institutes. They are professors, scientists, artists, journalists and activists. They are not without their political affiliations. Nevertheless, many of them have succeeded in retaining an identity of their own.

(iv) The intellectuals of the kind we are talking about continue to exist and assert the relevance of their agenda. In our times they often remind us of the desirability of the Nehruvian ideal, its ability to rescue India from the twin 'vices' of economic liberalization and religious fundamentalism. One is often reminded—and reminded even by the leftists—of the Nehruvian ideal of socialism, autonomy of the state and significance of the public sector. Likewise, Nehru's secular and scientific temper, the intellectuals tell us, ought to be seen as an inspiration, a way out from the growing communalization of politics. In other words, for the leftists, secularists and modernists (and they constitute a significant section of the intelligentsia) there is no escape from the Nehru nostalgia!

A major reason behind the popularity of Nehru amongst the intellectuals is that they continue to feel that the agenda he initiated —promoting secular humanism to fight cultural prejudices—has not yet exhausted its possibilities. Not just economists and scientists, but even the intellectuals in the cultural domain tend to accept the grand ideal of modernity. As random examples, we will talk about two films (we are talking about cinema because it is a powerful medium that fascinates many intellectual minds) to make our point. To begin with, a look at Satyajit Ray's *Ganashatru*—a film based on Ibsen's *Enemy of the People*. It is a film in which Ray speaks of the language of reason. A rational and enlightened doctor seems determined to fight the pathologies of institutionalized religion, the way it promotes ignorance and superstitions. Ray, it seems, wants us to see the light of reason. His doctor—the central character he portrays in his film—is doing a job which Nehru wanted every rational Indian to perform. Likewise, *Parama*—a film made by Aparna Sen—depicts the story of another kind of emancipation. Aparna Sen speaks of a woman emancipating herself from the 'traditional' role—the role of an 'ideal' Hindu wife and mother. A new woman is born; she realizes herself as a person. In other words, she debunks the traditional notion of womanhood. Both Ray and Sen, in a way, convey the Nehruvian message: much of our tradition ought to be overcome in order to celebrate modernity. These two films are just examples that tell us how many of our cultural intellectuals are essentially modernists eager to teach, awaken and enlighten their countrymen!

Not all intellectuals are, however, Nehruvian in spirit. The reasons are diverse and many. To begin with, as we have been witnessing, left, secular or progressive intellectuals are often criticized for their supposedly 'Western' views, their irreligiosity and their unwillingness to understand the cultural aspirations of the dominant Hindu community. The Nehruvians have been condemned as "pseudo-secular", or alien outsiders. As militant, Hindutva asserts itself, it finds its own ideologues, intellectuals and theoreticians. Their project is different from that of Nehru. They seek to rewrite history; they do not want to forget the 'glorious' Hindu tradition. For them, cultural tradition is more important than secular or scientific temper!

These 'rightists' or 'fundamentalists' do not get much intellectual recognition or respect from the Nehruvian intellectuals —the intellectuals whose voices are heard in almost all prestigious centres for learning. Because it is argued that they think and read less, but talk more. They are not 'objective', they are merely ideological. Their intentions are duious!

But, then, there are others whose intellectual worth can by no means be negated. It is from them that the Nehruvians are finding the real challenge. In our times one such challenge has come from the historians known primarily for their "subaltern" approach. The adherents of this approach would argue that the Nehruvian project is a clear case of "bourgeois/nationalist elitism."[73] What is, therefore, needed is to rescue the reading of Indian history from the dominance of this elitism. Ranjit Guha, the chief proponent of the subaltern school, speaks of the "poverty" of this bourgeois/nationalist historiography for it gives no space to the "autonomous domain" of the "politics of the people" According to Guha, it "fails to acknowledge, far less interpret, the contribution made by the people on their own, that is, independently of the elite to making and development of this nationalism."[74] In other words, we ought to realize the "failure of the Indian bourgeoisie to speak for the nation."[75] One knows that the subaltern historiography concentrates on the history of colonial India. Yet, its implications for our times are obvious as can be discerned from the points given below:

(i) The Nehruvian project of nation-building is suspected because subaltern people—peasants, tribals, oppressed castes —are not the authors of this project. Instead, it is expected to be performed by the professional elites, scientists, technologists, experts and English-educated intellectuals. This subaltern awakening can be seen in the assertion of the Dalits and the marginalized castes in India. As they overcome their silence and regain their agency, they critique the 'elitist/paternalistic' character of the nationalist project. This criticality can be seen in the emergent intellectual tradition as articulated by the scholars like Gail Omvedt, Kancha Ilaiah and G. Aloysius.[76]

(ii) This means an appeal to the intellectuals to come out of their enclaves to realize that those whom they want to teach, civilize and educate—subaltern masses—are also the active agents and "subjects of their own histories."[77] In fact, the environment that gave birth to the subaltern school of thought ought to be understood. It was in the late *sixties and early* seventies that we saw the emergence of the critical Left not happy with the existing communist states and orthodoxies. Instead, it was more sensitive to the outburst of Marxist-influenced peasant and tribal insurgencies in India. It was essentially an attempt to recover the hitherto absent voices. This Marxist influence notwithstanding, it should not be forgotten that the subaltern school was also undergoing a process of change. For example, it is possible to see the influence of post-modernism in the writings of contemporary subaltern scholars. Because they suspect modernity and its Enlightenment rationality. Not solely that. Instead of universal histories, they talk about the histories of fragments.[78]

This subaltern approach can be seen in divergent contexts:

militant leftists organizing the tribals and peasants for their rights or post-modernists working among the Dalits, women and minorities and retaining the autonomy of the domains of their struggle. As a matter of fact, the intellectual challenge of this kind comes as a severe blow to the monologue of the elites, even if they appear to speak a 'progressive' language!

A major component of the Nehruvian project of nation-building is science. Nehru put great emphasis on 'scientific temper'. He imagined a new India technologizing and modernizing herself. What is, however, interesting is that we are now witnessing a new intellectual current that challenges this modernity, debunks the politics of science and sees great wisdom in alternate traditions prevalent among non-modern, peripheralized Indians. Perhaps in Ashis Nandy's writings, this voice—the critique of modernity—asserts itself rather sharply. He tells us about the damage that colonialism did to our psyche, how its `secular hierarchies' (the human over the non-human and the sub-human, the masculine over the feminine, the adult over the child, the historical over the ahistorical, and the modern or progressive over the traditional or the savage[79]), its ideals of development and progress wounded our self-pride, how we internalized the West and sought to speak in the language of the colonial master. But then, Nandy speaks not simply of the loss of self; he also speaks of its recovery. We are asked to realize how, for example, Gandhi was gifted with an alternative agenda—the way he fought all `imperial categories', saw enormous possibilities in what the mighty West regarded as `weak', how he feminized the political sphere, rescued the notion of courage from the West's `hypermasculinity' and sought to emancipate the colonizers as well as the colonized. Nandy has been writing consistently about the discontents of modernity, the way it celebrates the rationale of domination and violence. Unlike modern/secular/progressive intellectuals who perpetually condemn people's superstitions and teach them the elementary lessons of science and reason, Nandy wants the modernists to look at themselves, see the pathologies of their projects, the way in the name of science, development and nationalism, people have been tortured and killed. It is in this context that Nandy says that science has become a "new reason of state'.[80] It is seen as "spectacular technology"[81] —something that can cure all ills! Not surprisingly, science legitimates the domination of the elites—the elites who run the Indian state and evolve an "instrumental-managerial" orientation towards Indian society. The danger is that science becomes a new religion because everything is justified in its name, and it can't be opposed! This certainly goes against the "culture of open politics". The task is, therefore, the "repoliticization of science"—the political audit of science by those outside the estate of science and by its victims.[82] The message Nandy conveys is clear. He wants to deprive the modernists of their cognitive privilege. He is for the recovery of all that has been lost because of the ruthlessness of science and technology. He wants our intellectuals not to be seduced by science and modernity, but to listen to the emancipatory voices of the victimized, the marginalized and the silenced.

A critique of this kind is gradually becoming popular. These days we are hearing a new intellectual voice—a voice which, for example, sees great possibilities in the Chipko movement (a movement initiated by the Himalayan peasantry towards forest protection), a voice which, at the same time, tells us to learn the necessary lesson from the gas leak at Bhopal—the dark side of modern technology. We are indeed witnessing the growth of new intellectuals sympathizing with hundreds of grass roots groups involved in environmental issues. They are supporting the movements against deforestation, against the construction of big dams, against a model of development that is inherently violent and ecologically insensitive. As a matter of fact, in this new intellectual voice one sees a departure from the Nehruvian paradigm of development and modernity. Ramachandra Guha helps us to understand this departure.[83] Generally speaking, as Guha says, economists and social scientists have not shown much interest in the environmental debate in India. Perhaps they might have feared that any task of ecological constraints to economic activity would be seen as a deviation from the primary task of rapid industrialization. The intellectual climate of Independent India, argues Guha, has been marked, in the main, by a profound indifference to human interactions with the natural environment. Things are, however, changing. There is a growing awareness of what Guha calls "social ecology" —a new sensitivity that imagines a harmonic relationship between man and nature, economy, culture and environment.

All this suggests that among the intellectuals there is a renewed interest in Gandhi. Perhaps the intellectuals we are talking about are rediscovering Gandhi. They, it seems,are eager to learn some important lessons from his world views in order to evolve a critique of the prevalent notion of modernity and development. In fact, in the intellectual domain an interesting debate is taking place between the Nehruvians (or even the leftists) and the neo-Gandhians. The debate is centred on modernity, development, culture, religion and social movements.

It is in this context that one understands the emergence of a large number of action groups working at the grass roots among the tribals, rural and urban poor, Dalits, women and similar other disadvantaged groups which have indeed succeeded in inviting many middle class intellectuals. It is not uncommon to see these intellectuals verbalizing the grievances of the marginalized sections of society. A sociological look at this phenomenon reveals the failure of the prevalent mode of development, its biases, its unevenness, its inability to alleviate the sufferings of the poor. It also reveals the failure of the state machinery and the mainstream political parties which are obsessed with the election arithmetic, to communicate with the people and understand their local or specific needs and aspirations. Not surprisingly, these groups tend to operate outside the institutional framework of both the government and established political parties.

Rajni Kothari articulates the intellectual philosophy beneath the rise of these grass roots movements. For Kothari, it is an attempt at "redefinition of politics".[84] At a time when the "erosion of democratic institutions and values" is complete, when the state, because of its obsession with "technological modernization", fails to cope with the needs and aspirations of the poor, what is needed is a new politics—a politics that would "kindle faith and energy in anti-establishment forces." Kothari sees emancipatory possibilities in these movements. Not solely that. These movements are also coping with the so-called "unpolitical" domain—culture, gender, age, technology, ecology, health, nutrition, education and pedagogy.

As Kothari says, the challenge is to create a "viable state and a democratic social order."[85]

One thing is clear that in these grass roots movements one is witnessing the birth of a new intellectual—an intellectual who reminds us of the Gandhian message. What are the qualities of this intellectual? He is not a 'professional' intellectual using his knowledge to establish his domination. He is not one of those who, in the name of 'scientific planning', reduce a large section of mankind into objects of experimentation. He is coming out of his enclave, trying to overcome the barriers of distance, centralization and expertized knowledge. He is continually listening to the people and collectively striving for a new practice. Kothari too, it seems, is eager to celebrate the arrival of this new intellectual, his engagement with the world, his "deprofessionalized cognitive role"[86] in order to make the transformation possible—"from government of humans to humane governance." Kothari's intellectuals, therefore, identify with "the victims of history"; they are "moved by passion and commitment".[87]

It is now possible for us to make the following four observations:

(i) The intellectuals in the pre-Independence era were largely social reformers and activists. In the process of the anti-colonial struggle for liberation they were perpetually reflecting on the destiny of India, her identity, her engagement with tradition and modernity, science and religion. These concerns have not died even after Independence. But now the intellectuals are also engaged in a more difficult task: how to strengthen the power of the nation-state and take it to the path of technological modernization. It is in this context that the Nehruvian philosophy helps us to understand the new role assigned to the intellectuals. And unlike the kind of social reformers many of these intellectuals are essentially professionals—economists and social scientists, technologists, artists and journalists—located in different institutes and centres for learning.

(ii) It is not that these professional intellectuals are indifferent to social reform and change. They take up issues like secularism against communalism, scientific temper against religious superstition, and invariably engage themselves in the task of social reconstruction. Moreover, as advisers and policy makers, planners and teachers they give a direction to the agenda of the nation-state. Yet, what should not be forgotten is that many of them are 'professional' in the sense that they are not very closely and directly involved with any socio-political movement. They love to operate from their own specialized institutes and centres for learning. Perhaps it is this distance owing to their professionalized behaviour, their technical idioms and the exclusivist character of the intellectual circle, that makes it difficult for them to emerge as authentic communicators, and come closer to the people, their immense sufferings and struggles, hopes and aspirations.

(iii) What is, however, striking about the intellectual tradition in contemporary India is that there is a renewed interest in Gandhi. True, there is also a critique of Gandhi in the new intellectual tradition. For example, Dalit intellectuals or subaltern historians like Ranjit Guha may not feel very comfortable with Gandhi. In Gandhi they may see a religious/bourgeois paradigm defined by caste Hindus. But then, what is striking is that there are many who have been influenced by Gandhi's radicalized self: his critique of techno-economic modernity and his sensitivity to the voices of the people. The rediscovery of Gandhi has led to the birth of new intellectuals—not just professionals, but activists involved in innumerable grass roots movements and taking up the issues the Nehruvians are not necessarily comfortable with—discontents of modernity, limits to growth, ecological and cultural struggles, decentralization and diffusion of power.

(iv) What can be said about the class character of the intellectuals? Ashok Rudra, for instance, would argue that the intelligentsia in India has been coopted and bought up by the two dominant ruling classes: industrial capitalists and big landlords.[88] As a result, the intelligentsia itself has become a third ruling class. These "manufacturers of ideology", according to Rudra, perform the functions that, in the ultimate analysis, serve the interests of these three ruling classes. Rudra's observations are not likely to be shared by all. Well, it is true that there are intellectuals (big scientists and technocrats, media celebrities and mega professors) who continue to get huge benefits from the system and remind us of Rudra's apprehensions. But there are limits to this generalization. There are intellectuals who do try to come out of their privileged circuits and the functions they seek to perform (like working among the marginalized sections of society and evolving a critique of the prevalent mode of development) are not conducive to the interests of the ruling classes. Moreover, there are intellectuals who, despite the 'benefit' they get from the system, retain their criticality and reflexivity. They may not be revolutionaries, but they are not necessarily conformists.

IV

Need for Self-Introspection

This brief, yet meaningful, reflection on our intellectual traditions suggests divergent possibilities. In fact, an awareness of our intellectual traditions would be of great help in order to make sense of the debates which are taking place in Indian social thought. These traditions provide the background that enables us to throw light on the emergent social reality in India. It is, therefore, important that intellectual traditions evolve, grow, prosper and, irrespective of internal differences, retain a set of ideals that we have already identified. But then, there are obstacles—the obstacles rooted in our own times—that seek to hamper the growth of the proper intellectual climate.

Commercialization of life

A look at the changing cultural climate shows that what one witnesses all around is a purely instrumental orientation towards life and this is what is affecting the mind of the middle class. This instrumentality. goes against what an intellectual climate needs—one's urge to go beyond merely practical or mundane interests and dedicate oneself to a serious enquiry into life's profound questions. Imagine the way this instrumentality is dictating one's career choices. These days there is an obsession with the careers that give immediate visibility, glamour and material success—computer, management and advertising. It is indeed sad to see that the youth who are performing well in their schools and colleges do not show much interest in teaching or research. It doesn't require any statistical evidence to tell that many of them do not want to become intellectuals, instead strive for professions as corporate executives or bureaucrats. Not surprisingly, a negative meaning is attached to the domain of thought and reflection. Anyone familiar with Indian colleges and universities knows how all sorts of serious enquiry are fast disappearing, why there is utter cynicism and despair amongst the students and the faculty regarding the intellectual climate. Perhaps the most damaging thing is that many of them who are still engaged in teaching or research do not have a positive attitude towards themselves. It is, therefore, hardly surprising that not many teachers are left who can encourage their students to take up an intellectual vocation.

This scenario ought to be altered if we need a healthy intellectual climate. For the intellectuals, it is important to realize the worth of what they ought to do. They must not allow themselves to be defeated by the prevalent instrumentality and commercialization of life. They need the power to see the hollowness of what is seen as practical, gorgeous or glamorous. Perhaps this requires a sort of spiritualization—an orientation, a faith, a conviction.[89]

Institutions in crisis

It is believed that political parties and universities are two important sources of intellectual thought. Both these institutions are, however, in crisis. To begin with, let us reflect on the state of the existing political parties. Enough has already been written about the erosion of political culture—the way political parties, because of their obsession with vote banks and immediate gain, fail to evolve an ideology, a world view, a coherent thought pattern. Gone are the days when one could see a Gandhi or a Nehru, a M.N. Roy or an Ambedkar relating politics to serious thinking. Gone are the days when one could see the cadres/comrades learning important lessons of economy and culture from the study circles. Even when exceptions exist in some radical organizations, the fact remains that the politician of today is not expected to be a thinker or a philosopher; his/her only task, it appears, is to manipulate and come to power at any cost. None expects works like *Hind Swaraj* or *Glimpses of World History* from contemporary politicians.

Things are not really better in colleges and universities for India lives in two worlds. While there are some prestigious colleges and universities, most of our centres for learning fail to create an environment needed for the development of intellectual tradition.[90] These overcrowded colleges and universities, together with the lack of funds and resources and disinterested students and teachers, look like factories distributing degrees and diplomas. Serious teachers and researchers still exist. They are, however, demoralized and discouraged. Moreover, metropolitan intellectuals are not particularly eager to initiate a dialogue with local intellectuals. As a result, their possibilities remain unexplored.

Things are not so good even in the so-called centres of excellence. Administrative interference and bureaucratization destroy a free and egalitarian milieu needed for a healthy intellectual tradition. Moreover, if privatization becomes the order of the day, it would affect and distort the intellectual climate. 'Meaningful' knowledge would be defined in terms of its marketability, its functional relationship with the needs of the industry!

And herein lies the challenge. The intellectuals we are imagining ought to acquire the strength to fight these distortions. It is for them to speak the language of sanity with courage and confidence, even when madness is all-pervasive.

Pathology of privilege

Not all intellectuals have got an equal access to the centre of power. Metropolitan intellectuals—scientists, economists, academicians, artists and journalists located in prestigious institutes of learning and communication—are relatively more privileged than innumerable local intellectuals. They are often consulted by the state and other agencies. They get more media coverage and have got more publications, more tangible projects, foreign trips and positions to demonstrate their intellectual worth. It is this privilege which may prove to be an obstacle to the path of an emancipatory intellectual tradition.

Privilege causes arrogance. Metropolitan intellectuals tend to look at local intellectuals with contempt. Far from sharing their experiences and understanding the miserable conditions under which they work, metropolitan intellectuals are more eager to 'advise' and 'educate' and retain the hierarchy. Barring a few remarkable exceptions, academic intellectuals from, say, the Delhi School of Economics or the Jawaharlal Nehru University feel themselves superior to those teaching in unknown colleges and universities. It is unlikely that these privileged intellectuals would prefer any egalitarian ideal.

This is a strange situation in which metropolitan intellectuals do not like to associate themselves with local intellectuals. They are, however, over-enthusiastic, as far as their association with Euro-American intellectuals is concerned. One knows how our professors do not want to lose any opportunity to visit abroad. One knows how they seek to study even specifically Indian problems—caste, communalism, poverty and unemployment—from Euro-American universities. Everyone engaged in the academic/intellectual milieu is asked: 'Have you been abroad?' In other words, for everything, be it the journals in which they want to publish or the 'contacts' they seek to cultivate for academic interactions, our metropolitan intellectuals remain pathetically dependent on the West. Only the naive would believe that this sort of dependence promotes an egalitarian intellectual tradition.

This also explains how ordinary people look at metropolitan intellectuals. They are often seen as opportunists with no coherence between what they say and what they do. Their 'radicalism', it is thought, is essentially a package portrayed in the form of a book or a research paper!

Such situations require to be altered. We need a new intellectual climate. Metropolitan or privileged intellectuals must undergo a process of self-introspection. Undue privilege, they must realize, is an enemy of freedom and honesty. They must realize that concrete life-practices are no less important than what they write in their books and research papers. They must also realize that dialogue is the essence of a healthy intellectual climate and the possibilities are alive not solely in the metropolis but also in the periphery.

Language that alienates

Another difficulty arises out of a temptation many intellectuals find difficult to resist of writing in a language that, far from bringing any clarity, further mystifies, conceals and hides the issue. This kind of writing is justified in terms of the 'complexity' of thought or the 'inevitability' of technical language or jargon. Granted, some theories are complex and simplification may lead to trivialization. Granted also that not everything can be expressed in ordinary language and technical concepts have their functions. Yet, for those writing on culture, polity, society and economy, it is not altogether impossible to write in a language that makes sense to the larger audience. After all, we have seen philosophers and thinkers arousing our collective imagination without simplifying or trivializing the essence of what they communicate. Imagine the intellectuals like Vivekananda, Gandhi, and Nehru and their communicative skills!

We do not need intellectuals who talk only among themselves and who derive pleasure in their isolation and complex writings, who seek to silence people by bombarding them with their bad prose. The intellectuals of our imagination are those who do not feel ashamed of their simplicity (simplicity is strength, not naivety) and honesty, who do not mind expressing themselves in whatever reaches the people, be it a newspaper or a little magazine or a broader politico-cultural forum.

Narrow specialization and its limits

Narrow specialization is yet another obstacle. There are specialists/experts who find it difficult to reflect on and relate to the issues of wider public interest. This is damaging for three reasons. First, it deprives one of the language. One needs to overcome the barriers of one's narrowly specialized area of interest and evolve an integral and holistic approach to thinking and action. Second, it legitimates one's irresponsibility, one's silence, one's indifference to the issues of public interest. For example, it is not uncommon to find many academic intellectuals arguing like this: "Gender is not my area. I, therefore, cannot say or do anything about the injustice done to women. Or, I have not done any research on social equality. So I cannot say anything about the desirability or undesirability of reservation". Third, as a result of all this, it kills the humanistic spirit of knowledge. It kills involvement and passion. As the specialists/experts isolate themselves, no communication is possible. There is no shared language, no public forum. There is no dialogue. Our ideals are different. One may have a special interest in a particular branch of knowledge. But an intellectual is one who despite this special interest, is in a position to widen his horizon and relate to and participate in the issues of wider public interest. It is easy to become a specialist. It is difficult to emerge as a communicator or an intellectual.

In this chapter, we have analysed how the intellectuals participated and are participating in the debates on tradition, modernity and nation-building. A look at these discourses has also helped us to examine the nature of their criticality, dialogic/communicative spirit and the degree of their organic relationship with the larger collective. We have also identified a set of obstacles to be overcome. In fact, there is no escape from continual self-introspection. It is this perpetual quest, critical spirit and reflexivity which would strengthen the intellectual tradition and take us to a world in which every act of communication is an act of emancipation, a world in which we learn to appreciate the meanings of tradition and modernity, science and religion and relate meaningfully to the past, present and future.

A healthy intellectual tradition, it should not be forgotten, is the fundamental prerequisite for the development of critical/humanistic consciousness we need to reflect on the destiny of modern India. The insights we have gained, particularly, the complexity of the nature of Indian responses to modernity, would help us to understand more meaningfully what the remaining part of the book is all about—secularism, gender, culture and social reconstruction.

NOTES

1. See, for example, Edward Shils, *The Intellectuals and the Powers and Other Essays* (Chicago : University of Chicago Press, 1972).
2. Antonio Gramsci, *Selections from the Prison Notebooks* (London: Lawrence and Wishart, 1971), p. 9.

3. Zygmunt Bauman, *Legislators and Interpreters: On Modernity, Post-Modernity and Intellectuals* (Cambridge: Polity Press, 1987).
4. Paulo Freire, *Pedagogy of the Oppressed* (Penguin Books, 1972), p. 65.
5. Gramsci, *op. cit.*, p. 10.
6. Karl Mannheim, *Ideology and Utopia: An Introduction to the Sociology of Knowledge* (London : Routledge and Kegan Paul, 1960), pp. 136-46.
7. *Ibid.*, p. 139.
8. *Ibid.*
9. Shils, *op. cit.*, p. 13.
10. Gramsci, *op. cit.*, p. 3.
11. *Ibid.*, p. 12.
12. *Ibid.*, p. 7.
13. Here what is important to recall is Marx's Eleventh Thesis on Feuerbach. Marx wrote: "The philosophers have only interpreted the world in various ways; the point is to change it". Karl Marx, *Theses on Feuerbach* in Marx and Engels, *The German Ideology* (Moscow: Progress Publishers, 1976), p. 617.
14. K.N. Panikkar, *Culture, Ideology, Hegemony: Intellectuals and Social Consciousness in Colonial India* (New Delhi, Tulika, 1995), pp. 8-9.
15. Quoted in Susobhan Sarkar, *On the Bengal Renaissance* (Calcutta: Papyrus, 1979), p. 16.
16. Quoted in Sumit Sarkar, *A Critique of Colonial India* (Calcutta: Papyrus, 1985), p. 3.
17. Quoted in Susobhan Sarkar, *op. cit.*, p. 80.
18. *Ibid.*, p. 82.
19. *Ibid.*, p. 79.
20. *Ibid.*, p. 77.
21. *Ibid.*, p. 101.
22. *Ibid.*, p. 103
23. Sumit Sarkar, *op. cit.*, p. 1.
24. *Ibid.*, p. 7.
25. *Ibid.*, p. 8.
26. *Ibid.*, p. 1.
27. Quoted in Partha Chatterjee, *Nationalist Thought and the Colonial World: A Derivative Discourse* (Delhi: Oxford University Press, 1986), p. 57.
28. *Ibid.*
29. *Ibid.*
30. Quoted in Tapan Raychaudhuri, *Three Views of Europe from Nineteenth Century Bengal* (Calcutta: K.P. Bagchi and Company, 1987), p. 14.
31. Chatterjee, *op. cit.*, p. 70.
32. Raychaudhuri, *op. cit.*, p. 17.

33. Swami Vivekananda, "The Mission of the Vedanta" in *The Complete Works of Swami Vivekananda*, Vol. III (Calcutta: Advaita Ashrama, 1991), p. 190.
34. *Ibid.*
35. Swami Vivekananda, "Vedanta in its Application to Indian Life" in *The Complete Works of Swami Vivekananda*, Vol. III, p. 243.
36. Swami Vivekananda, "The Common Bases of Hinduism" in *The Complete Works of Swami Vivekananda*, Vol. III, p. 370.
37. *Ibid.*, p. 380.
38. Swami Vivekananda, "The Work Before Us" in *The Complete Works of Swami Vivekananda*, Vol. III, p. 274.
39. K.N. Panikkar, "The Intellectual History of Colonial India: Some Historiographical and Conceptual Questions" in Sabyasachi Bhattacharya and Romila Thapar (eds.), *Situating Indian History* (Delhi: Oxford University Press, 1986), pp. 403-33.
40. Sri Aurobindo, *The Foundations of Indian Culture* (Pondicherry: Sri Aurobindo Ashram, 1959).
41. This statistical data has been collected from Sumit Sarkar, *Modern India: 1885-1947* (Madras: Macmillan, 1983), p. 65.
42. Quoted in A.R. Desai, *Social Background of Indian Nationalism* (Bombay: Popular Prakashan, 1982), p. 321.
43. M.K. Gandhi, *Hind Swaraj or Indian Home Rule* (Ahmedabad: Navajivan Publishing House, 1938), p. 55.
44. *Ibid.*, p. 53.
45. M.K. Gandhi, *An Autobiography of The Story of My Experiments with Truth* (Ahmedabad: Navajivan Publishing House, 1927), pp. 29-30.
46. *Ibid.*, pp. 295-96.
47. Bhikhu Parekh, *Colonialism, Tradition and Reform: An Analysis of Gandhi's Political Discourse* (New Delhi: Sage Publications, 1989).
48. Gandhi, *An Autobiography*, p. 383.
49. S.A. Dange, "Gandhi vs Lenin" in his *Selected Writings*: Vol. I (Combay: Lok Vangmaya Griha, 1974).
50. Parekh, *op. cit.*, Ch. 2, pp. 34-70.
51. Ashish Nandy, *The Intimate Enemy: Loss and Recovery of Self under Colonialism* (Delhi: Oxford University Press, 1983).
52. Quoted in K.N. Panikkar, *Culture, Ideology, Hegemony*, p. 22.
53. Rabindranath Tagore, *Crisis in Civilization* (Bombay: International Book House, 1941), p. 5.
54. *Ibid.*, p. 10.
55. Chatterjee, *op. cit.*, p. 100.
56. *My Discontents of a Culture* (Calcutta: Writers Workshop, 1988), pp. 38-42.

57. Jawaharlal Nehru, *The Discovery of India* (New Delhi: Jawaharlal Nehru Memorial Fund, 1983), p. 81.
58. *Ibid.*, p. 509.
59. Jawaharlal Nehru, *An Autobiography* (New Delhi: Jawaharlal Nehru Memorial Fund, 1984), p. 509.
60. *Ibid.*, p. 370.
61. *Ibid.*, p. 510.
62. *Ibid.*
63. *Ibid.*
64. *Ibid.*, p. 511.
65. Nehru, *The Discovery of India*, p. 50.
66. *Ibid.*, p. 110.
67. Nehru, *An Autobiography*, p. 406.
68. Bhikhu Parekh, "Nehru and the National Philosophy of India", *Economic and Political Weekly* (January, 5-12, 1991), pp. 35-47.
69. Nehru, *The Discovery of India*, p. 512.
70. *Ibid.*
71. Parekh, "Nehru and the National Philosophy of India", p. 46. Also see his "Jawaharlal Nehru and the Crisis of Modernisation" in Upendra Baxi and Bhikhu Parekh (eds.), *Crisis and Change in Contemporary India* (New Delhi: Sage Publications, 1995), pp. 21-56.
72. For further elaboration, see Sanjay Sethi, *Marxist Theory and National Politics: The Case of Colonial India* (New Delhi: Sage, 1995), especially, Ch. 6.
73. Ranjit Guha, "On Some Aspects of the Historiography of Colonial India" in Ranjit Guha (ed.), *Subaltern Studies I: Writings on South Asian History and Society* (Delhi: Oxford University Press, 1982), pp. 1-7. Also see his "Dominance Without Hegemony and its Historiography" in Ranjit Guha (ed.), *Subaltern Studies VI* (Delhi: Oxford University Press, 1989), pp. 210-309.
74. Guha "On Some Aspects", p. 3.
75. *Ibid.*, p. 5.
76. See Gail Omvedt, *Dalits and the Democratic Revolution: Dr Ambedkar and the Dalit Movement in Colonial India* (New Delhi: Sage, 1994); Kancha Ilaiah, *Why I am not a Hindu: A Sudra Critique of Hindutva Philosophy, Culture and Political Economy* (Calcutta: Samya, 1996); G. Aloysius, *Nationalism without a Nation in India* (New Delhi: Oxford, 1997).
77. Veena Das, "Subaltern as Perspective" in Ranjit Guha (ed.), *Subaltern Studies VI* (Delhi: Oxford University Press, 1989), pp. 310-24.
78. Partha Chatterjee, *The Nation and Its Fragments: Colonial and Post-Colonial History* (New Delhi: Oxford, 1994).

79. Ashis Nandy, *The Intimate Enemy*, p. X.
80. Ashish Nandy, "Science as Reason of State" in Ashish Nandy (ed.), *Science, Hegemony and Violence: A Requiem for Modernity* (Delhi: Oxford University Press, 1988), p. 10.
81. *Ibid.*, p. 7.
82. *Ibid.*, p. 11.
83. Ramachandra Guha (ed), *Social Ecology* (Delhi: Oxford University Press, 1994).
84. Rajni Kothari, *State Against Democracy: In Search of Humane Governance* (Delhi: Ajanta Publications, 1988), p. 46.
85. *Ibid.*, p. 109.
86. *Ibid.*, p. 13.
87. *Ibid.*
88. Ashok Rudra, "Emergence of the Intelligentsia as a Ruling Class in India", *Economic and Political Weekly* (January 21, 1989), pp. 142-50.
89. Avijit Pathak, "On Teachers and Teaching: Reflections on Existing Pedagogical Practices" (*Mainstream*, April 19, 1994).
90. Romila Thapar, "The Academic Professional", *Seminar* (No. 222, February, 1978), pp. 18-23.

TWO

Limits to Secular Modernity: Religiosity and its Possibilities

Modernity continues to make the intellectuals think and reflect. Its promises are tempting. Yet, there is also an acute anxiety that the experiences of modernity are painful. Culture suffers, religiosity declines and, because of the global ambitions of modernity, there is a challenge to the uniqueness/specificity of our cultural identity. Indeed, the complexity of the intellectual response (with all its tensions, ambiguities and reactions) is likely to be reflected here. Because here we propose to talk about secularism and religion—something that invariably reminds us of the promises and anxieties involved in the process of modernization of a traditional society.

It is true that secularism as an ideal has always fascinated the liberals, modernists and socialists. Because, in this ideal, as it is thought, lies the vision of a new society: a society modernizing itself, overcoming many traditional fixations and embracing the age of reason. It is, of course, true that not every proponent of secularism is hostile to religion—the major component of a traditional society. There are many, particularly in India, who do not necessarily equate secularism with atheism, who would not mind, for instance, one's 'privatized' religion. This 'tolerance' notwithstanding, the fact remains that there is always a possibility of broken/distorted communication between the secularists and the believers. Secularism, particularly its militant brand, derives its strength from science—the most dominant and successful ideology of our times.[1] This cognitive power explains why many militant secularists look at man's religiosity with utter indifference and contempt. The consequences of this broken communication are disastrous. To begin with, because of excessive zeal for secularization, not many progressives are willing to understand the emancipatory ideals of religion. Likewise, there are zealots who utilize men's religious sentiments and seek to destroy the gains of positive secularism. It is in this context that this chapter acquires its relevance. It seeks to examine the possibility of religion in a world in which, as it is argued, there is no escape from secularization. The chapter, therefore, raises some theoretical/philosophical questions relating to science, modernity and secularism and the issues like life and death, finite and infinite, faith and transcendence.

I

Soft Secularism and its Gains

To begin with, it is necessary to reflect on secularism—the way its adherents justify its desirability without, however, denying religion or insulting the sentiments of the believers. This positive notion of secularism (we call it positive because it affirms more, negates less) is likely to reveal why even those who are by no means atheists (or extreme modernists with 'scientific temper') tend to give their consent to it. There are primarily three constituents of this loose, tolerant and soft brand of secularism.

Harmony in a plural society

Without secularism, it is argued, there is no way one can retain order in a plural society. Because beneath it lies a notion of justice that is inherently universal, that rescues man from the boundaries of religious traditions. Secularism does not permit differences (in terms of one's politico-economic rights) based on one's religious identity. It tends to arrive at a common universal point without which pluralism is likely to degenerate into mutually exclusive forms of life' perpetually engaged in conflict and war. In other words, in a plural society the antithesis of secularism is communalism—a pathological situation in which the majority community denies the right of the other groups to exist. Divergent religious communities can coexist only when there is a consensus, a shared practice, a way of seeing that asserts fundamental unity amidst differences. And secularism promises all that. It does not deny plurality; it promises harmony. It is this moral implication of secularism that fascinates many, particularly those who by no means want to hurt the minority communities. Far from being seen as anti-religious, it is regarded as a principle of harmony and togetherness, a peaceful way of coexistence. In fact, there is a close affinity between this positive meaning of secularism and the profound spiritual truth of oneness!

Growth of modern knowledge systems

Secularism, it is believed, widens man's horizon and brings about a kind of 'true consciousness'. Because it asserts very forcefully that there are problems which are by no means religion-specific and whose solutions require a collective endeavour that overcomes religious differences. There is an element of objectivity in hunger, malnutrition, poverty and disease because man's religious identity does not increase or reduce it. It is this awareness of trans-religious problems that helps to produce modern knowledge systems, viz., science, medicine, technology, etc. In other words, the success of secularism is that it separates this public/objective/universal domain of knowledge from one's religious beliefs and practices. In this context the appeal of secularism is both moral and practical. It is moral because in the public sphere man is more than his caste, creed and religion. It is practical because the realization of this universality promotes modern knowledge systems. It is in this context that Professor Andre Beteille's arguments in favour of secular institutions—universities, laboratories, hospitals, banks—become relevant.[2] He is certainly not a militant secularist. He believes that "no scientific or secular reasoning can displace religion from its pre-eminent domain of ideas."[3] Yet, he is in favour of secular institutions free from religious influences. Even those academics who are otherwise critical of secularism, Beteille insists, would not disapprove of the relevance of secular institutions.

Balancing the twin spheres

Another appeal of secularism is that it rescues politics from religion. Here the anxiety is that if religion is allowed to mingle with politics, it would create a conflict-ridden society and politico-economic problems would be reduced into communal categories. This does not mean that secular politics is free from conflict; in fact, conflict is its essence, but this time the nature of conflict is secular or material. While one's bourgeois/proletariat/middle class/peasant identity is a secular one, one's predominantly religious identity may degenerate into a communal one. This kind of secularism, it appears, legitimates the distinction between the sacred and the profane. Religion is sacred for spiritual salvation. Its politicization, it is feared, would trivialize it and make it too profane! Another point needs to be added. Beneath secularism lies a belief that all that politics is concerned about—distribution of power, wealth and education—has to be explained in terms of the phenomenal world and it has got nothing to do with one's religious or transcendental belief. In other words, secular politics derives its strength from two sources. It retains the 'purity' of religion. And it also promotes reason in the sense that the explanation for socio-economic conflicts has to be sought in this world only. Religion and politics can coexist occupying two different spaces. I can be religious as well as secular only if I retain my religion in my private sphere, make it purely sacred and do not allow it to evolve my political identity. This notion of secularism has got tremendous attraction in a society like ours where one needs both: religion as well as the promise of reason.

Here the notion of secularism is quite broad. It is not anti-religion. It is a moral and practical urge to give both religion and modern rationality their legitimate spaces. With this soft, tolerant and elastic view it is not difficult to brand innumerable varieties of people—Nehru, M.N. Roy, Gandhi, Ramakrishna, Vivekananda, Kabir—as 'secular'. Because what unites Ramakrishna and M.N. Roy or Nehru and Gandhi, as it is argued, is their tolerance and universality. They did not discriminate people on the basis of caste, creed and religion. Hence they were 'secular'. In other words, as far as this definition goes, all tolerant, peaceful and broad-minded people can be called 'secular'!

Two observations have to be made. First, particularly in troubled times like ours, this wider perception of secularism has got its relevance. When the communalists appropriate religion and try to see it as an antithesis of reason, the projection of Ramakrishna and Vivekananda as 'secular' does help to fight the politics of appropriation.[4]

The second point, that is secularism is everything, thus loses its specificity. Nehru and Ramakrishna—both were tolerant, granted. But, at the same time, one knows that there were fundamental differences in their world views. How does secularism cope with these differences?

As a matter of fact, the question that ought to be raised is: why should one be so eager to call people like Ramakrishna or Vivekananda 'secular'? Why can't one say that they were just religious/spiritual people? In fact, this excessive anxiety to see them as 'secular' is to give one's consent to the dominant scientific belief that it is good to be secular and there is something inherently regressive in religion. And hence Ramakrishna as a religious man does not fit well into the cognitive map of modern secularists. If they accept him at all, they have to accept him as 'secular'! The inherent strength of religion as such is not accepted; religion is accepted only if it affirms some 'secular' principles. This is the subtle domination of secular categories. The fact is that even soft or tolerant secularists (despite their willingness to 'accommodate' religion) are not free from this hierarchy of knowledge: science is superior to religion! and therefore, in order to have an adequate understanding of secularism, we must see its relationship with science, technology and the project of modernity. Only then would it be possible for us to understand militant secularism and its ruthless attack on religion. This would also help us to understand the ambiguities of soft secularism.

II

Beginning of a Militant Agenda: Secularism and Modernity

No understanding of secularism is complete unless its conflict-ridden relationship with religion is felt. As Byran R. Wilson says, secularism is a "process whereby religious thinking, practice and institutions lose their social significance."[5] To speak of secularism is to speak of the triumph of science over religion and reason over faith. Secularism is a celebration of man's reason, its ability to emancipate him from the influences of religious customs, beliefs and practices. Secularism, as its militant proponents would assert, means the inevitable "desacralization of the world—the world loses its sacred character as man and nature become the object of rational-casual explanation in which the supernatural plays no part.[6] This 'disengagement of society from religion' cannot be understood unless we look at the origin of militant secularism. As any careful reader of the history of Western civilization would argue, it was deeply related to a great historic project— the project of modernity sustained by scientific discoveries and the birth of industrial capitalism.

Well, one can argue that the roots of secular thinking could be found even in the religious sphere. For example, Calvinism—the religion of townsmen and traders of Europe in the sixteenth century—gave a new momentum to Christianity. Max Weber told us about the process of secularization (or rationalization) inherent in this "inner-worldly asceticism".[7] It eliminated magic and supernatural quest for salvation; instead, it created the religious motivations for seeking salvation primarily through immersion in one's worldly vocation. Indeed, it created an ethic which was pragmatic, rational, controlled and anti-emotional. It was the beginning of the process of secularization.

Despite these religious roots (or factors internal to Christianity), it should not be forgotten that secularism, in the ultimate analysis, began to challenge the authorities or religion. While examining the "social context of secularization" in the West, Byran R. Wilson gives tremendous importance to science. With the growth of science emerged a rational or pragmatic attitude towards society.[8] Science demystified and demythologized the world. Its inherent rationalism; as Wilson reminds us, was determined to equate religious beliefs with irrational and superstitious practices. This secular process of debunking religion could be seen in English utilitarianism, Comteanism, Marxism and pragmatism. Not solely that. For the man in the street, the gains of science were more concrete and tangible. This further led to the decline in the importance of religion. To quote Wilson:

The real danger of science to religion, however, was rather in

> the increased prestige of science and the decline in the intellectual prestige of religion. Since science had answers, and had positive tangible results, it came increasingly to command respect and approval. As governments became less concerned with the promotion of religion, so they became increasingly disposed to sponsor science, at first by prizes and awards, and later by ever-increasing endowments of scientific enquiry and scientific education.[9]

Wilson also speaks of the "entertainment industry", how it posed a challenge to religion, how "it replaced religion's attempts to awaken public sentiments by offering titillation of private emotions."[10] Moreover, there was another factor characteristic of the new industrial and scientific age—the process of democratization of society. Its deeper implications, Wilson argues, ought to be understood. Democracy did indeed reduce the importance of supernatural intervention in the world. Because democracy empowered man, it made him realize that the general pattern of life-circumstances could be affected by instrumental action and mass decision-making. In other words, democracy further challenged the "religious-moral interpretations" of the world.[11]

Secularism, as it developed in the West, is, therefore inherently sceptical towards religion. Not to see this conflict-ridden relationship with religion is to overlook the specificity of secularism. An example would suffice. Was Ramakrishna 'secular'? He was not. He was tolerant and universal. Yet, he was not secular. Because he was not anti-religious. His temper was not scientific. His mind was not the creation of the European Enlightenment. He transcended reason; he communicated with his dearest goddess—Ma Kali! When he spoke of unity, his inspiration was religious or spiritual, not scientific. It is this madness of faith that the secularists, honestly speaking, are uncomfortable with. Is it possible to imagine a secularist talking to Ma Kali and striving for *samadhi*? Herein lie the ambiguities of soft secularism. It wants the supremacy of science; yet, it wants to accommodate one's religiosity. To put it otherwise, it wants to be soft towards what it wants to disappear!

But militant secularism makes us aware of its specificity, its clearly articulated anti-religious agenda. Unlike soft secularism, militant secularism does not promote the principle of tolerance. Instead, it is for uniformity and homogeneity. For example, when a militant secularist says that he does not discriminate between Hindus and Muslims, it does not mean that he tolerates them or likes them equally as Hindus and Muslims. It means that he wants them to adopt modern, universal, scientific rationality and overcome their cultural and religious fixations and identities. This becomes clear when one reflects on the much talked about Uniform Civil Code. A secularist does not tolerate a Muslim with his personal laws, but he wants him to become modern and rational. Here is a project aimed at reducing all differences and arriving at the uniform and universal definition of man: man with objective reason and scientific temper! In fact, as we have been trying to argue, secularism is impossible to imagine without its modernizing, universalizing and homogenizing tendencies. As a result, what it fails to comprehend is that the rationality inherent in a cultural and religious community need not necessarily coincide with the rationality of secular modernity."[12] To see only 'revivalism' or 'backwardness' in these conflicts of divergent rationalities is to miss a great deal. This is primarily a conflict for a meaning, a life style, a set of symbols. For example, Salman Rushdie's text is not just another piece of literature; it is often seen as a threat to a world view that a particular community wants to retain. Likewise, the cry against the Uniform Civil Code may also be seen as a protest against the 'single vision' of modernity, even if it satisfies the rationalist and the progressive. In fact, secularism, because of its close affinity with the project of universal modernity, is not very comfortable with the right of a religious community to retain its cultural practices. The same kind of anxiety can be seen in a paper entitled "Secularism and Toleration" written by Partha Chatterjee.[13] He does not seem to be very happy with secularism because it may fail to assure the rights of cultural groups to protect their autonomous existence. The "liberal-democratic" principle of secularism fails to locate the individual in his/her cultural context. Instead, it treats all citizens equally regardless of race, sex, religion and other cultural particularities. And this is not a very sound practice for tolerating differences! Chatterjee, for example, refers to the Uniform Civil Code; the fact that both the

Hindu Right and the secularists want it makes him think. He argues that secularism is no less authoritarian; its implicit homogenization (or cry for uniformity) is not sensitive to cultural differences. He, therefore, argues that it is for the Muslim community to decide whether it wants the Uniform Civil Code. In other words, the religious community must be left to reform itself. Non-interference, for him, is preferable to the unacceptable arrogances of the state imposition in the name of secular uniformity. In a way, Chatterjee warns us of the tyranny of secularism.

Secularism creates its own hierarchy. Because the entire project of modernity is based on hierarchy and binary oppositions—reason versus faith, science versus religion, universalism versus particularism and technology versus myth. The urge is to establish the kingdom of reason. Secularism is thought to be desirable because it is what the project of modernity is all about: economic progress, technological development and universal science. And religion is an obstacle to be overcome. It is at this juncture that militant secularists would perhaps assert the relevance of Max Weber's understanding of the religion of India.[14] Unlike 'ascetic Protestantism', Asiatic religions, Weber argued, were by no means related to a "rational-purposive activity." In fact, in Asiatic religions Weber saw the danger of world-rejection—'absolute flight from the world'. To quote Weber:

> . . . the aim was the achievement of apathetic-ecstatic Godly possession of gnosis in opposition to everyday life as the abode of transient and meaningless drives. This, too, represents an orientation that is both extra-worldly and passive and thereby from the standpoint of inner-worldly ethics it is irrational and mystical, leading away from rational conduct in the world.[15]

In other words, the hidden message Weber conveyed was clear enough: 'If you want rationalization and progress, overcome your religion'. It is this conflict between progress and religion that militant secularists talk about.

Without secular and scientific temper modernization is impossible. Take a simple example. Modern medicine is impossible without the secularization of human body, without secular perceptions of life and death. If the body is seen as sacred or as a manifestation of the divine, its objectification is impossible. And without this objectification modern medical science cannot progress. As a matter of fact, secularism begins with a belief that there is no God, no transcendental realm to regulate man's life; he himself is responsible for his own destiny; he can alter it, control it, manipulate it. Secularism is a celebration of the release of this power: the power man enjoys in a godless world. The argument is that whereas religion belittles man, secularism makes him proud of the power of his reason and intelligence.

For a secularist—as we see him/her rooted in the process of rationalization of the world—religion is a mistake, an inferior brand of knowledge. He or she wants it to disappear. Without the abolition of religion, the argument goes, the project of modernization and emancipation will remain incomplete. Look at Marx and Freud—two great minds of the modern age. For Marx, religion exists primarily for its capacity to shield people from harsh realities and to bolster the prevailing distributions of power in society by making them appear to be natural and necessary. Marx who strove for the practical emancipation of people from oppression would argue that in a society without alienation and exploitation religion would cease to exist[16]. Likewise, for Freud, religion is mankind's "collective neurosis". It exists because man remains helpless before the facts of existence—death, sickness and separation. It is the memory of childhood that drives man to imagine God as a father-figure and a protector. Religion expresses man's utter helplessness, his inability to see the world as it is. Religion is, therefore, an illusion, a kind of wish-fulfilment. For Freud reason alone can fight this neurosis called religion.[17] To put it otherwise, be it Freud or Marx, a healthy society is not the one that celebrates religion. All this perhaps led Max Weber, another important sociologist of the modern era, to argue that "the fate of our times is characterized by rationalization and intellectualization and, above all, by the disenchantment of the world."[18] Indeed, in such a "godless and prophetless time" it is not at all easy to remain "religiously musical!"[19]

III

Religion and its Altered Modes of Functioning

Does it then imply that religion has lost its meaning and does not have much importance in a secular world? An authentic answer to this question is possible only if we understand the significance of religion and its deeper implications. But before we do that, let us try to examine how religion, as it appears, has responded to the process of secularization and altered its modes of functioning. This break-up is illustrated as follows:

(i) To begin with, it is not uncommon to see what can be regarded as a kind of "withdrawal symptom". Religion is forced to withdraw itself from the affairs of the real world. In the public sphere it accepts the superiority of science, the inevitability of secularization. It exists merely in man's private realm—without noise and without any urge to claim its authority. This is what can be called the privatization of religion. There are many sociologists of religion who have tried to understand this phenomenon.[20] For example, Thomas Luckmann, talks about "invisible" functions of religion. Luckmann is unwilling to equate religion solely with its formal organizations or its rituals and doctrines—things which have indeed lost their significance in a secular world. But that does not mean, as Luckmann argues, that the broad function of religion is in the decline. What is important to realize is that the meaning systems that relate experiences of everyday life to a "transcendental" layer of reality continue to locate individuals in their social order and these "symbolic universes", therefore, fulfil an essentially religious function. Because it enables individuals to transcend their "biological givenness" and thereby locate their practical actions in a broadly sacred context. For Luckmann, this means the proliferation of personal models of religiosity in response to the declining significance of church-oriented religion in modern societies. Likewise, Richard Fenn argues that in modern industrial societies what one witnesses is a kind of "quietistic" and "introversionist" form of personal religiosity. A religion of this kind, unlike traditional religions with strong ethical and moral motivations, does not challenge the predominance of instrumental rationality in the world of work and politics. As a matter of fact, both Luckmann and Fenn remind us of a situation in which the process of secularization is irreversible, a situation in which religion can exist only when it alters its mode of functioning, when, far from challenging the public policies prevalent in a modern industrial world, it remains confined to one's personal and private domain.

Regarding this state of affairs Peter L. Berger makes a very interesting observation.[21] Berger tells us that the experience of living in human society is the experience of living in a socially constructed meaningful order or "nomos". This rescues one from chaos, disorder and meaninglessness. This is indeed a "shield against terror".[22] For Berger, religion has been the "historically most widespread and effective instrumentality of legitimation".[23] With its "sacred cosmos" it legitimates the humanly constructed "nomos" and, as a result, "the inherently precarious and transitory constructions of human activity are given the semblance of ultimate security and permanence."[24] This enables man to cope with "marginal situations" like death, to believe that death is meaningful and it has got a place in a universe that makes sense. But, Berger reminds us, secularization has resulted in the "widespread collapse of the plausibility of traditional religious definitions of reality."[25] Religion, as a result, loses its monopolistic control. This leads to pluralism. In a typically market situation religions are bought and sold. So religion, if it exists, remains just a choice; it remains confined to one's private life. Not surprisingly, this "private religiosity" fails to fulfil the classical task of religion, that of, "constructing a common world within which all of social life receives ultimate meaning binding on everybody."[26]

(ii) Secondly, religion projects itself as something different, something that produces 'charisma' and performs miracles. And miracles do fascinate because the world is otherwise becoming too rationalized and regimented. In India, for instance, there is no dearth of religious "gurus" performing miracles! All these "gurus" sell their religion and compete with one another. With this marketization of religion the only function it serves is magical. It tends to charm the individual tired of the "disenchantment of the world".

(iii) Thirdly, religion seeks to manifest itself in divergent philanthropic activities, in good works and noble causes. Here religion seeks to fulfil the desire unfulfilled by the rational design of the bureaucratic state. It is not difficult to see many religious organizations and personalities engaged in this humanistic endeavour. The goal is meaningful work, not a debate with science. Instead, it uses science and technology to promote its cause: building up hospitals and schools, working for the flood-affected victims, etc.

(iv) Fourthly, religion becomes offensive. Religion opposes the fast growing secularization of the world. As a result, it begins to symbolize all that is lost: morality, identity and culture. This is generally called revivalism or fundamentalism. What is significant is that here religion breaks its silence, politicizes itself and begins to intervene in the phenomenal affairs of the world. It is this manifestation of religion which, for secularists, is the most damaging and threatening one.

The manifestations of religion are, indeed, worth examining. For instance, soft secularism accommodates man's private religiosity. This private religion, although more prevalent in the West, can be found even in India. It is not difficult to find some soft secularists with their private religiosity. Moreover, soft secularism would not feel uncomfortable with the 'humanistic' function of religion—the activities of, say, Mother Teresa, or Ramakrishna Mission. The proliferation of religious "gurus" (Sai Baba, Mahesh Yogi, Rajneesh, etc.) would, however, be seen with suspicion. But, it is the outburst of fundamentalism or revivalism that would be disliked most by secularists.

Yet, these manifestations (how religion 'adjusts' or its extreme reaction to the process of secularization) are not sufficient to comprehend the true significance of religion. This requires an understanding of the discontents of secular thinking. In fact, what ought to be realized is that secularists too need to grow humble; religion can still enlighten them.[27]

IV

Discontents of Secular Thinking and Necessity of Spiritual Religion

Enough has already been said and written about the virtues of positive secularism—the way it has emancipated reason, widened man's horizon and created a space needed for trans-religious communication. Moreover, the gains of modernization that accelerate the process of secularization are well known. But what is equally important to understand is the weakest aspect of secularism—its almost complete failure to accomplish what religion has been doing for ages: providing a meaning of existence. This needs explanation.

One problem man has always tried to resolve is the problem relating to the finitude of existence. Its fleetingness, its temporality and ultimately death cause a terrible crisis of meaning, seek to threaten man's world. Death denies all designs and patterns. Each death is a reminder. The world that man creates with his pride and intelligence collapses without much noise and without his will. And it goes without saying that man's secular mentality, because of its very nature, fails to cope with this crisis. As Leo Tolstoy once said, for civilized man, death is meaningless; his 'progressiveness' or his perpetually linear movement towards more and more makes it impossible for him to realize the meaning of death. Because death is meaningless, Tolstoy would argue, civilized and secular life as such is meaningless.[28]

Modern medical science, to take yet another example, tries its best to have control over human body. It can 'explain' its decay; it can cure it, manipulate it. But it cannot provide the answer to the question man raises: why this life after all, when death takes away everything and reduces him into nothingness? Moreover, there are accidents and tragedies that refuse to be explained rationally. The problem with secular rationality is that it is the philosophy of the finite. It cannot, therefore, transcend the suffering related to the finitude of existence. Secular rationality—with its science and technology—can reduce the degree of physical suffering. But then, suffering is not just physical. It is also existential born out of death and separation. Secularism is not very profound in having an appreciation of this kind of suffering and anxiety. It required a man like Gautama Buddha to renounce the world and evolve a meaning of existence. And in our times Clifford Geertz with his profound anthropological sensitivity asserts the necessity of the meaning that religion provides.[29] Geertz talks about three types of experiences—bafflement, suffering and evil—that threaten to reduce the world into a meaningless chaos. And without religion, argues Geertz, there is no way one can make sense of these experiences. Whereas the scientific perspective is essentially sceptical, religion is about faith. Faith, Geertz would argue, makes life meaningful.

Secular problems acquire a meaning only in the context of a meaningful existence. And meaningful existence, as we are arguing, is impossible without coping with the finiteness of our being, without transcending it. Religion has been doing this job. It can be argued that one of the positive functions of religion is to make the world meaningful. It generates that faith, that intensity, that unboundedness man needs to transcend the finiteness of his being and thereby make his suffering bearable.

Herein lies another important function of religion: to make man realize the infinite and, therefore, enable him to move, to expand. This is to help him to mediate between the finite and the infinite, between the temporal and the eternal. Sri Aurobindo, a great Indian saint and thinker, taught us about this spiritual journey. To quote him:

> Our spiritual evolution ascends, therefore, through the relative to the absolute, through the finite to the infinite, through all divisions to oneness. Man in his spiritual realization begins to find and seize hold on the satisfying intensities of the absolute in the relative, feels the large and serene presence of the infinite in the finite, discovers the reconciling law of a perfect unity in all divisions and differences.[30]

It can be said that in religion man finds what transcends him. It is this transcendence that, in the ultimate analysis, makes him conquer the fear and suffering of the finitude. Perhaps it is only with religion that man can overcome his excessive obsession with himself, with the pleasures of his little body and mind. It is this surrender before the infinite that purifies man. Barriers are overcome; love unfolds itself. This is unbounded energy.

Secular thinking cannot take man to this realm. Because with its purely scientific rationality man cannot transcend himself. Secularism is a philosophy of the finite. It sees what is visible. It does not comprehend the invisible. It fails to realize that there is a primary paradox in the human situation. Man is finite; yet, he intends to be infinite. He is small, egotistic, yet, he intends to embrace the universe. He lives in time, in history, yet, he seeks to experience timelessness and eternity. He is in the world preoccupied with his work and business; yet, he seeks complete nirvana, bliss, peace, happiness. In other words, he wants to have an experience of transcendence, an experience of unboundedness.[31]

To put it otherwise, secularism limits man's possibilities. This does not mean that secularists are selfish or incapable of expanding their horizons. Instead, we have seen many secularists sacrificing their little pleasures for a better world—for socialism/ communism/ collective liberation. But religion is more than that. It is beyond society. It takes man to what is inexplicable. It is the beginning of silence and bliss. It is also the beginning of prayer.

Interestingly, it was this religious experience with which Mahatma Gandhi sought to purify the domain of politics. Unlike what the secularists prescribe, Gandhi did not separate religion from politics. Gandhi believed that the politico-economic domain ought to be spiritualized and hence it must draw important lessons from religion. It can be said that, despite being an actively political man, Gandhi continually communicated with the transcendental realm. It was this voice from the invisible world that led Gandhi to mould his politico-economic viewpoints. Not surprisingly, in Gandhi one could see a critique of what promotes secularism: the project of modernity. In this project Gandhi could see the aggressiveness of a "Satanic civilization", the denial of God; he could see man's excessive preoccupation with his comforts and pleasures. "This civilization is irreligion, and it has taken such a hold on the people in Europe that those who are in it appear to be half mad. They lack real physical strength or courage. They keep up their energy by intoxication".[32] In other words, the secular project of modernity, for Gandhi, could not overcome man's finitude. It invariably led to violence, destruction and immorality. The following illustrations from the Gandhian project would reveal his religiosity:

(a) *Ahimsa* as a mode of existence and political protest, as Gandhi said repeatedly, was based on the spiritual realization of the unity of life—the unity that transcends the finitude of existence and takes one to the realm of the infinite.[33]

(b) Beneath his critique of materialistic civilization lay his firm belief that because of his narcissistic search for comforts, man denies God. To realize religiosity is to go beyond this narcissism and experience love in the act of *sarvodaya* and prayer.

(c) Never did Gandhi deny his faith. His faith transcended reason and, at times, surprised many rationalists. His faith was his strength. Without this faith, Gandhi argued time and again, satyagraha is impossible. To quote Gandhi: "The root of satyagraha is prayer. A satyagrahi relies upon God for protection against the tyranny of brute force . . . Satyagraha teaches us the art of living as well as dying. Birth and death are inevitable among mortals. What distinguishes man from the brute is his conscious striving to realize the spirit within...."[34]

In terms of the concrete political struggle Gandhi fascinated many secularists. But his message was that the process of secularization as such would not take mankind to a higher level. It must spiritualize itself. Without religiosity, for Gandhi, the fate of all civilizations is bleak. In Gandhi, as a result, one saw the strong and bold affirmation of religion, its relevance in the public domain.

All that we have said so far reveals that the secular world view has got its limits. Reason cannot accomplish what faith has been doing. The boundaries of reason—its inability to establish an effective communication between the finite and the infinite, the phenomenal and the transcendental—explains why secularization alone cannot make sense of human life. Faith would continue to assert itself.

These discontents of secular thinking and the necessity of spiritual religion perhaps explain the growth of new religious movements all over the world, and more particularly in the West that has experienced rather intensely what modernity (with its rationalization and secularization) is all about.[35] Many explanations are possible. What, however, cannot be denied is that in these religious movements there is a rebellion against the materialist utilitarian individualism of modern consumer society and the technical rationality of a scientifically dominated culture. This is against alienation and fragmentation (reason versus faith, science versus religion, time versus timelessness and individualism versus communitarianism). This is for a holistic conception of self. Faith makes these movements possible. In these movements one can see what Gandhi demonstrated: an anthropological protest against modernity.

It can, however, be argued that the way we are projecting religion aims at hiding many evil practices. The argument is that religion, as it is practised, is not spirituality or the unity of life. Practised religions have got other connotations: rituals, superstitious practices, oppressive institutions, subjugation of women, etc. As secularism emancipates reason, it becomes easier to fight these oppressive practices. There is indeed an element of truth in what the secularists say. In fact, as it is clear, we are not denying the possibilities of positive secularism. We are not denying the gains of modernity. What we are arguing is that these gains notwithstanding, there are discontents of secular thinking. And religion is not just what the secularists see in it. Religion too can be emancipatory. In fact, in the history of religion itself one can see this conflict—conflict between religion as ideology and religion as faith, between bondage and freedom. While attacking the weakest aspects of religion, one should not overlook its higher/nobler and spiritual aspects. From these spiritual aspects of religion, as our argument goes, secular reason can draw necessary lessons and humanize itself further. This is essentially what, for instance, Ashis Nandy pleads for.[36] Nandy who has been continually debunking the project of modernity wants us to see the shortcomings of secularism. For him, secularism is an alien category, a product of Western modernity. With its ruthlessness and instrumentality it destroys plurality and causes violence. Moreover, for Nandy, secularism is an ideology of statehood. To accept the ideology of secularism is to accept the ideologies of progress and modernity as the new justifications of domination. Again, for Nandy, a religion-based public morality is superior to modern/secular notions of public and political morality. He distinguishes religion-as-faith from religion-as-ideology. Religion-as-faith is inherently good. It is non-monolithic and plural. It provides the space for heterogeneity. But, says Nandy, religion-as-ideology is bad; it is a 'secular identifier' connected to the pursuit of secular interest. As he feels, it is religion-as-faith that can give one the strength to overcome communal violence as well as secular modernity. Not surprisingly, Nandy wants to recover the traditional culture of religious tolerance which, as he feels, is still alive in the life-practices of non-modern, peripheralized believers as distinguished from the modern secular rationalists and the semi-modern zealots. That is why, Nandy concludes that the state systems in South Asia may learn something about religious tolerance from everyday Hinduism, Islam, Buddhism and Sikhism. In other words, religion as faith—as spiritual reawakening, as fusion of horizons is full of possibilities. It is different from religion as—ideology of domination and power. The secular age should not be allowed to make us forget this distinction. Not to see the emancipatory potential of religion is to make us poorer.

V

Religion, Secularism and Contemporary India

The emancipatory potential of religion is nothing new to India. In fact, it is this awareness which gives a new meaning to India's road to modernity. This modernity, as the intellectual tradition tells us, is quite complex. Although it is not indifferent to the secular West, it is deeply sensitive to India's cultural and religious traditions. In other words, we have been repeatedly asked not to forget the possibilities inherent in our cultural and religious ideals.

Let us take, for instance, Swami Vivekananda who was extraordinarily critical, not a blind lover of tradition. Yet, what he did not want us to forget was the desirability of retaining our unique "national idea".[37] Each nation, according to Vivekananda, carries a corresponding national idea and if this idea disappears, the nation begins to decay. For us, the national idea is religion and it ought to be retained, even when modernity is tempting and secularization is the order of the day. "I ask in all seriousness which is easier to give up—our national character evolved out of thousands of centuries, or your grafted foreign character of a few hundred years?"[38] Indeed, without religion, for Vivekananda, there is no hope for India. And particularly at a time when the model of secular modernity seeks to homogenize the entire world, Vivekananda's "plan work for India" is worth remembering:

> This is my method—to show the Hindus that they have to give up nothing, but only to move on in the line laid down by the sages and shake off their inertia, the result of centuries of servitude... Each nation has a main current in life; in India it is religion. Make it strong and the waters on either side must move along with it.[39]

For Sri Aurobindo too, the national idea that Vivekananda wanted to retain was important. Aurobindo knew that for the average secular European mind, it was not easy to understand the depth of religion. The story of modern Europe, said Aurobindo, was the story of separation—separation of religion from life, philosophy, art, science, politics, and the greater part of social action and existence. But Aurobindo wanted us to see the limitations of secularization—the 'cult of reason'. While speaking of the fundamentals of Indian culture, he asserted the relevance of religiosity. "If reason is to play any decisive part", wrote Aurobindo, "it must be an intuitive rather than an intellectual reason, touched always by spiritual intensity and insight."[40]

In Gandhi too, we saw the assertion of the relevance of religion. Gandhi, despite his criticality, did not want India to forget her past which was nothing but her religious strength. Are all the scriptures of the world old women's tales of superstition? Is the testimony of the Rishis and the prophets to be rejected? Is the testimony of Chaitanya, Ramakrishna Paramahamsa, Tukaram, Ramdas, Nanak, Kabir, Tulsidas of no value?[41] A question of this kind revealed Gandhi's religiosity, its necessity to humanize the world. It also revealed his awareness of the dangers of Western modernity or secularism. To quote Gandhi:

> The tendency of the Indian civilization is to elevate the moral being, that of the Western civilization is to propagate immorality. The latter is godless, the former is based on a belief in God. So understanding and so believing, it behoves every lover of India to cling to the old Indian civilization even as a child clings to the mother's breast.[42]

From Vivekananda, Aurobindo and Gandhi, the message we got was clear enough. It was the message of spiritualized religion and its possibilities. And this message also reflected the necessity of retaining India's uniqueness: a religious society not totally carried away by secular modernity. Not surprisingly, despite the presence of the Nehruvians, the nature of Indian secularism was of a different kind.[43] One thing was clear. Even the 'official' brand of secularism that post-Independence India adopted was not militant in nature. Because never did it expect the impossible from the process of secularization: complete disappearance of religion. Instead, it accepted the presence of religion and it did not condemn it. The intention of the Indian Constitution was not to oppose religion, but to maintain the neutrality and impartiality of the state in matters of religion.

In other words, it may be argued that our secularism is soft in nature. And this softness has not always been appreciated by militant secularists. In this softness they would see our half-hearted modernity, the residue of the Gandhian legacy. They would see innumerable contradictions of this soft secular state. And particularly when militant Hinduism or *Hindutva* (with its aggressive communalism) is asserting itself, they find yet another reason for condemning this kind of softness to religion. In fact, the colossal growth of *Hindutva* has given a new meaning to the debate on religion, secularism and modernity. Before we understand the significance of this debate, let us understand some of the salient features of *Hindutva* as mentioned below:

1. In *Hindutva* the role of religion is primarily divisive. It does not have any spiritual mission that can see the unity of all religions. Instead, it alienates, separates and divides.
2. Far from providing a meaning of existence (enabling man to transcend the finitude of existence and thereby mediating

between the finite and infinite), *Hindutva* engages itself in crudely utilitarian projects: acquiring political power and creating a modern Hindu *rashtra*. It does not transcend the phenomenal world; nor does it spiritualize it. Instead, it remains obsessed with electoral victory or political power.[44] It can be said that a religion of this kind is different from, say, what Gandhi visualized. It was true that Gandhi too related religion to the domain of politics. But while Gandhi sought to spiritualize politics, the communal forces allowed the instrumental rationale of politics to rob religion of its spiritual mission. A religion of this kind, because of its totalitarian ambition, gives no space to breathe free air, to experience unboundedness.

3. A religion of this kind does not seem to be particularly bothered about the emancipatory traditions born out of true spirituality. Instead, its affinity with a patriarchal/oppressive social order is obvious. It can be seen as "a fascist concentration of negative traits, of resentment and frustration born in reaction to the space conquered by the oppressed and the underprivileged in India's political universe."[45] As a result, in the name of religion the communal forces negate all egalitarian projects: equality of women, human rights and socialist vision of society. All egalitarian projects are condemned as "Western" or "pseudo secular". What is forgotten is that even the religion they want to "protect" from the secularists, if interpreted and experienced properly, can give a new momentum to the project of equality.

It is this potential fascism hiding itself in a religious ideology that worries the secularists. They raise their voice against it. When religion has been so communalized, the glorification of religion or the critique of secularism, they fear, would further help the communalists to assert their voice. Even soft secularism, as the argument goes, would not help to combat this trend. Moreover, it is also argued that the stage of development which India is passing through is not so high that we can afford to tolerate the post-modern critique of enlightenment, rationality and secular thinking. India needs more modernization, science and rationality to fight all that is happening in the name of religion. Achin Vanaik, for instance, is one such secular thinker who is by no means willing to compromise with religion. He insists that secularization ought to be seen as a process through which religion loses its importance in defining our existence, politics and ways of engagement with the world. He celebrates modernity. In modernity he finds what he desires: the rationale for secularization. One may argue that modernity may lead to disenchantment; modernity deprives us of the meaning of existence; or, modernity cannot accomplish what religion has been doing: providing a meaning of existence! He does not agree. Because, as he argues, it is only in the modern age that the authentic search for meaning begins. He argues, modernity creates a situation conducive to the plurality of beliefs and life-practices. It is only in the world of abundance (abundance of choices) that the possibility of meaning arises. In fact, as he thinks, the pre-modern world heavily dominated by religion was essentially a closed system. It was static. There was no choice and hence no meaning. The superiority of modernity that he establishes makes it easier for him to assert his main thesis on secularization, as decline of religion is desirable.

With this positive engagement with modernity Vanaik critiques anti-secularists and post-modernists like Nandy and Chatterjee. They exaggerate the importance of religion and thereby tend to legitimate communalism. Communalism, Vanaik insists, cannot be fought without building modern, democratic and secular counter-institutions in civil society. Vanaik's answer is secular nationalism. Secular nationalism, as he sees, is future-oriented and emancipatory. It does not legitimate itself in the name of cultural past or Hindu civilizational unity. It is this fascination with secular nationalism that leads Vanaik to protest against those who despite their anti-communalism, tend to tap Hindu idioms or resources in order to mould Indian society. For example, it is clear to him that Indian nationalists like Vivekananda and Gandhi, despite their Hindu idioms, were by no means communalists. But, at the same time, he wants us to realize that they could be appropriated to serve the interests of *Hindutva*. Therefore, he is not with those who seek to oppose *Hindutva* from within the discourse of Hinduism and neo-Hinduism.

Not surprisingly, Sumit Sarkar—with his relentless urge to

fight the fascism of the *Sangh Parivar*—warns us of the dangers implicit in "current intellectual tendencies" that equate secularism with enlightenment rationalism and, therefore, reject it in the name of "popular" or "subaltern."[46] In other words, our context, as Sarkar would argue, does not permit even the slightest ambivalence towards secularism. Given the fact that *Hindutva* (with its "enduring hostility to reason and intellect")[47] as an ideology of domination and control ought to be fought at any cost. Sarkar's militant secularism may prove to be appealing to many of us, nevertheless, as we have repeatedly argued, secularism is not free from its discontents. And it would be naive to equate all those who speak of these discontents with the supporters (direct or indirect) of the fascism of the *Sangh Parivar*.

For Dipesh Chakrabarty, Sarkar's fear (to criticize secularism is to support communalism) does not make much sense.[48] Chakrabarty is eager to explore why the "hyperrationalism" of the project of modernity which, according to him, many militant secularists have inherited, fails to comprehend the significance of popular religiosity. To quote him: "Ours are cultures rich in these elements. Gandhi, Tagore and a host other nationalists have shown by their examples what tremendous creative energies these elements could unleash in us when mobilized for the purpose of fabricating new forms of life."[49] That is why, unlike Sarkar, Chakrabarty does not want to remain silent about the discontents of modern secular rationality.

The point we are trying to argue is that religion does matter. It is, of course, true that religion has been appropriated and falsified by the communalists. But then, the challenging task is to fight this appropriation and see its inherently humanitarian possibilities. This is perhaps the reason why many Indian social scientists refuse to remain contented with militant secularism. For instance, T.N. Madan's critique may be recalled.[50] In South Asia, argues Madan, "religion is constitutive of society" because its major religious traditions tend to claim "all of a follower's life".[51] Secularism is, therefore, an impossible credo! It is "the dream of a minority which wants to shape the majority in its own image, which wants to impose its will upon history."[52] This secular arrogance Madan dislikes. He wants the secularists to realize that religion is not just "superstition" or a "mask for communalism". Religion can humanize the world.

In other words, to borrow Sri Aurobindo's words, true religion has to be distinguished from religionism. True religion, said Aurobindo, is spiritual religion; it governs our being "by the higher light and law of the spirit".[53] But, then, religionism "lays excessive stress on intellectual dogmas, forms and ceremonies, on some fixed and rigid moral code, on some religio-political or religio-social system."[54] One can, therefore argue that communalism is religionism; it is by no means an affirmation of spiritual religion.[55]

One thing is becoming clear. Militant secularism is anti-dialogical; it does not understand the emancipatory potential of religion. As a result, it alone seeks to monopolize the right to fight communalism. Militant secularism is, indeed, exclusivist. It is arrogant. But in the prevailing intellectual tradition there is also a keen awareness of the discontents of aggressive modernity; there is a rediscovery of Gandhi. Perhaps this growing awareness reveals the trend. The secularists we see around are becoming soft; even the Marxists are trying to accommodate divergent religious traditions. In fact, what we are witnessing is humility, not arrogance. We are witnessing an effort to understand religiosity (instead of debunking it) and its emancipatory possibilities. For example, Rustom Bharucha—who has been writing on secularism and religion—is sympathetic to the question of faith.[56] Perhaps his primary agenda is to establish the necessity of fighting for the secular on the terrain of religious discourse itself. It requires a more sensitive appreciation of religion-as-faith and its resources.

Soft secularism has got many positive features. But then it is purely strategic. Its adherents speak of religion because religion does matter in India and soft secularists cannot afford to deny it. But, more often than not, they do not possess what sustains religion—the power of faith. What characterized Kabir, Ramakrishna, Vivekananda and Gandhi was their irresistible power of faith. Any attempt to appropriate them while denying their faith is bound to fail.

Yet, we would argue that soft secularism, its ambiguities notwithstanding, is a better alternative. At least, it is a beginning. With it begins the possibility of a dialogue. The characteristics of this dialogue are as follows:

(i) To begin with, we realize the gains of positive secularism. We realize how it emancipates reason, gives us the strength to fight the discontents of a traditional society.[57] It is this emancipatory reason that no great intellectual mind denied. Indeed, we realize how it evolves an art of living and political practice that is needed to retain pluralism, to protect the minority community from the possible onslaught of majority communalism.

(ii) But we also learn how to rescue modernity from its Eurocentric ambition, its scientism and its aggressive instrumental rationality. We learn how to make it humble, how to allow it to learn from alternate religious and spiritual traditions. We learn how to spiritualize modernity.

(iii) We begin to see the significance of religion. Religion, we realize, may help us to reshape our public policies. This assertion of religion is not communalism or fundamentalism, but the spiritualization of the economy, polity and culture. As religion is about love and unboundedness, it promises a society about which the young romantic Marx articulated in his own language:

Communism is the genuine resolution of the conflict between man and nature and between man and man—the true resolution of the strife between existence and essence, objectification and self-confirmation, freedom and necessity, the individual and the species. Communism is the riddle of history solved, and it knows itself to be this solution.[58]

Indeed, when a saint and a revolutionary, a mystic and a communist, a prophet and an activist begin to embrace one another, history begins to alter itself. A new religion is born, a new politics created. And a new man begins to sing the music of love and harmony!

That, in essence, is the outcome. The dialogue we are thinking about would lead to a more and more holistic attitude towards life. There would be no reason to fear and deny religion. There would be no reason to speak of religion in a strategic or diplomatic fashion. Because in the new world religion would unfold its potential. It would spiritualize the world, bring authentic harmony, universality and tolerance. Religion would be able to save itself from its self-proclaimed "protectors".

NOTES

1. When I say that science has become the most successful ideology of our times what I mean is that its cognitive arrogance has made it anti-dialogical; it refuses to listen to alternative modes of existence or plurality of epistemologies. Not solely that, in the name of 'value-neutrality', it seeks to justify an oppressive/technologized social order. For further elaboration, see, for instance, Paul Feyerabend, *Science in a Free Society* (London: Verso, 1982).
2. Andre Beteille, "Secularism and Intellectuals", *Economic and Political Weekly* (March 5, 1994), pp. 559-66.
3. *Ibid.*, p. 564.
4. Avijit Pathak, "Looking for a Creative Engagement with Culture", *Mainstream* (May 13, 1995).
5. Byran R. Wilson, *Religion in Secular Society* (Penguin Books, 1969), p. 14.
6. Malcolm B. Hammilton, *The Sociology of Religion: Theoretical and Comparative Perspectives* (London: Routledge, 1995), especially Ch. 15.
7. Max Weber, *The Sociology of Religion* (London: Methuen and Co. Ltd, 1966), see especially Ch XI and Ch XVI. Peter L. Berger too wrote about the role of Protestantism in the development of secularism. According to Berger, rational tendencies with Christianity were rooted in Judaism. They were contained, by Catholicism but unleashed by the Protestant Reformation. Berger also spoke about the peculiarities of the Christian Church—the institutional separation of religion. The concentration of religious activities and symbols in one institutional sphere defined the rest of society as 'the world', as a profane realm at least relatively removed from the jurisdiction of the sacred. As a result, 'the world' could all the more rapidly be secularized because it had already been defined as a realm outside the jurisdiction of the sacred. See Peter L. Berger, *The Sacred Canopy: Elements of a Sociological Theory of Religion* (New York: An Anchor Press Book, 1969), especially Ch. 5.
8. B.R. Wilson, *Religion in Secular Society*, see especially Ch. 3.
9. *Ibid.*, p. 68.
10. *Ibid.*, p. 61.
11. *Ibid.*, p. 58.
12. Avijit Pathak, "On Community Consciousness and Cultural Dialogue", *Mainstream* (Annual Number, October 26, 1991).

13. Partha Chatterjee, "Secularism and Toleration", *Economic and Political Weekly* (July 9, 1994), pp. 1768-77.
14. Weber, *The Religion of India: The Sociology of Hinduism and Buddhism*, (New York: The Free Press, 1958), see especially Ch. X.
15. *Ibid.*, p 337.
16. Marx articulated his understanding religion in his *Contribution to the Critique of Hegel's Philosophy of Right*. A brief and lucid analysis of the Marxian understanding religion can also be found in Malcolm B. Hamilton, *The Sociology of Religion*, see especially, Ch. 6.
17. Sigmund Freud, *The Future of an Illusion in Civilization; Society and Religion; Group Psychology; Civilization and Its Discontents* and Other Works (Penguin Books, 1985).
18. Max Weber, "Science as a Vocation" in Gerth and Mills (eds.), *From Max Weber: Essays in Sociology* (London: Routledge and Kegan Paul, 1948), p. 155.
19. *Ibid.*, p. 153.
20. Here we have talked about three sociologists of religion—Thomos Luckmann, Richard Fenn and Peter L. Berger. A precise and lucid analysis of Luckmann's and Fenn's perceptions of religion can be found in James A. Beckford, *Religion and Advanced Industrial Society* (London: Unwin Hyman, 1989), see especially, Ch. 4 and Ch. 5.
21. Peter L. Berger, *The Sacred Canopy*, see especially, Ch. 1, Ch. 2 and Ch. 6.
22. *Ibid.*, p. 22.
23. *Ibid.*, p. 32.
24. *Ibid.*, p. 35.
25. *Ibid.*, p. 127.
26. *Ibid.*, p. 134.
27. Avijit Pathak, "Beyond the Secular Critique" (*Mainstream*, April 3, 1993).
28. In his essay "Science as a Vocation" Max Weber referred to Tolstoy, his perception of life and death.
29. For an understanding of Clifford Geertz's perception of religion and meaning, see Malcolm B. Hamilton, *The Sociology of Religion*, Ch. 14.
30. Sri Aurobindo, *The Human Cycle* (Pondicherry: Sri Aurobindo Ashram, 1977), pp. 118-19.
31. Avijit Pathak, *Journey Towards the Sacred* (Calcutta: Writers Workshop, 1989), pp. 128-37.
32. M.K. Gandhi, *Hind Swaraj or Indian Home Rule* (Ahmedabad: Navajivan Publishing House, 1989), p. 33.
33. Avijit Pathak, "Uniqueness of Gandhian Art of Rebellion", *Mainstream* (January 27, 1990).

34. Quoted in: V.V. Ramana Murti (ed.), *Gandhi: Essential Writings* (New Delhi: Gandhi Peace Foundation, 1970), p. 49.
35. Malcolm B. Hamilton, *The Sociology of Religion*, pp. 206-15.
36. Ashis Nandy, "The Politics of Secularism and the Recovery of Religious Tolerance" in Veena Das (ed.), *Mirrors of Violence: Communities, Riots and Survivors in South Asia* (Delhi: Oxford University Press, 1990), pp. 69-93.
37. Swami Vivekananda, "The East and the West" in *The Complete Works of Swami Vivekananda*, Vol. V, (Calcutta: Advaita Ashrama, 1989), pp. 441-537.
38. *Ibid.*, p. 460.
39. Swami Vivekananda, "A Plan Work for India" in *The Complete Works of Swami Vivekananda*, Vol. IV, p. 373.
40. Sri Aurobindo, *The Human Cycle*, p. 125.
41. Quoted in V. V. Ramana Murti (ed.), *op. cit.*, p. 78.
42. M.K. Gandhi, *Hind Swaraj*, p. 57.
43. It is often argued that Nehru, unlike Gandhi, was more committed to the ethos of Western secularism. Perhaps his 'scientific temper his fascination with modern/European thinkers like Marx, Darwin and Freud led to this impression. Nehru was not free from his ambiguities. Yet, the dominant image of Nehru was that of a 'rational'/'secular' personality. Nehru's disciples were/are not very happy with soft secularism.
44. Regarding this kind of mundane use of religion, Sudipta Kaviraj makes an interesting observation: "It turns the Durkheimian conception of religious life upside down: instead of valuing the sacred side of life over the mundane, it is willing to make compromises on the side of its sacred practices for securing advantages in politics, the most mundane of all pursuits." Sudipta Kaviraj, "Religion, Politics and Modernity" in Upendra Baxi and Bhikhu Parekh (eds.), *Crises and Change in Contemporary India* (New Delhi: Sage, 1994), p. 312.
45. K. Balagopal, "Why Did December 6, 1992 Happen?", *Economic and Political Weekly* (April 24, 1993), p. 792.
46. Sumit Sarkar, "The Fascism of the Sangh Parivar", *Economic and Political Weekly*, (January 30, 1993), pp. 163-67.
47. Sumanta Banerjee, "Hindutva— Ideology and Social Psycho-logy", *Economic and Political Weekly* (January 19, 1991), pp. 97-101.
48. Dipesh Chakrabarty, "Radical Histories and Question of Enlightenment Rationalism: Some Recent Critiques of Subaltern Studies", *Economic and Political Weekly* (April 8, 1995), pp. 751-59.
49. *Ibid.*, p. 758.
50. T.N. Madan, "Secularism In Its Place", *The Journal of Asian Studies* (Vol. 46; No. 4, November 1987), pp. 747-59.

51. *Ibid.*, p. 751.
52. *Ibid.*, p. 748.
53. Sri Aurobindo, *The Human Cycle*, p. 166.
54. *Ibid.*, p. 167.
55. In fact, it is important to distinguish communalism or the kind of religion that the proponents of contemporary *Hindutva* propagate from the authentic/emancipatory spirit of religion. Reading Vivekananda and Gandhi (apart from Aurobindo) is like knowing this distinction. Vivekananda was extremely critical of any dogmatic approach to religion (an approach that equates religion with a particular book or the veneration for some person or a belief that it alone is the truth). Instead, he spoke of "no book, no Person, no personal God". Swami Vivekananda's, "Is Vedanta the Future Religion?" in *The Complete Works of Swami Vivekananda*, Vol. VIII, (Calcutta: Advaita Ashrama, 1991), p. 127. Gandhi too, despite his close affinity with Hinduism, talked about the necessity of transcending Hinduism. "I have been experimenting with myself and my friends by introducing religion into politics. Let me explain what I mean by religion. It is not the Hindu religion, which I certainly prize above all other religions, but the religion which transcends Hinduism, which changes one's very nature, which binds one indissolubly to the truth within and which ever purifies." Quoted in V. V. Ramana Murti (ed), *Gandhi: Essential Writings*, p. 94.
56. Rustom Bharucha, *The Question of Faith: Tracts for the Times Series* (New Delhi: Orient Longman, 1993).
57. Joseph Tharamanglam, "Indian Social Scientists and Critique of Secularism", *Economic and Political Weekly* (March 4, 1995), pp. 457-61.
58. Karl Marx, *Economic and Philosophic Manuscripts of 1844* (Moscow: Progress Publishers, 1977), p. 97. Regarding the spiritualization of Marx, see also, Avijit Pathak, "Towards Spiritualization of Marx" *Mainstream* (January 11, 1992).

THREE

Assertion of Femininity: Modernity and its Ambiguities

The complex character of our modernity and how the possibilities of religion continue to be explored in India have already been discussed. Indeed, in a politico-cultural environment in which the model of secular modernity is not allowed to deny alternate possibilities, the feminist question acquires a new meaning. To begin with, women's emancipation, it is often thought, requires a modern secular culture—a culture that rescues them from the bondage and oppression implicit in traditional religious institutions and social practices. Modernity or the process of secularization (or rationalization) demystifies the 'naturalness' of the male-female division and hierarchy and shows how gender is essentially a constructed category. It gives women the confidence to come out of all imposed 'ideals' and see the world with their own eyes. Yet there is no simple formula that equates modernity with emancipation. And in our own times we have seen that the feminist assertion is not always a celebration of modernity. It reveals the gender politics of modernity; it sees the supremacy of masculine or instrumental rationality in science; it sees a close affinity between patriarchy and capitalism. This is not to suggest that the traditional ideals of womanhood ought to be seen as sacred and sacrosanct. In fact, authentic feminism poses a challenge to both orthodox tradition and ruthless modernity.

It is in this context that this chapter has to be seen as a continuity. Like the previous chapters, it also examines the interplay of tradition and modernity, science, community and religion and thereby sees divergent possibilities and meanings in the feminist struggle for liberation. This chapter is not about any specific feminist movement or struggle. Instead, it deals with major cultural and civilizational issues related to the status of women, their identities and the deeper implications of the feminist awakening.

I

Cultural Ideals of Indian Womanhood

It is widely believed that radical changes are needed for the improvement of the status of Indian women, because our cultural tradition and its institutional practices, it is argued, are not particularly favourable to women. Women are oppressed. Or women are 'idealized' in a way that our culture fails to understand real women, their aspirations and dilemmas. Perhaps, as it is often thought, structural transformations (modernization of the economy, polity and culture), egalitarian values and cultural innovations would produce a new situation conducive to women's emancipation. An enquiry of this kind, however, requires an understanding of the cultural ideals of Indian womanhood.

Although one is tempted to see Indian women as oppressed, what is worth recalling is that in the Vedic society the status of women was not really very bad. Not simply because there were women like Gargi, Atreyi, Lopamudra and Apala who were the great philosophers of the times and were among the composers of the Rig Vedic hymns, but even the average woman found herself in a relatively egalitarian milieu. This is not to suggest that there was no element of patriarchy in the Vedic society. There was certainly an attitude of indifference towards the female child and marked partiality for the male child. For instance, the prayers for ten sons in the marriage hymn, without reference to any daughter, seem to indicate that the latter was less welcome than the former. Yet, once born, the daughter was entitled to all the privileges given to a boy. The girls, like boys, underwent the *Upanayana* ceremony at an early age. There was no glorification of child marriage. Widows were permitted to remarry and the highest education, including Vedic studies, was open equally to men and women. The Vedic word *dampati*, etymologically means the joint owners of the house used to denote jointly the husband and the wife. The woman was entitled to all the *samskaras* or religious sacraments like men, and not only were religious prayers and sacrifices jointly offered by the husband and the wife, but the wife alone could offer them in the absence of her husband. It would, therefore, not be wrong to say that, within the framework of the patriarchal system, the position of women in the Vedic society was remarkably good.

What was, however, tragic was that the later Hindu society failed to retain the Vedic ideals. Women lost their earlier status. Gradually, pre-puberty marriage became the normal rule. Women lost the status of a *dwija* or twice-born, and came to be regarded as Sudras. Naturally, like Sudras, they were declared unfit for reciting or even listening to Vedic hymns. In fact, as it has been repeatedly argued, the *Manu-Smriti* created a theoretical basis for the legal and social subordination of women. Never did Manu approve of the vision of a free and self-determining woman. Instead, as he argued, women were destined to remain dependent on the males of their families (father/husband/son).

Except *streedhan* (the property that was given to her before the nuptial fire in bridal procession), women were deprived of all property rights. Manu attached a negative connotation to womanhood. The creator "implanted in them carnal passions, love for ornament, impure desires, wrath, dishonesty, malice and bad conduct."[1] Not surprisingly, Manu gave husbands the right to beat their wives—if necessary, 'with a rope or a split bamboo'. But in Manu's world even an unfaithful or immoral husband ought to be worshipped by his wife. "Even though the husband be of bad character and seeks pleasure elsewhere he must be constantly worshipped as a god by a faithful wife."[2] In other words, Manu gave the blueprint of a world that a ruthlessly violent patriarchal social order would always love to retain.

India passed through many stages and it was difficult for women not to get affected by these societal transformations.[3] For instance, the Buddhist era witnessed significant changes. Buddhism, it should not be forgotten, was a protest against Brahminism. It could visualize freedom and equality for women in the religious sphere; even prostitutes were admitted in the

Buddhist order. Yet, the Buddhist era was not always favourable to women. For a long time, Gautama Buddha refused to admit women to his religious order. Moreover, he placed the nuns as a class in a position of inferiority to the monks. It was laid down, for example, that a nun, though a hundred years old, must stand in reverence even before a young monk just initiated into the order. Yet, what could not be denied was that, for a *bhikkhuni* in the order, it was a break, almost an experience of emancipation.

In the Puranic Hindu society the story of the subjugation of women repeated itself with more intensity. In the name of *pativrata dharma* woman was denied even the slightest independence. Their religious activity remained limited to the observation of some "vratas" only. Pre-puberty marriages were widespread and widows were not allowed to remarry whereas the horrible practice of sati was eulogised as an ideal.

The arrival of Islam was a significant event. Polygyny and the *purdah* were two of the most important social institutions of the Muslim conquerors of India. And these institutions did affect even the destiny of Hindu women. For example, before the Muslim conquest, the Brahmins had not followed the custom of sati, but following the conquests, instances of Brahmin women who practised sati were also recorded.

Yet, the cultural innovation that followed because of the fusion of these two religious systems gave a new meaning to the women's question. With the Bhakti movement the equality of men and women in the religious sphere was reasserted. Great women devotees like Mira, Jani, Muktabai and Gangubai were born. Another striking feature of the Bhakti movement was that no saint was permitted to take *sanyasa* without the consent of his wife. Moreover, the *bhaktas* emphasized salvation through devotion to a deity wherein no intermediary such as a pandit or a purohit was required. They used vernacular as a language of communication and it made easier for women to participate in the discourses of religion. Yet, there were ambiguities. Women, many *bhaktas* felt, were obstacles to the path of salvation. Imagine Tukaram saying: "Give me not the company of women ... for by them I forget God's worship and my mind goes beyond my control".

A discussion on Indian womanhood will, however, remain

incomplete, unless we speak of the ideals that seek to shape her being. These ideals include chastity, purity, gentle tenderness, devotion, patience and the ability to endure pain and suffering. From Sita to Damayanti to Savitri, we see the affirmation of these ideals.[4] In fact, the intensity of these ideals cannot be imagined without understanding the celebrated notion of motherhood. Nothing elevates the status of a Hindu woman more than her ability to become a good mother, a mother with all noble virtues. As Sudhir Kakar writes:

> For an Indian woman, imminent motherhood is not only the personal fulfilment of an old wish and the biological consummation of a lifelong promise, but an event in which the culture confirms her status as a renewer of the race, and extends to her a respect and consideration which were not accorded to her as a mere wife.[5]

The importance attached to motherhood explains why, for a Hindu woman, her son is seen as a saviour, a source of her improved status. Not surprisingly, Kakar relates this phenomenon to the "infantalization of the god"—the way "Krishna's very playfulness reflects the deep sensual comfort and security of the idealized bond of intimacy between Hindu mother and son."[6] "Krishna, the god of the legends", Kakar adds, "is the saviour of women not as an adult male and lustful partner, but as the son who is vital to the consolidation and confirmation of a Hindu woman's identity around the core of motherliness."[7]

The celebration of motherhood is certainly related to the worship of mother goddesses.[8] It should not be forgotten that in India from the age of the Indus civilization of Mohenjo-daro and Harappa down to the present time, the father-god is represented by the linga (the phallic symbol) and the mother-god by the *yoni* (the vaginal symbol). The representation of *Shiva-Shakti* by the *linga-yoni* is a popular religious practice in India. And in most of the ancient and modern temples of Shiva, the twins are worshipped in their symbolic representations. This symbiosis can be seen in all these constructs: Purusha-Prakriti, Brahman-Maya, Vishnu-Lakshmi, Rama-Sita and Krishna-Radha.

The worship of the mother goddess does not mean that a positive meaning is always attached to womanhood. A woman is often feared. Her potential destructiveness and uncontrolled passion cause terrible anxiety. "Thus underlying the conscious ideal of womanly purity, innocence and fidelity, and interwoven with the unconscious belief in a safeguarding maternal beneficence", writes Sudhir Kakar, "is a secret conviction among many Hindu men that the feminine principle is really the opposite —treacherous, lustful and rampant with an insatiable, contaminating sexuality."[9] Imagine, for example, the mythical meeting of Arjuna with the *apsara* Urvashi. Urvashi expresses her sexual desire for Arjuna frankly and directly. And Arjuna expresses the increasing helplessness of the child who desires the mother's comfort and care but instead is confronted with her sexuality: 'Return, O thou of the fairest complexion: I bend my head unto thee, and prostrate myself at thy feet. Thou deservest my worship as my own mother and it behoveth thee to protect me as a son.' Urvashi was deprived of her sense by wrath. She cursed Arjuna since he disregarded a woman who is pierced by shafts of *Kama*, the god of love. The point that Kakar makes is that the sexual presence of the 'bad mother' looms large in the Hindu psyche. Here is indeed a dual concept of womanhood. "The concept of the female in Hinduism." writes Susan Wadley, "presents an important duality: on the one hand, the woman is fertile, benevolent—the bestower, on the other, she is aggressive, malevolent—the destroyer."[10] What is the reason behind this duality? For Wadley, the female, according to Hinduism, is not just *shakti* (energy/ power); she is also *prakriti* (nature)—the undifferentiated matter of the universe. Moreover, as prakriti, she remains uncontrolled/ uncultured. And uncultured power is dangerous! This explains the deep-rooted fear and anxiety about her potential violence and destructiveness. If a woman decides her own sexuality, she can prove to be destructive and malevolent. But if she loses control of her sexuality by transferring it to a man, she is portrayed as consistently benevolent. It is, therefore, not surprising that "the benevolent goddesses in the Hindu pantheon are those who are properly married and who have transferred control of their sexuality (power/nature) to their husbands."[11] The implications of this duality are clear enough. Men must control women and their sexuality and power.

To summarize, the cultural ideal of Indian womanhood is full of ambiguities. To begin with, continual efforts were made to silence her and deny her autonomy. The 'ideals' imposed on her were often designed to repress her free and natural growth. On the other hand, in the cultural ideal one sees great respect to the potential of motherhood. Nothing would be complete without good mothers or benevolent mother goddesses. Again, women were seen as destructive— seducers or destroyers. Although these ambiguities were real, the fact was that the average woman in the post-Vedic society, apart from some remarkable exceptions during the Buddhist era and the bhakti movement, lived in a state of utter subjugation. As a result, the encounter of cultures (colonialism), the perceptions of a new and modern India and the resultant freedom struggle witnessed stimulating debates on the destiny and status of women—the debates which are equally relevant in our own times.

II

Imagining a New Woman

Colonialism created a situation in which cultures were continually reinterpreted. Chapter 2 shows that modern Indian intellectuals—from Rammohun to Gandhi—responded to the new age, looked at the West, its liberal, rational and scientific world view and reinterpreted their cultures and traditions. As a result, we saw the interplay of tradition and modernity, science and religion and the urge to create a new India—not indifferent to her past, yet aware of the many ugly practices and the resultant necessity of societal changes. As we would argue, these cultural experiments and innovations gave a new meaning to the women's question. The identity of a tradition, it should not be forgotten, was often equated with its notion of womanhood. Whatever sought to threaten the 'purity' of womanhood was seen as a danger, something that intended to colonize our cultures and traditions. Retaining the ideal of one's culture (or rescuing it from the evils of colonization) was like retaining the ideal of womanhood. Yet, the new age—or its creative and intellectual spirit—realized that much of our tradition ought to be altered. These twin urges, that of resisting the colonization of our culture, yet embracing changes, led to the imagination of a new woman: a woman willing to welcome the new age, while not forgetting her tradition, her ideal. In fact, in this new woman, modern India sought to see her identity—her experiments with tradition and modernity, secularism and religion.

Let us begin with Raja Rammohun Roy—widely regarded as the first modern champion of woman's rights. Roy dared to go against the views of orthodox Hindus, wrote powerful pamphlets against the custom of sati and supported its legal prohibition in 1829. What is, however, important to note is that his modernity (or his determined urge to abolish sati) was not a complete break from the Hindu tradition. Instead, he relied on the scriptures (not excluding the *Manusmriti*), drew his inspiration and found his reasons. He tapped cultural resources to fight his battle. For example, while offering Manu as his evidence Rammohun wrote:

> Manu in plain terms enjoins a widow to continue till death forgiving all injuries, performing austere duties, avoiding every sensual pleasure, and cheerfully practising the incomparable rules of virtue which have been followed by such women as were devoted to only one husband.[12]

In other words, as Rammohun argued, not sati—practice of burning widows alive on the pile and with the corpse of their husbands—but ascetic widowhood was what Manu pleaded for. Likewise, he produced similar proof from *Yajnavalkya* of the widow's right to live with her natal and marital family on the death of her husband. Rammohun relied on the Vedas and put forward his arguments against sati. To put it simply, his agenda was to demonstrate that sati was not commanded by the scriptures.

This dependence on cultural traditions and Brahminic scriptures has not always been appreciated by contemporary feminist writers and historians. Perhaps they think that this affinity with tradition (even for a progressive cause) was yet another source of bondage—looking at women not through their own eyes, but through tradition, Lata Mani, for instance, sees the absence of women, their agency in the entire debate on sati; instead, they became "sites upon which various versions of scripture or tradition or law were elaborated and contested."[13] Rammohun, Mani argues, did not base his support for the abolition of sati on the ground that it was cruel to women. Roy was essentially bothered about the "proper" interpretation of the scriptures. He was determined to defeat his opponents and prove that sati was not really 'commanded by the scriptures'.[14] It was not a secular discourse of reason. Instead, it was an exercise of reinterpretation of the scriptures; never did it allow women to articulate their voice or their experiences; women were just 'victims' and men like Roy were trying to "rescue" them from those incapable of understanding the "proper" meaning of the texts. Mani adds:

> What was at stake was not women but tradition. Thus, it is no wonder that even reading against the grain of a discourse ostensibly about women, one learns so little about them. To repeat an earlier formulation: neither subject, not object, but ground—such is the status of women on the discourse on sati.[15]

The use of tradition (and tradition being equated with the scripture) was responsible for Roy's ambivalence towards sati. As Mani would argue, it is not impossible to see the occasional glorification of 'voluntary'/'heroic' sati by Roy. Not solely that, Roy, because of his dependence on the scriptures, often pleaded for "ascetic widowhood" as an alternative to sati. This, certainly, was not a nice idea for a modern feminist to celebrate!

The women's question, as contemporary feminists are arguing, was deeply related to the religious discourse. Imagine a reformer like Ishwar Chandra Vidyasagar whose contributions to women's education was by no means insignificant, and who, even in those days, managed to secure nearly 21,000 signatures on a petition in support of the widow remarriage. But it should not be forgotten that, like Roy he too did not forget the scriptures. In fact, he justified widow remarriage by "correct interpretation" of *shastric* texts.

Dayananda Saraswati was another outstanding cultural innovator known for his passion for reformed Hinduism. While accepting the superiority of the Vedas, he looked at his own times and saw the all-pervasive corruption and degradation. His reformed Hinduism (which was against idolatry, casteism, child marriage and the vast bulk of popular religious practices), therefore, intended to create a new culture in which a healthy and pure stock of Aryans would assert and regenerate India. It was this mission that led him to imagine his ideal of womanhood. A woman's motherhood—her active role in the maintenance of the Aryan race, in the agenda of reformed Hinduism—was celebrated. And this also enabled him to deal with the sexuality of women. Here sexuality, far from being seen as something negative and threatening, was given a new meaning, endowed with a purpose, creating and nurturing a new race. To quote Uma Chakravarti:

> The traditional suspicion of women's sexuality was thus tempered, and the sexuality of women was transformed into a force which could be constructively channelized to serve in the regeneration of the Aryans... Dayananda had a theoretical framework within which he could confront the sexuality of women and successfully fit it into an ideology which was consistent within itself.[16]

Not solely that, since motherhood played a vital role in Dayananda's project, he was willing to accept remarriage for both men and women if there were no children from the earlier marriage.

As Dayananda's mission revealed, there was a growing realization that colonialism ought to be fought, a new race ought to be created and a new nation ought to be born. It was, therefore, necessary to imagine a new life project for the woman. With her potential strength of good motherhood and her ability to control and sublimate her sexuality, she could energize and inspire men, assume a new role and collectively fight for the liberation of the nation. For instance, this merger of religiosity, womanhood and patriotism was seen clearly in Bankim Chandra Chatterjee's celebrated novel *Anandmath*. Uma Chakravarti writes:

> Shanti in *Anandmath* is the prototype of the womanhood required by a nation in crisis... The Vedic woman who performed sacrifices to the gods by the side of her husband as an equal partner in the offering of the obligations ... is here dynamized into a figure who fights shoulder to shoulder with her husband in liberating the Motherland from its shackles . . . She would provide a model of womanhood, which came closest to a 'national' feminine identity during

the late nineteenth and twentieth centuries till India became independent.[17]

As a matter of fact, it was difficult to look at the women's question without locating it in the project we are talking about — the project of regenerating Hinduism, creating a new nation and retaining its specific identity that the powerful presence of the West sought to deny. The notion of womanhood was, therefore, a cultural and religious issue.

But, then, as has already been indicated, it is not easy for contemporary feminists to feel comfortable with this 'new' woman. There are two reasons for it:

1. To begin with, they would argue that what appeared to be 'new' was not really new; it was linked to the past—the religious ideal of womanhood; it was not free from the influence of the scriptures. As a result, this idealization ("a combination of the spiritual Maitreyi, the learned Gargi, the suffering Sita, the faithful Savitri and the heroic Lakshmibai"[18]), even though needed for supposedly noble causes like the creation of a new nation, was essentially a source of bondage. Ideals or even reinterpreted scriptures did not allow a self-determining, autonomous woman to emerge. This idealization was, after all, men's construction. They wanted women to fit into their agenda, their perceptions of nation, culture and religion. But what was missing in all these discourses was women's agency.
2. They also see the half-heartedness of this concern with the women's issue. Because most of the reformers were upper caste/upper class men, they often lost their initial zeal and enthusiasm. Imagine the paradox of Keshub Chandra Sen.[19] He pressed for a law to legalize cross-caste marriages within the Brahmo community and to raise the marriage age for females to 14 and for males to 18. Yet, Sen himself disregarded this law and married his 13-year-old daughter according to orthodox Hindu rites. Moreover, although Sen was an advocate of female education, he did not believe that girls and boys should have the same type of education. The curriculum at the Brahmo girls school reflected his perspective: the subjects included domestic economy, Hindu

ideals of womanhood and needle work. Keshub Chandra Sen's example, it would be argued, reflected the incomplete, half-hearted, contradictory character of the project of women's emancipation initiated by male Hindu social reformers.

The feminist intervention is important, because it is necessary to be aware of the questions they are raising. It is also desirable to realize that the presence of the religious ideal (often backed by the scriptures) may prove to be counter-productive, and may help the communalists and the conservatives to appropriate religion and thereby retain the practice of patriarchal subjugation of women.

Yet, there is no reason to be cynical about the contributions made by male social reformers like Rammohun and Dayananda, Vidyasagar and Bankim. The reasons are the following :

(i) Culture/tradition is not a fixed product. It is a continual process of discovery/rediscovery, a hermeneutic exercise of interpretation/reinterpretation. It is, therefore, wrong to believe that there is one and only one meaning of our tradition or our religious texts—the subjugation of women! There are possibilities, contestations and multiple interpretations. In fact, social reformers like Rammohun and Dayananda kept these possibilities alive and rescued our culture from the orthodox, monologistic interpretation. Any reference to culture or religion need not be feared or seen as an obstacle to progress. Moreover, they made us realize what many radicals are learning today: no emancipatory agenda is possible without tapping the indigenous cultural resources.

(ii) It is also necessary to be aware of the absurdity of a rigid distinction between tradition and modernity, religiosity and progress. In fact, a major contribution of our intellectual tradition was to go beyond these dualities. We have seen how religion can fight the discontents of fundamentalism as well as ruthless modernity. Likewise, the ideals of womanhood (motherhood or sublimation of sexuality) may also prove to be emancipatory. And not just male reformers, even women themselves can experience the potency of these ideals. In other words, the feminist critique should not be allowed to be reduced into an orthodox anti-dialogical, one-sided exercise of secular modernity.

In fact, a look at the views of Vivekananda and Gandhi—two outstanding critical/spiritual minds of modern India—and their discourses on women will help us to sharpen our arguments and throw a new light on the women's question.

Swami Vivekananda was against the early marriage of the girl; he laid great stress on the education of women. Yet, Vivekananda, despite his radical pronouncements, could not forget the ideal of motherhood. He wanted India to retain this ideal at any cost. "The ideal woman in India", said Vivekananda, "is the mother, the mother first and the mother last."[20] His strong commitment to this ideal led him to distinguish Indian culture from the individualistic ethos of the modern Western civilization.

In the Western home, the wife rules. But "a mother always lives in our homes, the wife must be subordinate to her."[21] Vivekananda continually spoke on behalf of the "marvellous, unselfish, all-suffering, ever-forgiving mother".[22] As he said, "the race that produced Sita—even if it only dreamt of her—has a reverence for women that is unmatched on the earth."[23] That is why, the new era required "fearless women—women worthy to continue the traditions of Sanghamitra, Lila, Ahalya and Mira Bai —women fit to be the mothers of heroes."[24] In other words, Vivekananda, the new age man, did not want to forget the cultural ideal—spiritual and religious characteristics of Indian women. "If we can preserve these beautiful characteristics and at the same time develop the intellects of our women", said Vivekananda, "the Hindu woman of the future will be the ideal woman of the world."[25] The message is clear. Tradition need not be forgotten in order to embrace modernity; spirituality ought to be seen as a strength in order to define our own project of emancipation.

A look at Mahatma Gandhi's contributions would make this point further clear. He was against child marriage. He held the view that the minimum marriageable age for the girl should be twenty years. He supported widow remarriage; he was against religious prostitution of women in the name of *Devdasi*. And, moreover, as historians have told us, it was possible for Gandhi to involve women in the struggle for liberation. Women participated in the non-cooperation movement of 1921 and civil disobedience movement of 1930 *en masse*. The visibility—or this participation in outside activities—led to the removal of various restrictions imposed by society on women.

The point we are trying to argue is that Gandhi's radicalism was not a complete break with the past. Instead, he was extremely critical of the evils of modern Western civilization. This critique of modernity was integrally related to his perception of femininity and its innate possibilities. It may be argued that modernity as a world view is terribly masculine in nature; its Baconian rationality aims at controlling and manipulating nature; it separates reason from emotion, thinking from feeling. Its 'liner'/'progressive' orientation means the imposition of the adult over the child, the male over the female. This dualism leads to violence and destructiveness. And this darkness Gandhi saw in colonialism, in the evils of modernity.

Gandhi strove for a different world view—a world view that would resist the process of masculinization of the world. As a result, his art of rebellion (*satyagraha*) was based on the qualities which were traditionally associated with women—love, receptivity, dialogue, patience, ability to endure pain and suffering and faith in life. Far from regarding these feminine qualities as weak, Gandhi radicalized their meanings and gave a challenge to the dominant principle of masculinity. "Strength", wrote Gandhi, "is moral power."[26] And, therefore, "woman is immeasurably man's superior."[27] This wavelength (and the feminization of his own personality) enabled Gandhi to communicate with women and thereby make them active participants in the non-violent struggle for liberation. For Gandhi, "woman is incarnation of ahimsa."[28] Men, Gandhi thought, should learn from this feminine principle, educate themselves, cultivate their 'soul-force'. In a way, Gandhi feminized the political sphere. Indeed, as social psychologists like Ashis Nandy argue, the Gandhian project does not see femininity/spirituality as an obstacle to be overcome; it is rather a source of immense potential and strength.[29]

Certainly in their visions—the visions born out of the dynamics of the modern era—a new woman was emerging. What kind of a woman was she? She was not Manu's woman: repressed, passive and invisible. She was educated, and acquired visibility. Yet, she was careful enough not to lose her femininity, her spirituality. Because femininity was no longer seen as weakness; it was a source of courage and strength. For instance, while commenting on the relevance of Mahatma Gandhi, Malavika Karlekar, a leading feminist sociologist wrote: "Gandhi too lauded the chastity of women, yet for him sacrifice and denial were sources of empowerment and not instruments of oppression in an unequal social order . . . Thus the Gandhian woman used her traditional qualities to build a new positive image of action, resistance and change."[30] In other words, despite the newly acquired confidence, she did not behave like a selfish or egotistic woman. She retained the spirit of motherhood. Motherhood, for her, was not an oppressive experience; instead, it was the affirmation of her strength—her ability to create and nurture life. It was a protest against uncontrolled passion, temptation, brutality and violence. She retained a splendid harmony of tradition and modernity. She was endowed with a mission. In her life modern India wanted to see her cultural identity, her departure from the materialistic West.

Indeed, as we reflect on the writings of Annie Besant and Sarojini Naidu—two prominent spokespersons of the early women's movement in India—we realize the imagination of this new woman. For example, Besant described women in the following fashion:

> Mothers, wise and tender rulers of the household, educated teachers of the young, helpful counsellors of their husbands, skilled nurses of the sick.[31]

And this innate strength—the strength rooted in our cultural traditions—ought to be realized and elevated for the liberation of India. "Indian women nursed on their old literature and its wonderful ideals of womanly perfection could not remain indifferent to the great movement for India's liberation."[32] Likewise, for Sarojini Naidu, "the true standard of a country's greatness lies . . . in the undying spiritual ideals of love and service and sacrifice that inspired and sustained the mothers of the race."[33] It was this lesson that Naidu wanted to recall while thinking about India's liberation and new identity.

In this exercise, Partha Chatterjee would see the "nationalist resolution of the women's question."[34] As Chatterjee feels, in order to cope with an alien power and its remarkable success in the material sphere, many nationalists felt, India must retain her spirituality and thereby keep her identity alive. Despite many changes the West brought with it, Indian women must keep their distinctive womanliness/spirituality alive. To quote Chatterjee:

> Once the essential 'feminity' of women was fixed in terms of certain culturally visible, 'spiritual' qualities, they could go to schools, travel in public conveyances, watch public entertainment programmes and in time take up employment outside the home. But the 'spiritual' signs of her feminity were now clearly marked: in her dress, her eating habits, her social demeanour, her religiosity.[35]

In other words, for the new woman, the entry into the public sphere did not mean the denial of her home, her inner world, her feminine essence.

As the discussion suggests, it was certainly a progressive journey though not without limitations a movement, even though incomplete, towards women's emancipation. Yet, two questions can be raised:

(i) The idealization of 'feminine'/`spiritual' qualities, it may be argued, implies the subjugation of women. Because this idealization (even when one attaches a positive meaning to it, as Gandhi did), it may be argued, is not sufficient to challenge a series of dualities implicit in the patriarchal social structure: male/female, public/private, world/home. For example, it may be argued that Gandhi's belief in complementary sex roles (nature, Gandhi believed, has created the sexes as complements to each other; equality of the sexes does not mean equality of occupations) meant that he was not always so supportive of women's participation in public life. The fear is that this ideology of complementary sex roles may be used by the opponents of women's movement to criticize efforts to improve the status of women. That is why, the question: Isn't it the fact that, for women, real emancipation requires a complete break with these 'feminine' virtues and their right to participate in a world which men and women must share collectively?

(ii) It may also be argued that freedom requires not 'spirituality' or 'religiosity' (heroic ideals of motherhood and sacrifice), but an equal access to modern rationality, its gospel of human rights, its science and technology. Any ambiguity towards modernity or any weakness towards tradition or religion, one may argue, would damage the feminist struggle for liberation. One may, therefore, question this tendency: equating the women's issue with the identity of tradition, culture and religion.

III

Feminist Challenge

Before we deal with these questions, we need to familiarize ourselves with some of the major concerns shared by Western feminists. One may feel that our problems are culture-specific and Western feminism (whatever its variety) cannot provide answers to our questions. But the fact is that cross-cultural communication is no less real and activists all over the world are continually meeting, sharing information, ideas and knowledge. Moreover, a look at Western feminism would also help us to examine the consequences of modernity—rationalization, democratization, industrial capitalism and technology—for the destiny of women. And, then, it would be easier for us to come back to our own context and reflect on the debates on the cultural/civilizational ideals of womanhood.

Anyone familiar with Western feminism would notice its sharp sensitivity to the politics of gender construction.[36] Gender is a product of human thought and culture—a social construction. This means that biological males and females are transformed by culture into men and women who are socially and psychologically conditioned to become masculine and feminine. To be truly masculine, it is thought, one should become strong, rational, competitive, proud and sexually active. And femininity is its complete negation; it is constructed as a formula for surrender. A woman must learn to mute her strength, her individuality, deny her own needs and respond to the world in an emotional and non-competitive fashion. Because of socialization these constructs are internalized and accepted as "natural". Any deviance from these expected models of behaviour is feared and suspected. "Real" men, therefore, should not encourage any "feminine" trait in their personalities. Likewise, if a woman refuses to accept her passivity and instead wants to act like a man by being competitive and self-directed, she is likely to be called bad, unfeminine, possibly a freak or an "unnatural" woman!

This imposed 'femininity' is, therefore, seen as a barrier; it conditions her, makes it difficult for her to widen her horizon and possibilities. Moreover, it subjugates her. Because 'femininity' is seen as something different from and inferior to 'masculinity'. She is inferior because she lacks all that men possess. She is defined and differentiated with reference to man and not he with reference to her. To quote Simon de Beauvoir: "She is the incidental, the inessential. He is the Subject; he is the Absolute—she is the Other!"[37] This "otherness" means that men and women are not equal; they cannot share the world!

A major event in the history of modern West—the transition from feudalism to capitalism—intensified this division.[38] In the feudal society men and women cooperated in producing a livelihood. Production and consumption were interrelated and both embedded in the economy of the household. Family life and work life were part of the same round of activity in the same locale. But things began to alter dramatically in the seventeenth century with the emergence of capitalism. As people were evicted from the land, they had to leave home to go to work. In the working class, it was men and women, in the bourgeoisie only men. This led to all sorts of dualities—consumption/production, home/work, public/private. For women, the spheres of consumption/home/domesticity/privacy became their natural habitats. And men were making a new world apart from the home: a world of business, politics, investment, law—a new capitalist and imperialist world. In other words, a look at the political economy of capitalism helps us further decipher the deeper meaning of the politics of gender construction.

Another event happened—the transition from Catholicism to Protestantism.[39] This transition helped women to enhance their social status. There is nothing in Catholicism, as many feminists argue, that can inspire a free/self-determining woman.

Because, according to it, women are evil; sex is evil. Or, there is an idealized version of womanhood: chaste, virginal, loving and other-worldly! But there is no attempt to understand a real woman, her individuality and autonomy. Protestantism, however, gives some space to women. She is not seen as evil; instead, she is a respectable companion of her husband. Moreover, Protestantism also makes it possible to redefine sexuality—the rejection of celibacy and the elevation of conjugal love. Yet, for women, as feminists argue, authentic freedom remained a distant dream. Because, as far as Protestantism is concerned, a woman cannot transcend her boundaries—the boundaries that define her role as a 'good'/ 'proper' wife. A woman ought to be cheerful, amiable and of equable temper, particularly towards her husband, "shunning all violence and rage, passion and humour." In other words, the feminist argument is that patriarchy itself was not challenged, merely shifted. The Protestant "improvements" were not free from their darker sides!

Understanding Western feminism, therefore, means understanding the changing world, its paradoxical consequences for women and divergent efforts to create a new world.[40] To begin with, what is important to recall is the contribution of liberal feminism. Being essentially liberals, the feminists of this kind gave supreme importance to equality of rights; each individual, irrespective of sexual differences, must enjoy the same rights. Not surprisingly, in the nineteenth century they fought for such basic liberties as women's right to property and vote. These liberal ideals—human dignity, autonomy, equality and individual self-fulfilment—did inspire a whole lot of feminists.

In the history of the feminist thought, Marxism was really a turning-point. Women's subordination, according to Marxism, ought to be explained in the form of oppression resulting from the institution of class society. With the invention of agriculture and the domestication of animals, the forces of production greatly expanded and a surplus was created. As these developments occurred in the male sphere of production, they gave men social dominance over women. Moreover, having acquired wealth, men now wanted to be able to control its disposal and in particular to be able to bequeath it to their biological offspring. In other words, men changed the old kinship system in a way that it became patrilineal rather then matrilineal. For Engels, " the overthrow of mother right was the world historic defeat of the female sex."[41] This lead to monogamy. This made women economically dependent on their husbands. This also deprived them of full participation in society at large. The story, according to Marxism, continues. Under capitalism women are oppressed primarily because their oppression benefits capital. Only the abolition of capitalist society (its inherent monogamy) will liberate women. This struggle is, therefore, intimately related to the working class struggle for socialism/communism.

But what gives a new twist to the feminist thought is what is popularly known as radical feminism—a product of the late 1960s. It does not remain contented with just legal equality. Nor does it equate the issue with the class question. Instead, it sees the biological basis of women's subordination and wants to overcome these conditionalities in order to strive for emancipation. For example, Shulamith Firestone speaks of two universal features of the human biological condition.[42] First, women are physically weaker than men because of their reproductive physiology. Second, infants are physically helpless relative to adults. As a result, women must depend on men for physical survival and infants must depend on adult women. To put it simply, these biological activities make it difficult for women to realize their freedom. The burden of procreation/motherhood and the resultant dependence on men explain their subordination. But Firestone is helpful; the grand success of modern technology, she feels, will help women to transform these biological conditionalities. With contraceptive technologies/test-tube babies, women are in a position to establish their victory over the "kingdom of nature" and eliminate the basic and hitherto biologically determined sexual division of labour. Radical feminism—as it sees the exercise of male power in such personal institutions as childbearing, housework, love and marriage—coins the slogan: "the personal is political". "Love", wrote Firestone, "is the pivot of women's oppression today."[43] Women are defined sexually in terms of what pleases men. Unlike Marxists, radical feminists assert that sexism is the main enemy of women.

Perhaps socialist feminism is an attempt to initiate a dialogue with both Marxism and radical feminism. Because socialist feminists believe that it is necessary to understand how it is structured by male dominance. Likewise, a full understanding of contemporary male dominance requires a recognition of the way it is organized by the capitalist division of labour. In other words, for socialist feminists, capitalism, male dominance and sexism are so integrally related that they are inseparable and consequently the abolition of any of these systems requires the end of all of them.

This discussion on feminism will remain incomplete unless we speak something of a new trend in contemporary feminism—its critique of science or its celebration of differences.[44] Broadly speaking, science is seen as a virtue, a necessary component of any emancipatory project. Without science, it is thought, modernization is impossible. Liberals, socialists, Marxists, radical feminists—all, it appears, accept modernity, its 'Enlightenment' promises. They, therefore, take science for granted; they want to use it—its rationality, secularity, technology for their emancipation. In other words, it is the agenda of modernity—or Enlightenment scientific rationality—that unites these feminists, irrespective of their differences. As science is seen as liberating, this sort of Western feminism cannot escape it. But then, what is striking is that a new trend of feminist thought has emerged in the West. It is not happy with science. Science, it may be argued, is not neutral; it has got its gender biases. It is essentially a 'supermasculine', 'activity', hostile to all that it regards as 'feminine'. We are asked to see 'rape' and 'torture' metaphors in the writings of Bacon and Machiavelli who were enthusiastic about the scientific method. Scientists and technologists, it should not be forgotten, see nature as a woman. And nature has to be conquered, manipulated and raped in order to establish man's superiority. The scientist as a man and nature as a woman are engaged in a relationship of power/powerlessness, domination/subordination. Science is, therefore, based on 'masculinist dichotomies': mind versus nature, reason versus emotion, objectivity versus subjectivity, abstract versus concrete. In each case one is told that the former must dominate the latter. Otherwise, human life will be overwhelmed by 'irrational' forces

–the forces symbolized in science as the 'feminine'. The message is clear. In science, as it is practised, women cannot find the path to emancipation. Emancipation requires a different path, a different culture, a different epistemology—a revolt against the 'Man of Reason', against the masculine definition of reality.[45]

It is in this context that post-modern feminism acquires its relevance.[46] It is a way of being, thinking and speaking that allows for openness, plurality, diversity and difference. Women are asked to realize and retain the difference. They need not feel ashamed of it; they need not overcome it. Instead, hope lies in this difference.

> Post-modern feminists take de Beauvoir's understanding of Otherness and turn it on its head. Woman is still the Other, but rather than interpreting this condition as something to be transcended, post-modern feminists proclaim its advantages. The condition of Otherness enables women to stand back and criticize its norms, values and practices that the dominant culture (patriarchy) seeks to impose on everyone, including those who live on its periphery—in this case, women. Thus, Otherness, for all of its association with oppression and inferiority, is much more than an oppressed, inferior condition. Rather, it is a way of being, thinking and speaking that allows for openness, plurality, diversity and difference.[47]

Post-modern feminism, particularly its French variety, shows how male sexuality, because of its pointedness and singularity, is boring and, therefore, masculine writing is essentially phallocentric. It fears multiplicity and chaos. But female sexuality is multiple and open, varied and rhythmic, full of pleasure and possibilities. Luce Irrigary, therefore, challenges the neutrality of science. She differentiates the plural, circular, vaginal, libidinal economy of women from the singular, linear, phallic libidinal economy of men.[48] Likewise, Julia Kristeva wants to be enlightened by the marginal discourses found in madness, the irrational, the maternal and the sexual.[49] What is striking is that equality is not equated with uniformity. Instead, it is believed that equality is possible only by retaining differences.

This brief familiarity with different streams of Western feminism does indeed help us to draw the following conclusions:

(i) A new woman is born. She asserts her agency, overcomes her silence. She is confident. She is perpetually critical. Never does she allow herself to fall into the trap engineered by men and their patriarchy. As a liberal, she regards herself as an equal citizen. As a Marxist, she sees the falsehood of monogamy, the way it subjugates women. As a radical feminist, she fights the politics of sexism inherent in the patriarchal system. The new woman takes nothing for granted. She challenges the ideals put forward by religions; she challenges the conventional role-definitions. And, as post-modernists have argued, she can even challenge even the supremacy of science.

(ii) She is a struggling woman. She does not wait passively. She does not beg justice. Instead, she is extraordinarily sensitive to her dignity. She struggles and achieves her due. As a liberal, she fights for egalitarian ideals. As a Marxist, she is struggling for socialism, for the abolition of class society. As a radical feminist, she struggles against sexism, strives for a society in which technological miracles would make it possible to abolish the biological basis of women's oppression. As a postmodernist, she struggles to resist the masculinization of the world; she struggles to retain her difference, to debunk science and put forward plurality and multiplicity.

It has to be examined how Indian women striving for an emancipatory practice can initiate a dialogue with this new woman (the creation of Western feminism)—assertive, critical, struggling and broadly secular.

IV

Feminist Journey to Emancipation: Overcoming Communalism

A meaningful dialogue generates new possibilities. It is also an occasion to cultivate our criticality and reflect on culture and modernity, science and religiosity, ideals of womanhood and the doctrine of individual rights. It is through this critical reflection that we can think of an authentic feminist intervention. Before we begin this search, it is, however, necessary to look at two disturbing trends—communalism and consumerism—affecting the destiny of women. Communalists appropriate religion and their invented tradition seeks to confine women to the boundaries defined by the dominant patriarchy. And consumerism—which looks gorgeous, glamorous and modern—creates new images—the images that seduce, oppress and deny alternate possibilities of living. In other words, women find themselves in a world in which tradition (or its religious scriptures) and modernity (or its technological promises) are designed in a fashion that makes the feminist journey to emancipation far more difficult.

Let us begin with communalism. One thing is certain. Beneath the politics of communalism lies an idealized notion of the community—how its 'purity', its 'cultural boundaries' have to be protected from its 'enemies'. And what is significant is that women are often seen to be the repositories of tradition and group identity. As a result, communal politics begins to affect women in two ways. First, women have to continually prove their 'virtues'—the 'ideals' of womanhood—in order to retain the specific 'identity' of the community. This means perpetual surveillance; i.e., a series of restrictions on their movements. Second, their 'honour' ought to be protected by men. This is like legitimizing the superiority of men. They must have complete control over the women of their community. They see themselves as saviours; at moments of crisis they rescue their women from the enemies! But women are hardly seen as active/reflexive agents. They are reduced to mere symbols —the symbols of tradition!

A striking example of this phenomenon is the way in contemporary India 'personal laws' have increasingly come to signify the 'authentic' traditions of particular communities.[50] Personal laws containing the 'scripturally sanctioned' notions of womanhood and the family, acquire great relevance. Any attempt, whether secular, progressive or otherwise, to challenge these laws is seen as a threat to the cultural specificity or uniqueness of the community. It is seen as a ruthless intervention by alien forces not sympathetic to the age-old tradition of the community. Not surprisingly, as one recalls the controversial Shah Bano case and its consequences, the 'representatives'of the Muslim community opposed the Uniform Civil Code and sought to retain their own personal laws. Likewise, as history tells us, in the Hindu Code Bill debates of the 1940s/1950s, Hindu communalists opposed women's right to property. This sort of intervention into the family ethos, they feared, would cause 'great psychological upheaval' to men, lead to 'mental disease and distress' and eventually create an 'effeminate race'. As a matter of fact, whatever seeks to alter the subordinate status of women and bring egalitarian values is suspected. In the name of retaining the cultural particularity of the community, its self-proclaimed male representatives refuse to give any space to women. This is not to suggest that the model of secular modernity—with its uniform/universal agenda—is the only option available for the feminists to put forward their case. Because we are not denying the significance of cultural pluralism. And the identity of the community is not unimportant; it resists the colonization of cultures. But, then, what is important to assert is that this community identity need not necessarily be equated with the way men define it; women's agency is equally important in the definition of group identity. The danger is that the communalists are not sensitive to this agenda: women's active participation in the discourses on culture, religion and community.

In fact, the politics of communalism seeks to hide this oppression in the name of great ideals. The RSS, for instance, represents Hindu women in overwhelmingly idealized terms. They are primarily the 'chaste mothers' of their sons. And 'modern', 'feminist', 'Westernized' women negate this ideal! The RSS degrades sexuality; but what is interesting is that it projects sexuality onto the others.[51] Thus, as it is argued, the counterpart of the chaste Hindu male is the Muslim male polygamist, and the chaste motherly Hindu woman is the Muslim woman as the potential wife. This is the beginning of stereotypes without which no community can retain its separation from its generalized others! Muslims are seen as rapists who, given a chance, would not hesitate to degrade Hindu women. This means that Hindu men must protect and rescue the honour of their mothers and sisters. Communal violence is justified because it protects the honour of women! Amrita Chhachhi is not wrong in arguing that "this sexual imagery of communal riots depicts Muslims as dirty, driven by uncontrollable lust, being ever ready to seduce, abduct and assault Hindu women."[52]

Not solely that, Beneath this communal politics lies a 'sympathetic' attitude towards Muslim women. They are just 'sacrificial goats' or 'unfortunate slaves'. And they must be 'protected' from their men. It is this 'sympathy' that leads Hindu communalists to oppose the Islamic personal laws and plead for the Uniform Civil Code. This is a clear case of the appropriation of secularism by Hindu fundamentalists. This time they need secularism to deprive the Muslim community of its specific identity. It may be argued that RSS motive was to divide Muslims along gender lines, and to use Muslim women to denigrate Muslim men. The RSS is fundamentally opposed to heterogeneity, autonomy and non-Hindu nationalist identities. It would like to see all women come under a uniform Hindu law, and, therefore, under Hindu nationalist male control.[53] The point to reflect on is that what characterizes this discourse is the absence of self-determining, autonomous, reflexive women. Everyone else 'represents' and 'protects' them. Never do they shape their own destinies.

A discussion on communal politics will remain incomplete unless some recent developments are mentioned. These days we are witnessing the emergence of the 'militantly communal Hindu woman'. What is worth examining is that these women, unlike their traditionally oppressed sisters and mothers, are not passive or invisible. Instead, as Tanika Sarkar has written,"hitherto homebound women are reclaiming public spaces and acquiring a public identity."[54] Indeed, we have seen how women like Uma Bharati and Sadhvi Rithambara and their innumerable disciples activated themselves in order to 'liberate' the 'occupied Janmabhumi' and restore the honour of Ram. Perhaps this is a 'reversal of roles'.[55] Because, as far as the epic goes, Ram and his army of monkeys rescued Sita. But this time 'Sita's sex is coming to the rescue of Ram'. This 'empowering self-image' of women activists is giving a new meaning to the politics of communalism.

Sarkar's study of the *Jagriti* — the journal of the *Rashtrasevika Samiti* — is quite revealing. Far from idealizing women as chaste mothers, the journal is sensitive to the 'problems of the newly mobile professional women.'[56] It denounces sati; it does not oppose intercaste/intercommunal marriage. Moreover, the journal cannot be accused of being sympathetic to the 'conventional women's topic' like beauty aids, cookery and child-rearing.

These changes notwithstanding, the fact remains that the newly emergent militant woman is by no means a liberator. The paradigm that defines her thinking/acting is closely linked with the politics of the authoritarian *Hindurashtra*. Needless to add, this goes against the spirit of freedom. There are two reasons for it. First, this sort of politics is based on hatred, separation, violence and narcissistic pride—all the vices of a ruthlessly violent patriarchal social order. This does not create an alternate ethos conducive to the emancipation of women—an ethos based on dialogue, receptivity, relatedness and reciprocal understanding. Second, the activity this politics demands from women is used to solidify all sorts of patriarchal values. That is why, the new Hindu woman, even when she appears to be strong and strives for work, education and employment, restores "the glories of an ancient past—a past which, as reconstructed through communal discourses, accords a particular role for women in the family and in the society: dutiful wives and self-sacrificing mothers." "Any additional roles that women may perform", it may be argued, "are ancillary to these roles."[57] Her agency, therefore, fails to challenge the structure of the patriarchy.

Once we grow aware of the gender politics implicit in communalism, we need to engage ourselves in a more challenging endeavour. For example, it is necessary to recall that an authentic project of emancipation must support the plurality of cultures and traditions. A ruthlessly uniform, homogenized world denies the ethos of freedom and self-determination. Neither men nor women can experience freedom in a world in which there is colonization and the hegemony of the dominant culture remains unchallenged. There is no easy solution. One cannot impose the model of secular modernity and its implicit package of freedom on specific cultures and traditions. Any imposition—even if it appears to be 'progressive'—leads to counter-reactions. This perhaps explains the complexity of the Uniform Civil Code—an issue generating divergent responses from feminists, modernists and traditionalists.

While colonization has to be resisted, there is, however, no reason to believe that culture is static or incapable of changing itself and learning from alternate traditions. Dialogue is what makes us humane. The challenging task is, therefore, to see the community identity as a process of restructuration and transformation. This is to think dynamically and see many possibilities in the culture of the community. An example would suffice. Hindu communalists talk about *matri shakti*, but, then, this appropriation of the ideal of motherhood, as many feminists have revealed, oppresses women. This, however, does not mean that this ideal is necessarily always negative, an instrument to be used for the patriarchal or communal design. Gandhi (or, for that matter, Vivekananda) gave a new meaning to this feminine ideal, radicalized it for the creation of a new society. Likewise, as Ashis Nandy has demonstrated, Tagore's characters, being aware of the civilizational strength of maternity, could debunk the structure of male/aggressive nationalism.[58] In other words, opposing communalism should not mean opposing the entire cultural tradition as such. Suma Chitnis, it seems, has shown remarkable sensitivity to this challenging endeavour. Although "the temptation to follow the paths blazed by Western feminists, in research as well as in action, may be irresistible"[59] She does not want to forget the specificity of the Indian situation. Our tradition, she argues, "contains several elements that can be developed towards establishing equality for women and towards a new assertion of the full dignity of their personhood."[60] For instance, as she writes, "feminists could work towards building new attitudes among women by highlighting the spiritedness, the intelligence and the resourcefulness of figures like Sita and Savitri."[61]

In fact, neither exiles nor outsiders, but critical insiders alone can afford to have a creative engagement with the community and its cultural tradition. It is at this juncture that many feminists ought to practise the exercise of rigorous self-introspection. Are they critical insiders? Or do they, because of their eagerness to initiate radical changes, insult the sensitivities of the community, not excluding its female members?

V

Consumerism: Yet, Another Obstacle

It is now time to look at consumerism. To begin with, it appears that consumerism empowers women. Because the dominant images prevalent in the consumerist culture portray women not as passive or invisible, but as active, assertive and visible agents having sufficient purchasing capacity to buy innumerable commodities in the market place. A look at contemporary India suggests the growing emergence of this "new brand of woman".[62] This phenomenon has to be examined carefully in order to understand its deeper implications.

Here is indeed an example of contentless freedom. Enough has already been said about the seductive logic of consumerism, the way advertisements as modern mythologies, seek to blur the distinction between the real and the mythical. Freedom, as a result, is equated with one's ability to say 'yes' to the perpetually constructed new needs. Beneath this notion of freedom lies nothing but bondage—absolute surrender before the logic of the market. For instance, the choice women exercise in the consumerist ethos is essentially limited: which brand of nail polish or detergent powder or washing machine to choose? But she does not have a choice of not choosing these products. She does not have a choice of leading a life free from the pollution caused by the abundance of commodities. In other words, the visibility of women seen in the consumerist culture is used to reduce women into consumers, not active doers or creators of an alternate polity and culture.

What is equally worth examining is that consumerism, despite its presentation of active and visible women, does not necessarily refute the principle of seclusion: women confined to the private domain, doing just domestic household work. Instead, consumerism technologizes and glamourizes this private sphere. The image it portrays is that of a smart, efficient, educated, technologized housewife having one and only one aim: to create a 'good' home to which men can return after their engagement with the public sphere. The duality—private/public—remains unchallenged.

Consumerism is also a process of objectification. This is more so, particularly in the context of women. Here is indeed an unholy alliance of the market and the patriarchy. One smells sexuality—female sexuality—in the world of commodities. Women—their bodies, gestures and expressions—are used to sell the products. The instrumental orientation to female body/sexuality, it goes without saying, is the denial of their freedom, agency and autonomy. But the irony is that, because of attractive packaging implicit in the ethos of consumerism, this does not look like oppression. Instead, it appears that here is a group of women who are sufficiently free and courageous to overcome all traditional taboos, who decide for themselves about their bodies and in the process earn money and grow independent. We live in an age in which consumerism, its sleekness, its technological miracles seek to legitimate this superficial notion of freedom.

Its manifestations can be seen in the growing popularity of beauty contests and fashion parades. See the way this ideology is gaining legitimacy. Beauty queens, one is often told, are the 'cultural ambassadors' of the nation. In fact, beauty queens portray the image of a nation in the making—a nation to fit well into the model of a liberalized/global economy. Despite this legitimacy, the fact remains that the entire process goes against the spirit of women's autonomy. Because it is wrong to say that in this process women gain the right to have control over their bodies. The notion of beauty—or the way women would dress, walk, smile and cultivate their body language—seems to be thoroughly homogenized. It seeks to deny differences and subjectivity. It is like doing what one has been told to do by the managers of the techno-capitalist world.

Moreover, in the entire process lies the objectification of women. This is like further promoting the pornographic mentality.[63] Not surprisingly, there is a continuity between beauty contests/fashion parades and the proliferation of pornographic literature. Yet, it may be argued that a 'moralistic' critique of the emerging trend may prove to be anti-women in nature. There are three reasons. First, moralists often evolve a negative or contemptuous attitude towards women (women are immoral, because they are equated with sex, desire and pleasure). Second, moralists often blame women for the pornographic mentality. Women, for them, are primarily seducers corrupting the culture. Seldom do they look at the pathology of the male gaze itself, its violence and destructiveness. Third, in the name of rescuing women from consumerism, they often idealize a role which is no less oppressive. In the name of protecting the 'purity' of women, they deny their autonomy and individuality.

That is why, the task before us is rather challenging. This is not to condemn women for consumerism. Instead, this is an attempt to understand and debunk the politics of a system that reconciles patriarchy, consumerism and global capitalism. This is to realize that there are multiple obstacles—not just the *Manusmriti* and its boundaries, but also those sleek images the 'market-friendly' technology construct. If religion can be appropriated by the communalists, technology too can be appropriated by the image-makers of the global market. Male violence, as a result, does not end. It changes its style, its colour — from oppression to seduction. It technologizes itself. Herein lies the necessity of the feminist intervention. And this intervention acquires added relevance particularly at a time when consumerism is becoming 'the order of the day' and affecting the life-practice of India's fast growing urban middle class population.

VI

Towards an Alternate Agenda

So where do we find ourselves today? As we look at the feminist resistance in India, we see its growing assertion and maturation. In the nineteenth century, male social reformers like Rammohun and Vidyasagar initiated the process. During the freedom struggle Gandhi brought dynamism and succeeded in mobilizing women for the collective struggle for liberation. But with the formation of the All India Women's Conference (AIWC) in 1927, a new trend set in. To begin with, its objective was modest: to promote education for women and create awareness about evil social customs. Gradually, it became more and more assertive. As Neera Desai and M. Krishnaraj summarized the achievements of the AIWC:

> It also created a very important role in creating a favourable climate for new social legislation. The Sarda Act (1929) forbidding child marriage, the Dissolution of the Muslim Marriage Act (1940), the bill for the better supervision of orphanages, rescue homes and marriage bureaus (1939) were all made possible because of AIWC pressure. It was successful in drawing attention to the need for reform in family law by various means, including persistent lobbying on the Hindu Law of Marriage and Succession until its eventual passage in 1955.[64]

What is, however, remarkable is the assertion of multiple autonomous women's groups—the groups that began to emerge in the late 60s and 70s.[65] The groups like Saheli, Sahivar, Manushi, Stree Shakti, Nari Samta Manch, Vimochana, Chingari, Mahila Sangharsh Samiti continue to attract active, assertive and imaginative women. And they take up various issues like atrocities against women, rape, alcoholism, wife-beating, dowry harassment and murder, violence in the family, problems of working women, traffic in women, oppression of lower caste, lower class and minority women, media distortion of women's image, personal laws, health issues and problems of women in slums, etc.

In fact, living in contemporary India is like being aware of these groups, the questions they raise, the sensitivities they generate. When the feminist intervention is real, it is desirable to imagine a world view, a philosophy. Because no struggle can become meaningful without a long term objective, without evolving a world view, an ideal, a perspective or a philosophy. No matter whether one is fighting against rape or alcoholism or dowry harassment, one should have an idea about the new woman one is imagining. One should have an idea about the new society. These visions or ideals convey the faith in those for whom one is fighting. Ideals make us humane; liberation is impossible without 'utopian' ideals.

This chapter begins with this search. Therefore, the quest for an alternate agenda. And this is the product of a dialogue born out of our familiarity with tradition and modernity, science and religion, gender, technology and patriarchy, nationalist awakening and contemporary feminist assertion. Here is a list of the salient features of the new world we imagine—a world that takes the feminist question pretty seriously, alters itself and strives for a new language of communication between the hitherto unequal partners.

Naturalness of love

Recall the radical feminists like Shulamith Firestone. They are not always wrong in revealing the falsehood of love. Because in this relationship, as it is thought, women are defined in a way that suits men. Women must provide emotional support to men, inspire them to perform in the public domain 'behind every successful man there is a woman'. And men would give them 'security', protect their 'honour' but the reverse is not true. Women are always dependent, they are not the doers. Love legitimates this story of bondage. As J.S. Mill said, "men do not want solely the obedience of women, they want their sentiments". A women should not be a forced slave, but a willing one. Yes, feminists are reawakening us. They want this slavery to end. Does this feminist revolt mean that love is an impossibility? The fact is that it is not. There are two reasons for it.

First, even in a patriarchal society not everything is about domination and violence. Rape, bride-burning and dowry death notwithstanding, there are innumerable silent stories and experiences of authentic love—men and women understanding one another, sacrificing their little/egotistic interests for collective fulfilment. Second, there are men who, despite all patriarchal privileges, do feel for women, they do not want merely the sentiments of women, they too give themselves. Even now many Indian mothers, wives and sisters will not refute this story. The fact is that love is the most natural experience. Despite all constraints or imperfections, it seeks to fulfil itself.

That is why, the point we are trying to make is that the feminist revolt against the pathology of love should not mean the denial of authentic love. This means striving for conditions and situations conducive to reciprocity, equality and dialogue. It is certainly not desirable if we find ourselves in a society in which men and women fear, suspect or hate one another and depend solely on contractual legal rights. An ideal society reaffirms the naturalness of love, faith, trust and mutual dependence. Cynicism is not the essence of the feminist critique. A rebel woman is filled with the intensity of love, faith and optimism.

Sexual freedom

Sexual freedom is a major issue. To choose one's own sexual life, it is argued, is to come out of a system that denies this choice or reduces women into sexual properties. The conventional sexual morality has always favoured men, it gives them the privilege to define women's sexuality in a way they want. No space is given to active, assertive or choosy women. This has led to strange categories of 'good' women and 'bad' women. While 'good' women are sober, silent and polite, 'bad' women are overtly sexual without much restraint and control!

The feminist revolt is challenging this morality. It debunks the narratives of 'happy' marriages and families. It reveals how women are tortured, oppressed and even raped by their husbands. And how economic powerlessness makes them silent and forces them to bear this humiliation.

Indeed, we are seeing a new assertion. Economic empowerment enables them to choose their own sexuality. Moreover, as it is argued, the new technologies of reproduction have made it easier for women to separate sexuality from procreation. There is no doubt that the feminist revolt has got its meaning and relevance. It frees sexuality from a repressive moral system. It softens the environment and creates a situation conducive to a relatively more healthy and egalitarian relationship between the sexes.

This is, however, not to suggest sexual permissiveness. Chaos is no answer to a repressive moral system. The answer is real communication. It should not be forgotten that the ever-expanding marketization of sexuality and the celebration of endless hedonistic relationships are fast polluting the socio-cultural environment, particularly in the advanced, post-industrial Euro-American world. There is no reason to believe that this chaos has elevated the status of women; perhaps women have been devalued further.

That is why, sexuality has to be seen as a dialogic

communication. Whatever disrupts this communication, be it a repressive moral system or the marketization of sexuality, has to be fought. A free woman is, therefore, capable of saying 'no' — no to a system that denies her choice and, at the same time, no to a system that reduces sexuality into just hedonistic pleasure and sensation. "A free person cannot allow himself or herself simply to be swept away by the impulses of nature. Nor can one blindly submit to a conventional form of existence. An unconditional, lifelong commitment must be in harmony with our deepest aspirations, as human persons, to choose freely what will promote our happiness."[66] Indeed, the recovery of dignity and freedom is possible only in a life-affirming, enduring and enriching relationship. Because "committed love transcends fleeting encounters or the merely conventional 'relating' to one another."[67] It is this real act of courage—to experience sexual relation as a lasting, mutual bond—that can rescue feminism from being vulgarized and trivialized.

Desirability of actively chosen ideals

Ideals, feminists have often reminded us, that norms are often engineered to subjugate women. Real women are tortured, ideals are worshipped. Moreover, ideals ('good' wives or sisters or mothers) make it difficult for a woman to cultivate her likes and dislikes and become a person in her own right. Ideals are suspected. For instance, a dominant theme in Western feminism is its critique of motherhood as an ideal, how it is constructed, how it conditions her, constrains her and makes it difficult for her to give the time and energy needed to enter the world outside.

While all efforts have to be made to create situations conducive to women's participation in the larger world, the point we are trying to state is that the desirability of ideal motherhood can by no means be negated. The reason is that motherhood is about life, its creation, protection and growth and no machine or technology can replace this great endeavour. A society without good mothers would be disastrous: full of crippled, injured, fractured beings.

This great function of motherhood led many Indian visionaries to reassert its importance—woman as mother goddess, mother Earth; she is *shakti*, the benevolent protector of life! And it would be too simplistic to say that an Indian mother is merely a myth without much power and authority. Sudhir Kakar's study shows how in Hindu families mothers play a leading role and how the all—pervasive presence of 'good' mothers created a 'maternal-feminine' orientation towards the world.[68] Indeed, as we look at many popular Hindi films (and these films do reflect our collective sentiments and wishes), we see the centrality of 'good' mothers. As a matter of fact, what we are trying to stress is that no society can survive without a positive and respectable orientation towards motherhood. Instead of denying the significance of motherhood, its importance has to be asserted and, at the same time, conditions have to be created so that it becomes easier for women to reconcile the twin spheres: the home and the world. It is equally necessary for men to realize the power of motherhood, surrender humbly before this power, redefine their 'masculinity' and, therefore, restore real equality in society.

Feminine ideals have often been equated with certain qualities: unconditional love, patience, perseverance and ability to endure pain and suffering. In the age of the feminist revolt these ideals, it is obvious, are suspected. As the emergent woman tells us, these ideals are expressions of passivity, weakness and submissiveness. After all, for many women, these ideals were imposed; they did not choose these ideals!

Even then a question remains: What happens if someone chooses these ideals? An ideal, if passively received, symbolizes one's weakness. But the same ideal, if actively chosen, becomes one's strength and courage. Therefore, it is not at all desirable to say that great Indian women like Sita, Savitri and Damayanti were necessarily weak. They chose what they practised. Their intensity revealed their almost infinite courage and strength. Moreover, these ideals do matter. Because no dreamer of a sane society would deny that we need love, not hatred; faith, not mistrust; perseverance and commitment to a life-long objective, not instanteinity and depthlessness. And the association of these ideals with women does not deny their relevance.

As we are arguing, when women themselves begin to choose these ideals, things alter dramatically. The rationale of patriarchy gets eroded. What is really illuminating is that there are some Western feminists—and Susan Griffin[69] is one of them—who, instead of devaluing, celebrate womanhood and see the discontents of the so-called 'masculine' virtues like hard objectivity, aggressiveness, separative mentality and conquering instinct. As Griffin suggests, women's special closeness with nature has given them special ways of knowing and conceiving the world. The human ideal is, therefore, that of a woman who has been able to develop her full human powers—the powers that have been suppressed by the patriarchy.

There is yet another point. Men too must practise these ideals. Gandhi's life was an effort to learn from these 'feminine' ideals — closeness with life and nature, perseverance and ability to endure pain and suffering. He altered the stereotypes and feminized the political sphere.[70] He was trying to teach men how to redefine their masculinity by realizing their innate femininity. His non-violence was not passivity; it was an active engagement with the world. Only a naive person would call him weak!

That is the point we want to stress. Ideals, when actively chosen and practised by men and women, no longer act like tools for oppression. Instead, ideals liberate the world. The feminist project cannot afford to miss this point.

Beyond the dualities

There are feminists who challenge the divisions: feminine/masculine, private/public, home/world. Because in these divisions lies an attempt to keep women in a dark, invisible world. They are not encouraged to participate in what is supposed to be called 'men's domain'. As more and more women are crossing the wall, entering the public space, becoming scientists, doctors, executives and even police officers, the rationale of the conventional gender construction gets eroded.

This is of great significance. It gives women the required confidence, the courage to demonstrate that they are not inferior. It should not be forgotten that in the dualities—masculine/feminine—there is also a hierarchy. Femininity is regarded as inferior. Imagine Freud describing women as "castrated" men suffering from "penis envy".[71] This negativity, according to Freud, explained their inferiority, their jealousy, their weak superego. Women's entry, therefore, into the public domain is indeed challenging the negativity associated with femininity.

This urge to overcome the barriers has, however, led many women to deny completely the meaning and significance of what is generally regarded as the feminine work. Perhaps their anxiety is that even the slightest glorification of the feminine work would reinforce the dichotomies and oppress them further. This contempt for the feminine work manifests itself sharply when Simone de Beavouir says, "Woman's work within the home gives her no autonomy. It is not directly useful to society. It does not open out on the future; it produces nothing".[72] Instead, as Beauvoir adds, "eating, sleeping, cleaning — the years no longer rise up towards heaven, they lie spread out ahead, grey and identical. The battle against dust and dirt is never won."[73]

Beauvoir's deep anguish is not difficult to understand. Yet, there is a danger. When feminists deny the significance of the feminine work, they, in fact, begin to give their consent to the male logic—the way it establishes the supremacy of the masculine work. It is this awareness that perhaps leads some contemporary feminists to refute Simone de Beauvoir and argue that women's realm—the private sphere of the home and child-rearing—is just as humane and therefore, 'rational' as the public sphere of men. Women need not and should not renounce this realm in favour of the male realm of rationality and abstraction.

Indeed, the real task is not to deny the feminine work, but to rescue it from its negativity, its exclusion and its marginalization. The task is to see its real potential, make men realize it and participate in this domain. There is no reason why women's work —creating a home or nurturing life—should be seen as inferior to men's work—official, industrial or productive work. Life would lose its rhythm, beauty and poetry without the intensity and intimacy which a true home is all about. While imaging a new woman, Indian visionaries were not wrong in thinking of a symbiosis of the home and the world.

Another point we wish to add is that if men just 'idealize' the feminine work without ever participating in it, it would lead to utter hypocrisy. Not solely that, it would lead to the marginalization and subjugation of women. What is, therefore, needed is not the denial of the feminine, but a true dialogue between the masculine and the feminine. To put it otherwise, feminism is an invitation, it invites men to the feminine sphere, it asks men to overcome their conditionings, realign themselves with a feminine ego-ideal[74] and become truly integral and holistic. Likewise, when women join the public sphere, they need not unlearn all that they have already learned from their private or domestic world. Because it is this rich, powerful experience that can alter the existing character of the alienating public domain and make it more humane and integrated. In other words, the kind of feminism we are proposing seeks to challenge men's monologue. It proposes a meaningful dialogue which, it is hoped, can alter what men have constructed —a patriarchal, bureaucratic, techno-capitalism. It can imagine a new possibility—"a society transcending the existing dualities: nature versus culture, development versus environment, reason versus emotion, thinking versus feeling, public versus private."[75]

Critical engagement with modernity

Any project of freedom is somewhat related to the agenda of modernity. Because the history of modernity is the history of revolt—revolt against traditionalism, burden of the past, institutionalized religions and their oppressive practices. Moreover, rationality, equality, universality and individual rights acquire great relevance in the project of modernity. Modernity has indeed given a new momentum to women's quest for liberation.

Yet, what ought to be emphasized is that this relationship with modernity is never a simple one. There are feminists who are becoming increasingly sceptical about science—a major component of modernity. Moreover, there are eco-feminists who see a close affinity among science, patriarchy and capitalism—the way the objectification of nature is inseparable from the objectification of women.[76] A new consciousness has emerged which is critical of the kind of science that disrupts the symbiotic relationship between the subject and the object, reason and emotion, thinking and feeling, human being and mother Earth. Again, there are feminists who are also seeing the oppressive dimension of modern technology—particularly, the ever-expanding reproductive technologies and the resultant objectification and medicalization of the female body. Likewise, we have seen how consumerism—another feature of contemporary mass culture—degrades and devalues women. In other words, the feminist thinking is critically engaged with the project of modernity. The relevance of this critique has to be stated for one more important reason. Modernity, because of the excessive importance it attaches to formal, legal or individual rights, tends to undermine the communitarian foundations of human culture. Thus, 'freedom' is gained at the cost of growing loneliness. Freedom without relatedness! That is the crisis.

This critique does not mean mindless rejection of modernity. Nor does it mean unconditional glorification of traditionalism. Creative dynamism should characterize new feminism. Only then would it be possible to reinterpret tradition and modernity—not as fixed or closed systems, but as dynamic possibilities.

Wider horizons

Women differ among themselves and hence it is not easy to have a perfect consensus on the nature of their agenda. For instance, in a society like ours there are many divisions possible—upper caste women and lower caste women, rich women and poor women, urban women and rural women. Their experiences and struggles differ. Take an example. Consumerism affects largely urban, affluent women, but poor women are bothered more about poverty, familial oppression or problems related to illiteracy and malnutrition. Moreover, there is no reason to believe that women, irrespective of their class affiliations, are always powerless. It does not require much sociological imagination to realize that rich/urban/elite women are relatively more closer to the centres of power than poor men.

These complexities notwithstanding, it is possible to speak of a broader feminist struggle. There are two reasons. First, the rationale of patriarchy transcends class divisions, it affects women of all classes in terms of their economic status, political participation and human agency. Second, there is a growing realization that all women—rich or poor, urban or rural—must unite to fight the gender politics of the prevalent system. The issues affecting them in some way or other are many: illiteracy, economic powerlessness, bride burning, dowry death, female infanticide, sexual harassment, pornography, consumerism, communalism and technological manipulation of the female body.

A feminist need not be an exclusivist in her thinking and practice. This is particularly important to remember because there are many militant feminists who tend to believe that feminism is only for women and about women and men have got nothing to do with their struggles. This sort of feminism excludes men; it doubts their motives. Well, it is true that there are men who negate feminism. Feminism, they are fond of saying, is a fashion, an upper class phenomenon; it is the ultimate expression of unhappy, frustrated women! Yet, it should not be forgotten that there are men (not just men like Rammohun and Gandhi) who take feminism pretty seriously, and seek to actively participate in their struggles. Moreover, what is worth remembering is that the destiny of men and women is so integrally related that feminism affects men equally. It is a reminder. It is a process that inspires men to redefine the dominant notion of masculinity, understand the feminine sphere and strive for a dialogic communication with women. To miss this point is to deny the deeper implications of feminism and its broader significance. If feminism becomes exclusivist, it damages itself.

The feminist struggle is deeply related to many other struggles taking place all over the world. We have seen how an unholy alliance of capitalism, patriarchy and technocracy subjugates and devalues women. As a result, the wider struggles against capitalism, against technocratic manipulation of nature are related to the feminist struggle against patriarchy. To sum up, a mature feminist is one who, despite her awareness of a broadly shared feminist agenda, is not insensitive to class divisions and hierarchies. She does not think that men are necessarily incapable of understanding women's issues. She invites men and widens the horizons of the struggle. And she knows that a real restructuring of society is possible only when the feminist struggle is related to many other struggles against domination and exploitation.

The kind of feminism we are imagining, it is now easy to understand, can be characterized by its cultural sensitivity, its openness to the possibilities inherent in our cultural traditions. It knows that creative Indian minds initiated a process—tapping cultural resources for social reconstruction—that cannot be negated. Moreover, the feminine/spiritual ideals, if given a new meaning suitable to our times, can revolutionize the world or heal the wound caused by aggressive modernity, its colonization zeal, its ruthless masculinity and violence. In other words, the agenda of feminism confirms the necessity of critical modernity meaningfully related to our cultural traditions and the possibilities of authentic religiosity and spirituality in a humane egalitarian world.

NOTES

1. Quoted in Ramesh Chandra Majumdar, "Ideal and Position of Women in Domestic Life" in Swami Madhavananda and Ramesh Chandra Majumdar (eds.), *Great Women of India* (Mayavati: Advaita Ashrama, 1953), p. 19.
2. *Ibid.*
3. Neera Desai, *Women in Modern India* (Bombay: Vora and Co., 1957), especially Ch. I and Ch. II.
4. See Shivaprasad Bhattacharyya,"Great Women in Sanskrit Classics" in Swami Madhavananda and Ramesh Chandra Majumdar (eds.), *Great Women of India,* pp. 238-52.
5. Sudhir Kakar, *The Inner World: A Psycho-Analytic Study of Childhood and Society in India* (Delhi: Oxford University Press, 1981), p. 79.
6. *Ibid.*, p. 153.
7. *Ibid.*
8. Shashi Bhusan Das Gupta, "Evolution of Mother Worship in India" in Swami Madhavananda and Ramesh Chandra Majumdar (eds.), *Great Women of India,* pp. 49-86.
9. Sudhir Kakar, *op. cit.*, p. 93.
10. Susan Wadely,"Women and the Hindu Tradition" in Rehana Ghadially (ed.), *Women in Indian Society: A Reader* (New Delhi: Sage Publications, 1988), p. 24.
11. *Ibid.*, p. 28.
12. Quoted in Lata Mani, "Contentious Traditions: The Debate on Sati in Colonial India" in Kumkum Sangari and Sudesh Vaid (eds.): *Recasting Women: Essays in Colonial History* (New Delhi, Kali for Women, 1989), p. 103.
13. *Ibid.*, p. 115.
14. *Ibid.*, p. 104.
15. *Ibid.*, p. 118.
16. Uma Chakravarti, "Whatever Happened to the Vedic Dasi? Orientalism, Nationalism, and a Script for the Past" in Kumkum

Sangari and Sudesh Vaid (eds.), *Recasting Women: Essays in Colonial History*, p. 57.

17. *Ibid.*, pp. 53-54.
18. *Ibid.*, p. 79.
19. Jana Matson Everett, *Women and Social Change in India* (New Delhi: Heritage Publishers, 1981), p. 52.
20. Swami Vivekananda, "Women of India" in *The Complete Work of Swami Vivekananda*, Vol. VIII, (Calcutta: Advaita Ashrama, 1964), p. 57.
21. *Ibid.*
22. *Ibid.*, p. 58.
23. Swami Vivekananda,"On Indian Women : Their Past, Present and Future" in *The Complete Work of Swami Vivekananda*, Vol. V, (Calcutta: Advaita Ashrama, 1964), p. 231.
24. *Ibid.*
25. Swami Vivekananda, "Women of the East" in *The Complete Work of Swami Vivekananda*, Vol. VIII, p. 198.
26. Quoted in R.K. Prabhu and U.R. Rao (eds.), *The Mind of Mahatma Gandhi* (Ahmedabad: Navajivan Publishing House, 1967), p. 163.
27. *Ibid.*
28. *Ibid.*, p. 167.
29. Ashis Nandy, *The Intimate Enemy: Loss and Recovery of Self Under Colonialism* (Delhi: Oxford University Press, 1983), pp. 52-55.
30. Malavika Karlekar,"The Relevance of Mohandas Karamchand Gandhi: A Contemporary Perspective" in *Indian Journal of Gender Studies* (Vol. 2, Number 1, Jan-June, 1955), p. 46.
31. *Speeches and Writings of Annie Besant* (Madras: G.A. Natesan, 1921), p. 73.
32. *Ibid.*, p. 336.
33. *Speeches and Writings of Sarojini Naidu* (Madras: G.A. Natesan, 1925), p. 16.
34. Partha Chatterjee,"The Nationalist Resolution of the Women's Question" in Kumkum Sangari and Sudesh Vaid (eds.), *Recasting Women*, pp. 233-53.
35. *Ibid.*, pp. 247-48.
36. Lucy Gilbert and Paula Webster, "The Dangers of Femininity" in Evelyn Aston-Jones and Gary A. Oslon (eds.), *The Gender Reader* (Boston: Allyn and Bacon, 1991).
37. Simone de Beauvoir, *The Second Sex* (London: Picador, 1988), pp. 13-29.
38. For a brilliant analysis, see Roberta Hamilton, *The Liberation of Women: A Study of Patriarchy and Capitalism* (London: George Allen and Unwin, 1978), pp. 23-49.

39. Roberta Hamilton has also analyzed this transition and its effect on the destiny of women, *Ibid.*, pp. 50-75.
40. For a brilliant analysis of divergent trends in Western feminism, see Alison M. Jaggar, *Feminist Politics and Human Nature* (Sussex: Rowman and Allanheld, 1983).
41. Fredrick Engels, *The Origin of the Family, Private Property and the State* (New York: International Publishers, 1972), p. 120.
42. Shulamith Firestone, *The Dialectic of Sex: The Case for Feminist Revolution* (New York: William Morrow, 1970).
43. *Ibid.*, p. 137.
44. Sandara Harding, *The Science Question in Feminism* (Milton Keynes: Open University Press, 1986), especially Ch. 3, Ch. 5.
45. Susan Hekman, "The Feminist Critique of Rationality" in *The Polity Reader in Gender Studies* (Cambridge: Polity Press, 1994), pp. 50-61.
46. Rosemarie Tong, *Feminist Thought: A Comprehensive Introduction* (Boulder: Westview Press, 1989), especially Ch. 8.
47. *Ibid.*, p. 219.
48. *Ibid.*, pp. 226-29.
49. *Ibid.*, pp. 229-31.
50. Maitrayee Mukhopadhyay, "Between Community and State: The Questions of Women's Rights and Personal Laws" in Zoya Hasan (ed.), *Forging Identities: Gender, Communities and the State* (New Delhi: Kali for Women, 1944), pp. 108-29.
51. Paola Bacchetta, "Communal Property/Sexual Property: On Representations of Muslim Women in Hindu Nationalist Discourse" in Zoya Hasan (ed.), *Forging Identities*, pp. 188-225.
52. Amrita Chhachhi, "Identity Politics, Secularism and Women: A South Asian Perspective" in Zoya Hasan (ed.), *Forging Identities*, p. 86.
53. See for instance, Ratna Kapur and Brenda Cossman, "Communalising Gender/Engendering Community: Women, Legal Discourse and Saffron Agenda", *Economic and Political Weekly* (April 24, 1993), pp. WS 35-42.
54. Tanika Sarkar, "The Woman as Communal Subject: Rashtrasevika Samiti and Ram Janmabhoomi Movement", *Economic and Political Weekly* (August 31, 1991), p. 2062.
55. *Ibid.*, p. 2058.
56. *Ibid.*, p. 2061.
57. Ratna Kapur and Brenda Cossman, *op. cit.*, p. WS 41.
58. Ashis Nandy, *The Illegitimacy of Nationalism: Rabindranath Tagore and the Politics of Self* (Delhi: Oxford University Press, 1994).
59. Suma Chitnis, "Feminism : Indian Ethos and Indian Convictions" in Rehana Ghadially (ed.), *Women in Indian Society*, p. 95.

60. *Ibid.*, p. 91.
61. *Ibid.*
62. Rajeshwari Sunder Rajan, *Real and Imagined Women: Gender, Culture and Postcolonialism*, (London: Routledge, 1993), especially Ch. 6.
63. Avijit Pathak, "Emerging Sexual Permissiveness", *Indian Express*, New Delhi, (9 December, 1994).
64. Neera Desai and Maitherye Krishnaraj, *Women and Society in India* (Delhi: Ajanta, 1987), p. 337.
65. Vibhuti Patel, "Emergence and Proliferation of Autonomous Women's Groups in India: 1974-1984" in Rehana Ghadialy (ed.), *Women in Indian Society*, pp. 249-56.
66. Cornelius F. Murphy, Jr., *Beyond Feminism: Toward a Dialogue on Difference* (Washington: The Catholic University of American Press, 1995), pp. 147-48.
67. *Ibid.*, p. 144.
68. Sudhir Kakar, *The Inner World*, p. 109.
69. Susan Griffin, *Woman and Nature: The Roaring Inside Her* (New York: Harper Colophon, 1980).
70. Clymes Augustine and A.K. Sharma, "Feminist Resurgence in India: Towards a Gandhian Framework," *Gandhi Marg* (Oct-Dec., 1992), pp. 489-502.
71. Sigmund Freud, *New Introductory Lectures on Psychoanalysis* (Penguin Books, 1979), Lecture 23.
72. Simone de Beauvoir; *The Second Sex*, p. 475.
73. *Ibid.*, p. 470.
74. Cornelius F. Murphy Jr., *op. cit.*, p. 96.
75. Avijit Pathak, "Men and their Paradoxical Feminism", *Mainstream* (January 1, 1994), p. 24.
76. For insightful discussions on eco-feminism, see Maria Mies and Vandana Shiva, *Eco-Feminism* (New Delhi: Kali for Women, 1993).

FOUR

Culture as an Arena of Struggle: Debates on Tradition, Modernity and Revival

Perhaps this is the time to talk about culture because culture is a way of life and we are repeatedly reflecting on its meaning and its possibilities. As a matter of fact, be it secularism or feminism—we seek to understand a way of life, an orientation to the world. It is therefore, important to have an understanding of culture. And particularly in this rapidly changing time not many would disagree that dramatic changes are taking place in our culture. These changes, it is believed, are not necessarily desirable. Instead, it has often been argued that there are dangers to our culture. There are divergent perceptions about this danger. Nevertheless, it is not altogether impossible to identify a set of concerns shared by many:

(i) Because of the encounter of cultures—an encounter in which the modernity of the West emerges as the dominant voice—we are losing our traditional and cultural ideals. This is, affecting almost every sphere of our existence—interpersonal relationships, family, marriage, kinship and sexuality.

(ii) The new forces of globalization—particularly, the ever expanding technologies of mass communication—are creating an ethos of consumerism, an ethos that seeks to deny all cultural memories and reduces the richness of life into images of mass consumption. This depthlessness, it is feared, is denying all that is sublime and spiritual about our cultural tradition.

(iii) With the increasing political manipulation of religious symbols, the cultural ideal of tolerance is disappearing. This has led to intolerance, the growing conflict of religious communities and traditions.

But before we go further, it is necessary to cope with two important questions:

(a) What is the deeper meaning of culture?
(b) What are the contents of Indian culture we are dealing with?

I

Understanding Culture

To begin with, what has to be accepted is that culture is not 'natural' in the sense that man is born with culture. Culture is not something innate or instinctive. Culture has to be learned, communicated and transmitted. It is our culture that speaks of what is distinctively human about us. This does not mean that there is no physiological/biological foundation of culture.[1] The point we are trying to state is that even our physiological drives and impulses are being shaped and modulated by culture. In other words, to understand man is to understand his culture— the way it shapes his thoughts, ideals and behaviour patterns.[2]

Culture is a meaningful zone each community ought to evolve in order to make sense of the world. In fact, there are many ways of leading one's life. But it is man's culture that teaches him the specific way to lead his life. As Clifford Geertz would argue, "Undirected by culture patterns—organized systems of significant symbols—man's behaviour would be virtually ungovernable, a mere chaos of pointless acts and exploding emotions, his experience virtually shapeless".[3] Culture, therefore, restores order and harmony and rescues man from the task of redefining the world every time. To put it simply, culture is a community's routinized response to a specific situation. Perhaps it would not be wrong to say that to know the culture of a community is to know how the members of the community would behave and respond to specific situations.

What are the contents of culture? Well, culture can be anything —music, literature, cinema, religion, customs, behaviour patterns.

Culture can be seen even in material objects—artefacts and technologies. But the fact is that culture is more than these discrete pieces. Culture is the total way of life of a community. And all the cultural artefacts reflect this way of life. Moreover, culture is shared. It is in the realm of culture that men communicate, understand one another and use shared symbols, codes, language and behaviour patterns. It is through his relationship with people—parents, community members, peer groups, teachers, colleagues, religious and scientific leaders, poets and artists—that man learns his culture. Learning culture is essentially a life-long process.

What does an anthropologist or a sociologist see when he or she studies culture? Not just individual manifestations of human behaviour, because no two actions or responses are identical. That is why, an anthropologist or a sociologist wants to examine whether these differences in individual manifestations notwithstanding, there is a pattern. To speak of culture is to speak of this pattern, an abstraction, an ideal type construction. Culture is not just what men do. Culture is a way of doing: it is an ideal, a guideline, a map. Clyde Kluckhohn wrote: "Culture is like a map. Just as a map is not the territory itself, so also a culture is an abstract description of trends towards uniformity in the words, acts, and artefacts of human groups".[4] What is equally important to remember is that each culture retains its distinctiveness because of its selective character. Each culture emphasizes certain aspects of human existence and ignores others. Each culture has got its priority list. To understand a culture is to understand its basic ideals, aspirations and motives. "If we are interested in cultural process," wrote Ruth Benedict, "the only way we can know the significance of the selected detail of behaviour is against the background of the motives and emotions and values that are institutionalized in that culture."[5] And it is this basic ideal that can be seen in all the components of that culture — customs, behaviour patterns, religion, science, literature and education. The point being emphasized is that culture is more than the sum of its traits. Each culture carries its specific ideal that manifests itself in its diverse components. To understand a culture is to understand its distinctive ideal.

Cultures, therefore, differ. But these differences notwithstanding, there is no reason to think that each culture is exclusivist in nature. The fact is that cultures do overlap. Moreover, any culture has to be seen as a living tradition. This means that there are possibilities of innovation, multiplete interpretations and contestations. In other words, our sensitivity to the basic ideals that distinguish a culture does not mean that we are absolutizing these differences. The point we wish to add is that, for any culture, its dialogic spirit is no less important than its identity for its growth and survival.

II

Great Cultural Ideals

It is very difficult to generalize about Indian culture. There are two reasons. First, what strikes one is the diversity of traditions, life-practices, religious symbols, languages and ethnic identities. Second, there is nothing static about Indian culture. It is continually evolving, changing and experimenting with itself. Because of this complexity it is extremely difficult to speak in general terms about Indian culture. Moreover, in an intellectual climate in which any grand generalization is suspected, no formulation about Indian culture is likely to remain complete. We, therefore, ought to understand the limitations of what we are arguing for. In our efforts to understand Indian culture we are perhaps emphasizing only some aspects of it, while ignoring others. These limitations notwithstanding, it would not be difficult to identify a set of salient features of our cultural ideals—the ideals which, as many of us fear, are in the process of disappearing because of 'cultural invasion'.

There is another important reason why we are talking about cultural ideals. Ideals play a very important role in the constitution of culture. Because culture is not simply mundane, in culture there is a goal to strive for, an ideal that sensitizes us, arouses our aspirations and makes us distinguish the desirable from the undesirable. To negate the ideal in the name of empirical everydayness is to do injustice to the meaning of culture. Culture without its ideals is impossible to imagine. Moreover, ideals are not necessarily invisible; ideals create the background through which we define and evaluate our everyday living. For example, the Ayodhya episode may be real and empirical. But it is precisely because of our cultural ideals of plurality and spirituality that we become critical of the Ayodhya tragedy and imagine alternatives. In other words, it is in the cultural realm that we see a meaningful relationship between the ideal and the empirical. That is why, it is important to identify our cultural ideals. These ideals, to use the Weberian language, are like 'ideal types': not necessarily the replica of the reality, but a way of approaching the reality. Our task is to understand and interpret how and why the prevalent reality resembles or differs from our constructions. Moreover, these ideals as guidelines would help us to intervene in the cultural domain and initiate a new project on the future cultural agenda.

Ethos of peaceful and/or group existence

What is striking about our culture is the way it locates the individual in the network of intensely powerful group relationships —family, kinship, village and caste. A major reason behind the cultivation of this group identity (for reduction of individualism) is perhaps India's agricultural economy. A country which consists mainly of plains, is well irrigated and has ample sunshine for the greater part of the year is suitable for agriculture. Not surprisingly, for almost five thousand years India has continually maintained and developed an agricultural economy. Perhaps it would not be wrong to say that agricultural communities all over the world tend to retain the ideal of group existence. The unit of life is the village community. As a result, culturally speaking, Indians are known for their deep loyalty to the village, the family and the *jati*.[6] Another major feature of an agricultural community is its relatively closer relationship with nature, its easy merger with the rhythm of cyclic seasons. An attitude of peace and harmony, therefore, becomes a distinctive feature of an agricultural community. Not surprisingly, while trying to understand the bases of Indian culture, S. Abid Husain wrote:

> The Indian mind . . . has developed in an environment which is blessed by a warm climate, a rich soil, abundant productivity and easy communication. Its normal relationship to nature is not, therefore, one of struggle but of harmony. Its

> fundamental moral consciousness does not regard the world as full of forces of evil, which man must fight and overcome, but as a place where the law of goodness and justice operates and to which man has to adapt his life.[7]

Inward-looking spiritual orientation

What distinguishes our cultural ideal is its inward-looking, spiritual character. As one reads the works of two great commentators of Indian culture—Anand K. Coomaraswamy and Sri Aurobindo—one sees the emphasis they put on the spiritual dimension of our culture. The cultural ideal is not to remain fixated at or contented with the mere materiality of existence—the temporality of egotistic desires and pleasures. The goal is to go beyond, realize the ultimate reality and experience the oneness with the universe. As a result, not the achievement in the phenomenal, but the realization of the ultimate spiritual truth becomes our cultural ideal. "Indian culture", wrote Sri Aurobindo, "has been from the beginning and has remained a spiritual, an inward-looking, religio-philosophical culture. Everything else in it has derived from that one central and original peculiarity or has been in some way dependent on it or subordinate to it; even external life has been subjected to the inward look of the spirit."[8]

All this does not mean that Indian culture negates the vitality of life. In fact, the ancient civilization of India founded itself very expressively upon four human interests—*dharma, artha, kama* and *moksha*. No aspect of life was considered unimportant; nothing was denied or repressed. To quote Sri Aurobindo: "Indian asceticism is not a mournful gospel of sorrow or a painful manifestation of the flesh in a morbid penance, but a noble effort towards a higher joy and an absolute possession of the spirit."[9]

This fundamental spiritual ideal can be seen in all spheres of cultural creation. As an example, let us see how Sri Aurobindo saw the presence of this spiritual ideal in Indian art. An Indian artist, according to Sri Aurobindo, is not bound to an imitation of nature; his goal is to portray a spiritual and a psychic beauty. For example, take the Indian sculpture. Generally, there is the objection to such features as the multiplication of the arms in the figures of gods and goddesses, the four, six, eight or ten arms of Shiva, the eighteen arms of Durga! But then, "art is not anatomy, nor an artistic masterpiece necessarily a reproduction of physical fact or a lesson in natural science."[10] For Aurobindo, art should not be limited by the "narrow prejudices of the natural realistic man."[11] The meaning of art is deeper; it is to elevate our profound spirituality. As a result, it has to be realized that even the dance of Shiva is not a dance of death and destruction, Natrajya expresses the rapture of the cosmic dance: eternal and infinite bliss. Likewise, even in the figure of Kali it is possible to see the deeper meaning of this fierce aspect of destruction: a spiritual urge to slay the *Asuras*, the powers of evil in man and the world. Anand K. Coomaraswamy too spoke in the same language. "Indian art is a spiritual discovery than a creation."[12] The mere representation of nature, according to Coomaraswamy, is never the aim of Indian art. The goal is to portray the ideal world of true reality, not the phenomenal world perceived by the senses.

If we look at Indian literature, it affirms the same intensity of the spiritual ideal—the ideal articulated in the Vedas and the Upanishads; the mighty structures of the *Ramayana* and the *Mahabharata*; Kalidasa and Bhavabhuti and Bhartrihari and Jayadeva and the other rich creations of classical Indian drama and poetry and romance, the *Dhammapada*; the Jatakas, and the *Panchatantra*; Tulsidas, Vidyapati, Chandidas, Ramprasad, Ramadas and Tukaram, the songs of Nanak, Kabir and Mirabai. This ideal could be seen even in the Puranas which were often discredited and depreciated. Because, as Sri Aurobindo told, "the Puranic religions are only a new form and extension of the truth of the ancient spirituality".[13] For Aurobindo, in the Puranic culture "there is no essential change, but only a change of symbols".[14] Not to see it is to misinterpret, for instance, how some Puranas revealed the sex symbolism or the intense sensuality implicit in the sport of Krishna with the Gopis. The fact is that, as our culture emphasizes, the love of man for woman or for nature is not different from his love for God. And herein lies the power of our culture, for it does not distinguish the sacred from the profane. "All love is a divine mystery; it is a recognition of unity!"[15] It would not be wrong to say that Indian music, painting, sculpture, literature—in fact, all the components of our culture—emphasize this ideal, the deeper meaning of existence, not just the materialistic aspirations of the temporal man.

It may be argued that the spiritual ideal we are talking about remains codified only in some classical, literary, religious texts; it does not necessarily tell about in some classical, the real cultural practice of people. But then culture is not just what men do; culture is also an ideal, a way of doing and living. Moreover, the ideal is not just an ideal, it seeks to manifest itself in concrete life-practices. Imagine an epic like the *Ramayana*— an epic that can indeed be regarded as an agent of the almost incalculable power in the moulding of the cultural mind of India. Sri Aurobindo wrote:

> The idealism of characters like Rama and Sita is no pale and vapid unreality, they are vivid with the truth of the ideal life, of the greatness that man may be and does become when he gives his soul a chance and it is no sound objection that there is only a small allowance of the broken littleness of our ordinary nature.[16]

Indeed, the *Ramayana* embodied for the Indian imagination its highest or tenderest ideals of character, made the qualities like strength, courage, gentleness, purity, fidelity and self-sacrifice familiar to it. Not solely that. The *Ramayana* gave a divine touch to the ordinary things of life—conjugal, filial, marital and fraternal feeling, the duty of the prince and the leader and the loyalty of the follower and the subject.

Accommodative space

Indian culture is not just Hindu culture. The great strength of Indian culture is its dynamism, its creativity, its ability to accommodate and synthesize multiple currents and traditions. The great lesson of Indian culture is how to remain open without denying the basic fundamentals. In fact, as one looks at history, one sees how, for instance, the Vedic Hindu culture itself emerged out of a meaningful convergence between the Aryans and the pre-Aryans. In fact, the cumulative growth of Indian culture witnessed many voices of dissent; it drew important lessons from Buddhism and Jainism. Perhaps this ability to cope with new challenges manifested itself rather sharply in the dialogue between Hinduism and Islam. With the arrival of Islam in India it was difficult to remain indifferent to its intensely powerful message of social democracy and equality. It was a religion centred upon this world and gave equal importance to empirical and transcendental considerations. Not surprisingly, Islam attracted many lower caste Hindus and they chose to change their religion.

The powerful presence of Islam gave birth to a unique cultural innovation in Indian society. What comes to mind immediately is the emergence of Muslim sufis and Hindu saints of the Bhakti school. They went beyond forms and rituals as they could see the essence and, therefore, preached the fundamental unity of all religions. In fact it was a great religious and cultural movement that emphasized the beauty of love and devotion, rescued religion from the monopoly of the select few and took spirituality nearer to the experiences of the subaltern masses. In other words, this cultural innovation was filled with the message of egalitarianism.

This accommodative spirit could be seen in many other spheres also. The *Ramayana* and the *Mahabharata* were translated in Persian. In the thirteenth century, the mixture of Persian with a dialect of western Hindi spoken in and around Delhi gave birth to a new language called Urdu. The great Hindu-Muslim cultural assimilation was also seen in music and architecture. For instance, a look at the general design of the Jama Masjid in Fatehpur Sikri shows that its imposing lofty gate is the characteristic of the classical simplicity of medieval Persia, but its domes reveal the influence of the Jain style.

The point to reflect on is the accommodative spirit of Indian culture, its ability to look at itself, its perpetual movement, its innovation, growth and dissent. And again it was the encounter with the West that gave Indian culture yet another opportunity to face new challenges and thereby experiment with itself. It is true that the ethos of Westernization—its secularity, rationality and individualistic concerns—came to India with colonialism. Colonialism was certainly not a very happy experience to celebrate; it was brutal, arrogant and insensitive to our cultural heritage. Colonialism was also an attempt to establish the superiority of the West over the non-West in terms of culture and power. Not surprisingly, a fight against colonialism in the domain of cultural ideals and civilizational values was not very easy. There were two possibilities: either self-exclusion and orthodoxy or mindless imitation of the West.

Yet, India went beyond these two possibilities and a new cultural innovation began to emerge. It was seen in the Brahmo Samaj movement led by Raja Rammohun Roy. Here was an attempt to build up a new culture out of the best of the civilizations of the East and the West. It was also seen in the neo-Hindu movement led by Swami Vivekananda. In fact, the spiritual ideal of Indian culture was not forgotten; it was seen as an answer to the evils of mindless materialism. But the criticality of Western rationality was also accommodated and it helped to evolve a critique of many ugly practices prevalent in our culture: be it women's oppression or untouchability. This awareness reflected itself in all spheres of our intellectual traditions—literature, philosophy and social movements. Be it Bankim Chandra Chatterjee or Rabindranath Tagore—the spirit was seen everywhere.

This spirit could be seen even in Jawaharlal Nehru's search for a new India. His modernity or scientific temper, as his *Discovery of India* reveals, could not fail to see the strength of this ancient civilization. He found inspiration in the Upanishads, in the *Bhagavad Gita* and in the sermons of Gautama Buddha.[17] All this perhaps suggests the ability of this culture to cope with the changing time without, however, denying its basic *swadharma*. Likewise, Gandhi's Hinduism was open enough to accommodate the spirit of Christianity and the ideals of Tolstoy and Ruskin. As Professor Nirmal Kumar Bose once wrote that it was Gandhi's extraordinary creativity that enabled him to keep himself rooted in the past, yet to carry India forward in directions radically different from the ancient tradition.

All these three ideals of Indian culture ought to be seen primarily as ideals, as abstractions. It was nobody's contention to argue that Indians were always group-oriented, peaceful, spiritual and tolerant. India too witnessed war, violence and hatred. India was also full of people with crudely materialistic and individualistic ambitions. Moreover, as some great historians and philosophers argued, it is possible to perceive the cultural map of India from an altogether different perspective. Recall D.D. Kosambi's reflections on the culture and civilization of ancient India. He debunked the idealism of Hindu philosophy. To take a few random examples from his mega work, he saw the Vedic god Indra primarily as a "violent, patriarchal, bronze-age barbarian"[18] fond of the powerful intoxicant *soma* and leading his Aryan followers to a ruthless victory. Kosambi could even argue that "Krishna's philandering with the milkmaids, dalliances with mother goddesses, killing of his own uncle and invariably crooked advice in the *Mahabharata* epic hardly inspire confidence in any morality he might preach."[19] In other words, unlike Sri Aurobindo, Anand K. Coomaraswami and S. Radhakrishnan, Kosambi saw nothing spiritual or emancipatory in the cultural ideals we have talked about. Likewise, Debiprasad Chattopadhya, it would appear, was reasonably sympathetic to the opponents of Indian idealism—*Lokayatas, Jaina, Mimamsaka* and *Nyaya-Vaisesika*. For instance, Chattopadhyay wrote, "... if there is anything in traditional Indian philosophy that has successfully stood the test of advanced scientific knowledge, it is the proposition of the *Lokayatas*, viz. that consciousness— ordinarily understood as the differentia of the spirit or soul is only a product of matter."[20] The *Lokayatas* talked of enjoying life rather than evading it. As a matter of fact, the point we are trying to argue is that it is possible to visualize a different perception of India—a perception that negates and falsifies idealism and spiritualism and asserts materialism.

These differences notwithstanding, we can always plead for our case. There are two reasons for it: First, we have repeatedly said that culture is not just what men do, but also a guideline, an ideal, a way of doing and living. And it is impossible to visualize Indian culture without the all-pervasive influence of a religio-spiritual ideal and its accommodative space. There have been continual efforts to keep this ideal alive. Even a Marxiologist like Dhurjati Prasad Mukerji would accept that "in India the mystic tradition did play an important part in society and its chief exponents were the social revolutionaries of their days."[21] For Mukerji, the mystic/spiritual tradition continued even in our age, in the life-practices of Ramakrishna, Gandhi and Tagore. Second, the ideals we are talking about are emancipatory and may help us to evolve a new orientation to the future. And this is important to recall, particularly at a time when the possibility of cultural invasion can no longer be denied.

III

Onslaught of Modernity

The ideals of modernity (and we mean aggressive modernity), are strikingly different from the ideals we have just talked about. When the forces of modernity are becoming irresistible, it is not difficult to visualize the threat to our culture. But, to begin with, let us understand the phenomenon called modernity. Modernity cannot be comprehended without understanding the ideals of the European Enlightenment. It is true that the Enlightenment project cannot be simplified. It is also true that modernity has got many currents—for instance, democratic liberalism or Marxian socialism. Yet, it is not altogether impossible to identify some of the striking features of modernity.

(i) Here is a view that history is an open project. There is nothing static; men are perpetually engaged in making and remaking the world. There is a linear progression of history.

(ii) It is future-oriented. We change our destiny; we can improve our lot.

(iii) It is rational in the sense that it has got a clear perception of means-ends relationship. This should not be forgotten in the name of 'non-rational' factors like emotional or affective ties or religious orientation to the world. Modernity implies the acceptance of what is called value-neutral, scientific, universal rationality.

(iv) Modernity is secular in the sense that it explains the phenomenal world in terms of scientific theories. It does not require any religious/spiritual/moral revelation in order to make sense of the world.

(v) It is in conflict with nature, not solely because its rationality is against natural instincts/impulses/sentiments. It is in conflict with nature because it wants to have complete control over nature. Progress means man's increasing capacity to establish his supremacy over nature.

(vi) It attaches supreme importance to science and technology as tools of domination or victory over nature.

(vii) It is universalistic in spirit. Its 'context-free' rationality suspects all 'undesirable' differences that may hamper the growth of secularity, science and technology.

A world view of this kind has got an unambiguously distinctive notion of a hierarchical relationship between the teacher and the taught. The West—with its Enlightenment experiences—is superior—cognitively, materially and culturally—to the non-West. To grow modern is to learn the knowledge system of the West. It is true that with colonialism began India's encounter with modernity. Well, it can always be argued that the colonial state was not particularly eager to modernize the country; instead, it was often seen to be forming alliances with feudal and traditional elements only to perpetuate its own order. Yet, it should not be denied that with colonialism the presence of Western ideas began to become increasingly visible.

We have already analyzed, how Indian thinkers responded to these ideas. Despite a dialogue with the West, India did not lose her critical orientation towards modernity. Gandhi's *Hind Swaraj* was perhaps the brightest illustration of this criticality. He raised his voice against Western modernity, its irreligiosity, its barbarism. And he wanted India to remember her spirituality and soul-force. His was a qualitatively different cultural/civilizational agenda based on the principles that seldom coincide with the goals of modernity. Ashis Nandy has rightly argued "... of all the major critics of modernity, Gandhi was one of the few to offer a radical critique of urban-industrialism and modern science. "Indeed, Nandy is right in seeing Gandhi's rigorous critique of secular scientific world view, its possessive individualism, its implicit technicism and technocracy. But, then, we saw how, gradually and steadily, the spirit of decolonization began to fade away, how post-Independence/post-Gandhian India choose to accept the inevitability of modernity. In Nehru we saw this remarkable turning-point, the articulation of the agenda of modernity. He symbolized the arrival of modernity. And this modernity as Yogendra Singh would argue, is more that the "sub-culture or little tradition of Westernization; it is indeed a great tradition of modernization,"[23] with industrialization and urbanization, increased network of communication and growth of nationalism. Its cultural significance is enormous.

The assertion of modernity is posing a real challenge to the three cultural ideals which have been talked about. First, the ethos of an urban or industrial form of living goes against the ethos of an agricultural society—its group orientation, close affinity with local communities and family-kinship ties. The ethos of a future-oriented, dynamic, achievement-based view of life disrupts the relatively peaceful character of a non-modern living. Second, the externalization of modernity, its secularity and logic of technological manipulation of nature for man's continual material well-being goes against what we have regarded as the spiritual or inward-looking dimension of India's cultural ideal. For instance, it has often been argued that the Hindu mind being shaped by the Vedas and the Upanishads is not particularly comfortable with the most fundamental feature of modern scientific and technological enterprise—the process of objectification of nature. It has often been argued that the ancient Hindu sages who sang the Vedas were worshippers of nature and not its explorers. Moreover, there was a spirit of humility and self-surrender before nature. In other words, here was a cultural tradition that saw nature as an expression of the cosmic order, not something to be objectified for domination.[24] It is this tradition that the instrumental rationality of modernity challenges. Third, the ethos of modernity seeks to threaten the accommodative space of our cultural tradition. The reason is that the cognitive arrogance of modernity (the assertion that all non-modern forms of living are necessarily backward), its scientism and universality are not comfortable with heterogeneity, plurality and differences. As a result, the homogenizing impulses of modernity may go against the accommodative/dialogical spirit of our cultural ideal.

Modernity, as Yogendra Singh has argued, is responsible for the cultural metamorphosis Indian society is passing through. For Singh, modernity implies "introjection of the value of equality in place of hierarchy, of individualism as replacement of holism, of historicity in place of continuity and of techno-scientific rationalism in place of the principle of transcendence.[25] The resultant cultural transformation can be seen in forms of living, behaviour patterns and relationships. Some broad generalizations are not impossible. For example, traditional sanctions are fast losing their importance in shaping the behaviour of the individual. It is not difficult to see how the intensity of family-kinship bonds is declining. The achievement-oriented individual is seeing his future in his engagement with the phenomenal world. Society is filled with violence and competitiveness. Modernity with its ethos of equality and uniformity is also denying the traditional role-differentiations. For instance, we see the assertion of the marginalized or subaltern castes, their refusal to accept the forward caste hegemony. Likewise, it may be argued that women exposed to modernity are no longer contented with their traditional roles. They are fast entering the public sphere. This has certainly led to the redefinition of family, motherhood and all that is associated with women.

There are, however, two points to note:

(i) We are not necessarily attaching a negative connotation to modernity. As oppressed groups like women and lower castes argue, modernity, because of its ethos of equality, has indeed played an emancipatory role. In fact, in a society like ours, as the progressives would argue, the state is required to act like an agent of modernization. It is often assumed that a 'secular' state—with its agenda of 'scientific temper', techno-industrial development and economic progress—must fight all sorts of 'pre-modern' pathologies located in a traditional society. Moreover, if we are really sincere about the ideal of accommodative space we are talking about, we must accommodate the positive features of modernity. To borrow Nandy's poetic language: "India, to be India, has to have the courage to be non-India—it is part of her dharma to be microcosm of the world."[26] As a matter of fact, far from negating modernity, what we are proposing is that if modernity is allowed to destroy the fundamental ideals of our culture, it would indeed be a case of cultural invasion, a threat to some of our noblest aspirations. Not surprisingly, we see the reflection of this anxiety in many sociological writings. Imagine, for example, T.N. Madan's intervention. "Modernization of culture should not mean sameness, for sameness is dullness of the mind and deadens creative faculties."[27] He reminds us of the Faustian character of modernity (the notion of growth as an unlimited good) and how it leads to destructive consumerism. He wants to remind us to what Gandhi wanted: limitation of wants and a harmonic relationship with the world. The fact is that unless we tap our own cultural resources, modernity, far from being emancipatory, may prove to be an oppressive experience.

(ii) It is equally important to remember that the assertion of modernity is not the end of the traditional culture. In fact, as sociologists are arguing, tradition has often used modernity to project itself in a new fashion. Some random examples would suffice. The rationale of popular democracy has been used to enhance the power of caste associations and identities. As the matrimonial columns reveal, modern newspapers are popularizing the idea of traditional or arranged marriage. Religion is also used for secular goals like political power. "It is, therefore, important", as Yogendra Singh has argued, "to conceptualize both tradition and modernization as sets of values and role-structures which interact as they come into contact, and between them a selective process of assimilation and syncretism starts."[28]

Here is indeed a complex situation. Modernity may be experienced as an agency of colonization. Again, its possibilities may be accommodated for emancipatory purposes. It may also give a new momentum to tradition. In our everyday existence, this complex interplay of tradition and modernity has perhaps led to a kind of cultural schizophrenia. More often than not, many of us experience ourselves as conflicted personalities with dilemmas, tensions and anxieties.

To understand all this one can only recall Ashis Nandy's remarkably brilliant analysis of commercial Hindi cinema.[29] Commercial Hindi films, despite their apparent superficiality and melodramatic gestures, respond to the psychological needs of the uprooted, people torn between tradition and modernity, people who still seek answers in their cultural traditions in order to make sense of the world. He is not wrong when he says that the commercial cinema in India, unlike many 'art' films which are ruthlessly hostile to the norms of our cultural traditions, tend to reaffirm the values being more and more marginalized by the language of the modernizing middle classes, values such as community solidarity, non-competitive and non-contractual human relations, priority of maternity over conjugality, priority of the mythical over the historical. Not surprisingly, in the commercial cinema, a modern, Western-educated, slickly-dressed woman is often projected as aggressive and openly seductive. But then, the shy, nurtural, submissive village girl has got a heart of gold. Likewise, to quote Nandy, "the ultra modern, arrogant, super-competent, Western-educated, professional has to ultimately turn to his twin—a rustic, good-hearted, spirited boy from the backwards of India to defeat the hard-hearted smuggler or black-marketeer who in turn is a negative model of modernity."[30]

Nandy's study is merely an illustration. One can give many other examples from the phenomenology of everyday existence itself. The fact is that as modernity is becoming overwhelmingly powerful, the fear of cultural invasion is becoming more and more acute. There is confusion or proliferation of split identities. And there are divergent attempts to 'rescue' our cultural traditions.

IV

Globalization, Consumerism and Mass Culture

This reflection on cultural invasion leads us to examine what is called globalization. "Globalization as a concept", wrote Ronald Robertson, "refers both to the compression of the world and the intensification of consciousness of the world as a while."[31] Perhaps the global culture is becoming a reality because, modernity as a grand system is bringing all cultures together and leading to a set of uniform responses and expectations. Moreover, with the new technologies of communication, the cultural messages of modernity are spreading everywhere. In India, for instance, we have seen the gigantic expansion of the new technologies of communication. As a result, all the words, images and symbols the metropolitan West emits are entering our world. This leads many to argue that gone are the days of cultural exclusion. India cannot remain insulated and we ought to integrate ourselves with the 'global village'.

While trying to understand the global culture Arjun Appadurai makes an interesting observation.[32] He talks about ethnoscape'—landscape of persons who constitute the shifting world in which we live : tourists, immigrants, refugees, exiles and other moving groups and persons. He also talks about 'technoscape' —the global configuration of technology that moves at high speeds across various kinds of previously impervious boundaries. And finally, he talks about 'mediascape' which refers to the distribution of the electronic capabilities to produce and disseminate information which are now available throughout the world. In other words, the point that Appadurai wants to make is that the combination of ethnoscape, technoscape and mediascape lead to the globalization of culture.

What is the cultural significance of globalization? Perhaps there is no single answer to such a complex question. For example, Appadurai is not willing to equate globalization with homogenization. Because he sees the tension between cultural homogenization and cultural heterogenization. ". . . The central feature of global culture today is the politics of the mutual effort of sameness and difference to cannibalize one another."[33] In one of his articles Anthony D. Smith has written about the difficulty in implementing the project of a global culture—a uniformly streamlined packaging.[34] The reason is that, as Smith would argue, a global culture is essentially "memoryless"—widely diffused in space and cut off from any past. But then, Smith seeks to remind us, collective identity is based on shared memories and a sense of continuity between generations: . . . "Given the depth of such memories, the project of a global culture . . . must appear premature for some time to come."[35]

It is possible to have a continual debate on the potency of globalization—whether it can homogenize the world or whether differences can still be retained. But, as it exists, what is really happening in the name of globalization is primarily domination or invasion. Authentic globalization requires a meaningful, egalitarian and dialogic exchange of cultures. This means that each culture expands its horizon without, however, denying its uniqueness and specificity. But this is not what is happening. The fact is that culture cannot be separated from power. In the world capitalist system the tremendous techno-economic power that the Euro-American world enjoys leads it to define and dictate the contents of the global culture. Not surprisingly, the contents of this packaged culture are utterly insensitive to the richness of our cultural traditions. This is essentially the American mass culture. With its hedonism and violence it shows its insensitivity to the kind of cultural ideals we have talked about.

Before more is written about consumerism and mass culture, let us understand the rationale of the new technologies of communication—particularly, the rationale of the visual media. Because it is primarily through the visual media that the global culture is transcending the boundaries of national societies.

As we are trying to understand the rationale of the visual media, we can do it by distinguishing, say, the power of books from the power of television. Three simple but meaningful observations can be made. First, particularly in the context of a society like ours where the level of literacy is not very high, books have their limits; not many can enter the world of books. But watching television does not require the literary skill; everyone can watch and enjoy the visuals. That is why, unlike printed words, visual images are much more successful in spreading the cultural messages of the 'global village'. Second, the kind of critical faculty which one needs to read books is not necessarily required while one watches television. To read a book is to think and argue with its author; it is an activistic and thoughtful process. But watching television is a relatively more relaxed, passive and non-critical exercise. Third, images with colour and glamour, images talking and smiling and persuading are intensely seductive. Images make one mad and blind. To sum up, these three observations suggest that with the gigantic spread of the visual media, the possibility of cultural invasion has indeed become acute and widespread.

It is at this juncture that we need to be careful about the danger of overreaction. As we are talking about cultural invasion —particularly, through the new technologies of communication— we are perhaps underestimating the hermeneutic faculty of the viewers, the consumers of media products. As John B.Thompson has argued, "...the reception of media products is fundamentally a hermeneutic process."[36] This means that this process of reception is a situated activity, a skilled accomplishment. Depending on their biographies, their social locations and collective memories, they attach their specific meanings to the globalized cultural products and symbolic forms. For Thompson, "the globalization of communication has not eliminated the localized character of appropriation... Its growing importance attests to the dual fact that the circulation of information and communication has become increasingly global while, at the same time, the process of appropriation remains inherently contextual and hermeneutic."[37] Perhaps Thompson seeks to suggest that the receivers of this media culture need not necessarily be brainwashed. They can retain their criticality and tap their own cultural resources while receiving these media products. In other words, do not feel paranoid; do not feel obsessed with the fear of cultural invasion!

Doubtless to say, Thompson's point makes sense. But, at the same time, it would be unrealistic not to see any threat of cultural invasion. The fact is that the packaged global culture does systematic violence to our cultural sensitivity. And at a time when images are seductive; it is difficult not to get carried away by this spectacular, media-induced culture. One thing should, however, be kept in mind. The danger is coming not only from the foreign media. In fact, what is striking is that even Indian television—because of its eagerness to cope with the foreign TV and therefore survive in this competitive world—is fast emulating the same rationale. Be it Doordarshan or Star TV or Zee TV—one can clearly see the emergence of a new cultural package. Let us understand it.

(a) This is consumerism. The first principle of consumerism is that it is based on man's 'having' impulses.[38] Have more and more of everything: money, sex, fun, pleasure. Consumerism, in other words, is based on the multiplication of human needs. With consumerism, it seems, one can no longer distinguish the real needs from the constructed ones. Each new need—be it the new model of a car or a refrigerator or an item of fast food—ought to be satisfied and fulfilled at any cost.

(b) Consumerism is not just the consumption of things and commodities. In a consumerist culture one buys a car not simply to satisfy the need for transportation, but because it symbolizes and signifies a mode of living, a style It is understood as success! Consumerism, therefore, means the proliferation of images and signs.

(c) This preoccupation with consumption, it is obvious, can become a dominant trend only when capitalism reaches a certain level of affluence, only when it succeeds in creating the new middle class having sufficient leisure time and the purchasing capacity. In this regard consumerism can be said to be the culture of late capitalism.

(d) The ethos of consumerism appears to generate uniform life-styles and expectations and, theoretically, everyone can participate in it. Yet, the very rationale of consumerism makes one perpetually anxious and insecure. Life is equated with having. Not to have, therefore, means lagging behind. While describing this 'insecurity innate in having' mode of existence Erich Fromm wrote:

> If I am what I have and if what I have is lost, who then am I? Nobody but a defeated, deflated, pathetic testimony to a wrong way of living. Because I can lose what I have, I am necessarily constantly worried that I shall lose what I have. I am afraid of thieves, of economic changes, of revolutions, of sickness, of death, and I am afraid of love, of freedom, of growth, of change, of the unknown. Thus I am continuously worried, suffering from a chronic hypochondriasis, with regard not only to loss of health, but to any other loss of what I have, I become defensive, hard, suspicious, lonely, driven by the need to have more in order to be better protected.[39]

This is the beginning of neurotic restlessness for new things, new fashions and new images. This insecurity gets intensified because consumerism separates man from history, from all cultural linkages and memories. There is nothing to rely on except the immediate or instant achievement. This is depthlessness.

Indeed, in recent times we have seen the arrival of this new cultural package in India. In order to make our point clear, we wish to reflect on three events: music as a piece of technological spectacle (Michael Jackson in Mumbai); food as an image of success (McDonald's in New Delhi) and beauty as an item of consumption (Miss World Contest in Bangalore). What is interesting is that it is the ethos of techno-capitalism that manifests itself in this culture. Technology, it is thought, is spectacular. Technology performs miracles! Not surprisingly, technology shapes even the phenomenology of everyday existence. As a matter of fact, Michael Jackson is a creation of this mind-set. He symbolizes that music is no longer music; it is a piece of technological spectacle as gorgeous as man's journey into the space. He conveys a message: even man's intimate musical moments of joy and sorrow can no longer be experienced in their profound simplicity. Again, food can no longer be perceived as pure nutritional need; it is often mingled with an image that defines one's identity, one's distinctive mark. Eating out is almost like a pilgrimage to a constructed space that inflates one's ego. McDonald's is precisely that. In a way, it symbolizes the American image of success. As a matter of fact, it is this hunger for consumption that objectifies everything. In this process of objectification, sexuality, for example, becomes a major instrument. A woman, her rhythm and poetry, her intelligence and body language—everything can be quantified and graded. It is this 'perfectly measured' beauty that we are asked to consume. A humane way of looking at women gets corrupted. We become hungry consumers and they become consumable commodities.

This culture has finally arrived in India. There are primarily two reasons. First, we are witnessing how 'official' India with its gospel of economic liberalization is eager to alter its self-image. This means almost a mindless entry into the global capitalist system; this is to accept its premises, projects and life-patterns. And globalization is impossible without the fundamentals of techno-capitalism. The changing cultural climate reflects the new image of India. Second, the aspirations of the emergent middle class have to be understood. Here is a class without any living memory of the ideals of the freedom struggle—the ideals that, for example, Gandhi articulated so well in his celebrated *Hind Swaraj*.

As we understand the meaning of consumerism, it becomes easier to comprehend what it means in the context of India. Anyone familiar with the media scene knows how consumerism is becoming the dominant culture. The men and women we watch on television, the way they eat, drink and smoke, the way they love and hate—everything seems to suggest that gone are the days of old values. There is only one aim—to have more and more of everything. We are also watching images; advertisements, to use Jean Baudrillard's words, take us to a "hyperreal" world in which there is no distinction between the real and the unreal. Life tends to be equated with all that those glamorous and gorgeous people do on the screen—the way they eat and sing, drive and travel. This mythologization of `success' can be seen in the growing popularity of fashion shows beauty contests and `look of the year' spectacles.

With consumerism—the culture of late capitalism—enters India, a country where there is a wide cleavage between the consumptionist middle class and the downtrodden, one can see its disastrous consequences. There is a democratization of images, but no democratization of resources to fulfil the desire intensified by the images. A contradiction of this kind leads to violence, imitative tendencies and all sorts of pathological complexes. In other words, consumerism denies the basic simplicity of the life-ethos that used to be a major feature of an agricultural society. Consumerism denies the great cultural strength of people, the ability to find joy and meaning not in things and commodities, but in harmonic relationship with one's community, with nature, with its rhythm and beauty.

To put it otherwise, the narcissistic ethos of the consumerist culture is against the group ideal of our culture. Moreover, consumerism, unlike our culture, does not know what it means to have a fusion of the sacred and the profane. Consumerism stimulates vital desires, but it does not know how to integrate these desires with the higher dimension of existence. Imagine, for instance, the fundamental difference between Krishna's love with Radha and the image of love the advertisement of the Kama Sutra condom projects. The fusion of Krishna and Radha tends to take us to a world of perfect joy, bliss and happiness. But the love implicit in the Kama Sutra condom is crudely utilitarian as it is based on the principle of 'having', not 'being'. It does not give itself, it just possesses!

There is another aspect to this culture. It is mass culture. And one can see how it differs strikingly from the rich folk tradition of Indian culture. The folk tradition is participatory. There is no qualitative differences between the entertainer and the entertained, the creative artist and the community which enjoys artistic forms. The whole community participates in artistic creations. But in mass culture there is no participation; people are just consumers or passive receivers. An example would suffice. In *Ramlila* as it is performed in innumerable villages and localities, the entire community participates. But how difficult it is when people watch Ramanand Sagar's *Ramayana* on television. Here is a striking metamorphosis—from an active participant to a passive consumer!

The folk tradition is organically related to people's struggle, their collective dreams, hopes, aspirations and anxieties. This means that there is no leisured class that creates the folk cultural forms. But as far as mass culture goes there is no organic relationship with people's everyday life. Culture is manufactured, sold in the form of attractive packages—the way fast food, soft drink and cosmetics are sold. Here is yet another transformation: from a struggling being creating culture to a consumer in the market place buying culture. Even when the urban middle class shows its eagerness to preserve the folk culture, it comes as a packaged item cut off from its soil. Culture becomes just an artefact with no live experience. With the consumptionist possession of the folk cultural form, it gets reduced into a decorum or a piece of fashion.

Not surprisingly, with 'mass culture' begins what is called "culture-industry".[40] It manufactures culture like consumable commodities. And like any other industry it uses every new form of technology to 'improve' its product. Technology enters almost every aspect of mass culture. Music, film, sports—everything gets reduced into a great technological spectacle. People are seen talking more and more about technics, but not about life. Not solely that, the 'culture industry' tends to create uniformity, some kind of standardization of tastes and responses. Be it a TV serial or a one-day-cricket match, culture becomes an item of mass consumption. In other words, we see the emergence of the non-critical, non-reflexive, homogenized mass of people. This is perhaps the beginning of authoritarianism.

V

Colonization of Religion

An understanding of culture would remain incomplete unless one talks about religion. Because when one is speaking of cultural decay in India, what comes to one's mind is also the decay in the religious sphere. It is true that the proponents of secularism often evolve a critique of religion, particularly the way it is allowed to enter the public sphere. The major thrust of this critique is that religion is essentially divisive, it is ritualistic, it is full of superstitions and, in the ultimate analysis, it is not conducive to the growth of secular and scientific rationality needed for modern democracy.

But we wish to argue that cultural sanity and religion are not necessarily incompatible with each other. As a matter of fact, the deeper experience of religion—spirituality, fusion of horizons and reduction of purely egotistic desires and impulses—is conducive to a healthy, peaceful, communitarian cultural practice.

This, however, does not mean that religion, as it is practised, does always conform to the ideal we are talking about. History has witnessed the recurrence of the conflict between the spiritual ideal of religion and the institutions of religion with—hierarchical and oppressive practices. History has also witnessed dissents and revolts. From Buddha to Kabir and from Chaitanya to Gandhi—the story is the same everywhere. This was a protest against empty ritualism, against institutionalized hierarchies and oppressions. This was also a reminder that the essence of religion, far from restricting man's possibility, ought to widen him, expand his horizon.

Today when we speak of the crisis, what comes to one's mind is the political manipulation of religion. To put it simply, religion is used for non-spiritual pursuits like acquisition of state power or creating a nationalist ideology. It can, of course, be said that the religious reformers we admire—for instance, Vivekananda and Gandhi—did try to broaden the scope of religion and give a political connotation to it. For Vivekananda, the agenda of a new India depended heavily on organized Hinduism. He wanted the Hindus to become aware of the great ancient ideals; he wanted them to develop "muscles of iron, nerves of steel and gigantic wills", to cultivate "manliness" and create a strong nation. Not surprisingly, Vivekananda's religiosity was not just committed to a purely transcendental realm. It sought to transform the larger society, fight untouchability and excessive ritualism. Likewise, Gandhi sought to reconcile religion and politics. In religious and spiritual ideals Gandhi found the strength needed to evolve the tools of political protest—ahimsa and satyagraha.

Vivekananda and Gandhi have often been hijacked by the proponents of contemporary *Hindutva*. Yet, the fact remains that the aggressive politics of *Hindutva* does not coincide with their ideals. They wanted to activate man's spiritual energy and create a society based on egalitarian values like tolerance and compassion. What we are witnessing today is, however, different. The goal is not to activate spirituality for egalitarian values. Instead, the aim is to reduce religion into an exclusivist identity that, far from uniting, separates one group from the other and causes violence, hatred and intolerance. This is a strange situation. One need not be a believer or a spiritualist, yet in religion one can see one's community identity. This is despiritualized religion. This is not a faith. This is an ideology, cleverly designed to 'unite' one group at the cost of separating it from its invented 'other'. This is what is called communalism or religious nationalism. This radiates not love, but hatred; not tolerance but intolerance; not the ethos of equality, but the principle of hierarchy. The popularization of this kind of religion has done severe damage to our cultural fabric. It is fast losing the great heritage of tolerance, spirituality and accommodative space. The Ayodhya episode symbolizes this fall.

Religion becomes extraordinarily conscious of its externalities. It is hardly experienced as a meaning needed to cope with the riddles of existence: life and death, finite and infinite, birth and separation, desire and suffering. It is incapable of creating its Ramana Maharshis and Ramakrishnas. Instead, with its *Bajrang Dal* brand it appeals to those who in this mass society have already become insensitive to the deeper questions of existence. As a matter of fact, the Ayodhya episode negates "the Hindu view of life" — the cultural ideal about which Radhakrishnan once wrote:

> . . . Hinduism does not believe in bringing about a mechanical uniformity of belief and worship by a forcible elimination of all that is not in agreement with a particular creed . . . Its scheme of salvation is not limited to those who hold a particular view of God's nature and worship. Such an exclusive absolutism is not fair to God or man to assume that one people are the chosen of God, that their religion occupies

a central place in the religious development of mankind, and that all others should borrow from them or suffer spiritual destitution.[41]

With its intolerance, the Ayodhya episode also demonstrates the packaging of religion in the name of an exclusivist nationalist ideology. The use of religion as a nationalist ideology, it goes without saying, has not been appreciated by many great minds. Nationalism as an ideology, it is thought, is very much 'modern' in the sense that its ethos is primarily the ethos of standardization and uniformity. As a result, it seeks to become violent and exclusivist; it is not very comfortable with differences, plurality and diversities. Religion, therefore, loses the spiritual ideal of seeing unity in differences. Instead, its ruthlessly violent and 'unifying' mission causes terror, arouses passion and blind loyalty. Ashis Nandy has argued in one of his recent books[42] that both Tagore and Gandhi, two outstanding personalities of modern India, saw the "illegitimacy" of this sort of nationalism. They saw its danger and violent implications. Both of them were patriotic, yet their patriotism was not based on exclusivist nationalism. Instead, their vision of India, Nandy argues, was based on great cultural and civilizational ideals of femininity (or maternity), love, spirituality and tolerance. Nandy further argues that particularly at a time when we are witnessing the evils of this sort of religious nationalism, it is necessary to grow aware of the alternate voice that came from visionaries like Gandhi and Tagore..

The damage to culture can also be seen in the way religion has been colonized by the logic of money. This is not to argue that in the past religion was necessarily 'pure' and 'free' from commercialization. What we are trying to argue is that in our times capitalism further adds to the commercialization of religion. The meaning of capitalism is that money can buy everything. Not surprisingly, more money means more religion! This unbounded faith in the power of money can be seen in the religious festivals in our times. Undoubtedly, festivals are important as they bring us closer and help us to break the monotony of existence. In festivals there is indeed a jump from necessity to freedom. But the festivals we are seeing around are fast losing that spontaneity, that innocence and pure joy. Instead, one smells the power of money. Festivals become gorgeous. Like TV serials, religious festivals too are now sponsored by big multinationals. For instance, anyone who has seen the Durga Puja festival in Delhi or Calcutta would agree that with this sort of commercialization of religion, the externality of the festivals has acquired great importance, but man's inner resources have been systematically denied. This is the denial of one's spirituality and ability to find joy in ordinary things of life. This is to quantify religion, to measure its "success" in terms of its money power. The point we are trying to state is that with the growing despiritualization of religion, our culture is fast losing its noblest ideals and strengths. It is affecting people's life-practices.

VI

Limits to Cultural Relativism

The awareness of cultural invasion—or this increasing sensitivity to the threat to Indian culture—does not mean that one is pleading for the 'purity' of our culture. In fact, there is no such 'purity'; it cannot be retained because cultures are continually overlapping. Even Sri Aurobindo who wrote so passionately about the fundamentals of Indian culture saw the desirability of cultural interchange. To quote Sri Aurobindo, "Any attempt to remain exactly what we were before the European invasion or to ignore in future the claims of a modern environment and necessity is foredoomed to an obvious failure."[43] Moreover, it has to be remembered that all the changes taking place in the cultural domain are not necessarily undesirable. In fact, this discussion will remain incomplete unless we speak of some of the positive changes which Indian society has experienced because of the ongoing process of cultural transformation.

This means that this cultural transformation, or, to put it in other words, the assertion of modernity, has posed a challenge to some of the unhealthy features in our culture. What are these unhealthy features? To begin with, what comes to one's mind is the principle of hierarchy in our culture. Its striking manifestation is the vertically arranged *varnas/jatis*. The pathology of casteism is its most negative aspect. This means that excessive importance is attached to one's ascribed status; one's status is determined by the accident of birth in a *jati*. Likewise, another ugly feature of our cultural practice is the ritual of purity and pollution. One comes in close contact and touch and eat only with those of equal ritual status, not with other groups. Its extreme manifestation is the practice of untouchability. Again, the doctrine of karma (broadly speaking, this means that the deeds of one's previous life influence one's present life) tends to cause a fatalistic or defeatist attitude towards life.[44]

It is true that all the great innovators of Indian culture—be it Buddha or Kabir or Gandhi—sought to fight these ugly cultural practices. But perhaps it is modernity—and modern/secular institutions—that did quite a lot to alter these practices. It is not anybody's contention to argue that with modernity all these ugly practices have disappeared. In fact, modernity has often helped these practices to acquire a new meaning. Yet, what is undeniable is that the ethos of modernity is leading to some significant changes. As it is based on equality and individualism, it begins to challenge the principle of hierarchy and ascribed status. As modernity seeks to restore the human agency and makes one future-oriented, it challenges the notion of karma and fatalism. Moreover, modern institutions—factories, hospitals, universities—or, modern modes of transportation and communication—cannot function with the principle of purity and pollution.

And modernity is indeed having its visible impact on the cultural practices of people. For instance, the hitherto oppressed groups are challenging the principle of hierarchy, purity and pollution. They are overcoming their silence, regaining the human agency and forcing the larger society to become increasingly sensitive to the ideals of equality, democratization and diffusion of power. In fact, the newly acquired confidence of the marginalized groups—oppressed castes and women—is a positive gain. This should not be overlooked.

The fact is that there are limits to cultural relativism. To absolutize relativism is to believe that a culture can remain insulated and retain its 'purity'. Moreover, to absolutize relativism is to believe that cross-cultural communication is difficult and it is impossible to have an ethical judgment.[45] But, as our arguments suggest, because of cultural encounters, there are changes in a culture and, at times, these changes are healthy and desirable. This means that we are not pleading for postmodernity and the way it absolutizes differences and promotes relativism. Not to accept postmodernity should not, however, be equated with the unconditional celebration of modernity and the resultant uniformity and homogeneity of cultures. This is important to understand. Although we accept the gains of modernity in some spheres of our collective existence, we are not willing to allow it to colonize our cultural traditions and deny the ideals we have talked about. To quote Sri Aurobindo once again: "We can still think in the essential sense of the great spirit and ideals of our past, but the form of our thinking, our speaking, our development of them has changed by the very fact of new thought and experience."[46]

But then, there are sociologists—Ernest Gellner is one of them—who, in the name of resisting cultural pluralism, speak of the inevitability of the homogenized or uniform culture. Because, it is argued, modern nation-states all over the world are engaged in the project of nationalism (or modernity) which invariably requires a standardized, literate culture overcoming variations, differences and local traditions.[47] Moreover, Gellner tends to suggest that no culture can remain indifferent to the "superiority" of Western or industrial culture.[48]

An argument of this kind ought to be fought and opposed. There are three reasons. First, cultural pluralism need not be equated with absolute relativism. Plurality and differences can be retained even without being utterly relativistic. In other words, we are for dialogue, not for uniformity or imposition of one particular culture on the rest of the world. Because dialogue means the possibility of what Gadamer would call the 'fusion of horizons'; dialogue means that, despite being rooted in one's own cultural tradition, one can grow up, learn from alternate possibilities and expand oneself. Dialogue means that cultures can grow and change is possible, although this change need not be imposed. In other words, dialogue means decolonization: not the imposition of Euro-centric modernity, but a critical engagement with it without losing the fundamentals of one's own culture. Differences are respected; but the possibility of cultural exchange and the resultant transformation is not denied. Second, the so-called inevitability of modern/industrial/western culture does not necessarily mean its absolute desirability. Some of the contents of this modern culture—its consumerism or its technologized mentality—have done severe damage to ecology and the mental health of the human species. What is, therefore, needed is not a surrender before modernity, but a critical reflection or a voice of dissent against the pathologies of modernity. Third, there are indeed emancipatory potentials in a non-modern culture. In the name of universal modernity, these alternate cultural ideals should not be abolished.

This takes us to the moot point. A new cultural agenda needs to retain its criticality in order to have a meaningful dialogue with modernity. It also needs the strength to realize the emancipatory potentials of the cultural ideals we have talked about. For instance, the peaceful/group ideal that our culture emphasizes can revolutionize our world—a world collapsing because of the strains of modernity, its aggressive individualism and the resultant alienation of man from man. Likewise, the cultural ideal of spirituality can restore the harmony that the dualistic principles of modernity have damaged. Similarly, the integral vision of life (merger of the sacred and the profane or the ability to raise the lower to the higher) can bring sanity to the pleasure-seeking, consumptionist, hedonistic man. Moreover, the accommodative spirit of our cultural ideal can democratize the world which is fast becoming homogenized and one-dimensional. As a matter of fact, the ideals we are talking about are not for any nostalgia for the past. Our cultural agenda is not regressive. It is progressive and seeks to create a new world. That is why, this cultural agenda has to be distinguished from what we have been witnessing these days—the emergence of a closed, orthodox, intolerant mentality and everything in the name of 'protecting the cultural heritage'! In other words, the agenda we are talking about seeks to tap the cultural resources in order to create a new society: emancipatory, communitarian, ecologically sensitive and spiritually cultivated.

To accomplish such a cultural project is to fight against the dominant economic ideals prevalent in our age. As development is equated with multiplication of needs and technologization of almost every sphere of our life, all cultural ideals experience severe threat. That is why, the challenging task is to say 'no' to the so-called inevitability of the global capitalist system. The task is to strive for alternate economic propositions based not on the ideal of unlimited consumption, but on a harmonic lifestyle. The task is to prevent the market from colonizing the lifeworld. Cultural recovery is impossible without an alternate agenda for politico-economic development.

The question is: who will be the new agents—the creators of this new world? Perhaps not much can be expected from the expanding middle-class. The sociology of this class has to be studied further. Meanwhile, one thing can be said about this class. Here is a class not at all filled with idealism, with a vocation, a mission. The spirit of decolonization has faded away. The class has also lost the urge or the confidence to assert the cultural ideal of India. Instead, here is a consumptionist, pleasure seeking, cynical class without the courage to say 'no' to false globalization and imperialism of thoughts, categories and life-practices. Moreover, the all-pervasive corruption in almost every sphere of life has made this class utterly opportunistic. To borrow Matthew Arnold's words, here is a group of "philistines" who believe that "greatness and welfare are proved only by being rich".[49] They are the enemies of "sweetness and light". Likewise, the intellectuals being born and brought up in an institutional milieu whose dominant ethos is primarily Western are not organically related to popular feeling. This alienation makes it difficult for them to represent authentically the voices of people and, thereby, lead a movement needed to fight the cultural invasion. In other words, we live in an age in which it is becoming increasingly difficult to find authentic leadership, organic intellectuals and cultural innovators. And it is this stage of void that is utterly suffocating.

Yet, the voice of sanity is never dead. For example, when one reflects on the last three films made by Satyajit Ray—one of the finest minds of the Indian cinema—one sees the all-pervasive corruption/opportunism that has inflicted the middle class. Yet, even in such a dark world Ray saw a possibility in the honesty of a doctor, a musical man and an anthropologist. Indeed, there are movements taking place—movements against corruption, brutality of development, and the marketization of sexuality. The question is, when and how do these movements overcome their marginalization, assume a truly pan-Indian character and restore all that we have lost and in the process of this recovery create a new future.

NOTES

1. For example, B. Malinowski pleaded for the biological foundations of culture. See his *A Scientific Theory of Culture and Other Essays* (New York: The University of California Press, 1965).
2. Ralph Linton, *The Cultural Background of Personality* (London: Routledge and Kegan Paul, 1947), especially Ch. I, Ch. II and Ch. V.
3. Clifford Geertz, *The Interpretation of Cultures* (New York: Basic Books, Inc; Publishers, 1973), p. 46.
4. Quoted in Richard Kluckhohn, (ed.), *Collected Essays of Clyde Kluckhohn: Culture and Behaviour* (New York: The Free Press, 1962), p. 45.
5. Ruth Benedict, *Patterns of Culture* (London: Routledge and Kegan Paul, 1971), p. 35.
6. Humayun Kabir, *The Indian Heritage* (Bombay: Asia Publishing House, 1955); S. Abid Husain, *The National Culture of India* (New Delhi: National Book Trust, 1956).
7. S. Abid Husain, *The National Culture*, pp. 18-19.
8. Sri Aurobindo, *The Foundations of Indian Culture* (Pondicherry: Sri Aurobindo Ashram, 1980), p. 52.
9. *Ibid.*, p. 75.
10. *Ibid.*, p. 236.
11. *Ibid.*, p. 276.
12. Anand K. Coomaraswamy, *Essays in National Idealism* (New Delhi: Munshiram Manhorlal Publishers Pvt. Ltd., 1981), p. 19.
13. Sri Aurobindo, *op. cit.*, p. 311.
14. *Ibid.*
15. Anand K. Coomaraswamy, *op. cit.*, p. 31.
16. Sri Aurobindo, *op. cit.*, pp. 292-93.
17. Jawaharlal Nehru, *The Discovery of India* (New Delhi: Jawaharlal Nehru Memorial Fund, 1983).
18. D.D. Kosambi, *The Culture and Civilization of Ancient India: An Historical Outline* (Delhi: Vikas Publishing House Pvt. Limited, 1970), p. 78.
19. *Ibid.*, p. 207.
20. Debiprasad Chattopadhyay, *What is Living and What is Dead in Indian Philosophy* (New Delhi: People's Publishing House, 1976), p. 610.

21. Dhurjati Prasad Mukerji, *Sociology of Indian Culture* (Jaipur: Rawat *Publications, 1979), p. 7.*
22. Ashis Nandy, *Traditions, Tyranny and Utopias: Essays in the Politics of Awareness* (Delhi: Oxford University Press, 1987), p. 158.
23. Yogendra Singh, *Modernization of Indian Tradition* (New Delhi: Rawat Publications, 1988).
24. Ramakant Sinari, "Science Technology and the Hindu Weltanschauung" in B.D. Nag Chaudhuri (ed.), *New Technological Civilization and Indian Society* (Simla: Indian Institute of Advanced Study, 1990).
25. Yogendra Singh, *Essays on Modernization in India* (New Delhi: Manohar, 1989), p. 183.
26. Ashis Nandy, *Traditions, Tyranny and Utopias*, p. 153.
27. T.N. Madan, *Culture and Development* (Delhi: Oxford University Press, 1983), p. 43.
28. Yogendra Singh, *Modernization of Indian Tradition*, p. 214.
29. Ashis Nandy, "An Intelligent Critic's Guide to Indian Cinema" in K.S. Singh (ed.), *Visual Anthropology and India* (Calcutta: Anthropological Survey of India, 1992), pp. 43-76.
30. *Ibid.*, pp. 70-71.
31. Ronald Robertson, *Globalization: Social Theory and Global Culture* (London: Sage Publications, 1992), p. 8.
32. Arjun Appadurai, "Disjuncture and Difference in the Global Cultural Economy" in Mike Featherstone (ed.), *Global Culture: Nationalism, Globalization and Modernity* (London: Sage Publications, 1990).
33. *Ibid.*, pp. 307-08.
34. Anthony D. Smith, "Towards a Global Culture" in Mike Featherstone (ed.), *Global Culture*, pp. 171-91.
35. *Ibid.*, p. 180.
36. John B. Thompson, *The Media and Modernity: A Social Theory of the Media* (Cambridge: Polity Press, 1995), p. 40.
37. *Ibid.*, p. 174.
38. For a brilliant analysis of 'having made of existence, see Erich From, *To Have or To Be* (London: Abacus, 1982).
39. *Ibid.*, p. 111.
40. For a brilliant analysis of 'culture-industry' see T.W. Adorno and Max Horkheimer, *Dialectic of Enlightenment* (New York: Herder and Herder, 1972), pp. 120-67.
41. S. Radhakrishnan, *The Hindu View of Life* (Bombay: Blackie and Son Publishers, 1983), p. 37.
42. Ashis Nandy, *The Illegitimacy of Nationalism: Rabindranath Tagore and the Politics of Self* (Delhi: Oxford University Press, 1994).

43. Sri Aurobindo, *op. cit.*, p. 392.
44. For further elaboration, see S.C. Dubey, *Indian Society* (New Delhi: NBT, 1990). Also see Yogendra Singh, *Modernization of Indian Tradition*.
45. For an illuminating discussion on confrontation of cultures, see Bimal Krishna Matilal, *Confrontation of Cultures* (Calcutta: K.P. Bagchi and Company, 1988).
46. Sri Aurobindo, *op. cit.*, p. 393.
47. It is not our contention to argue that Gellner was altogether unwilling to permit cultural differences. But the fact remains that he was largely inclined to the 'convergence thesis' : the belief that because of modernity there would be a certain measure of global cultural convergence. See Ernest Gellner, *Nations and Nationalism* (Oxford: Basil Blackwell, 1983), especially Ch. 8.
48. See Ernest Gellner, "The New Idealism—Cause and Meaning in the Social Sciences", in Anthony Giddens (ed.), *Positivism and Sociology* (London: Heinemann, 1978), pp. 129-56.
49. Matthew Arnold, *Culture and Anarchy* (London: Cambridge University Press, 1971), pp. 101-02.

FIVE

Conflict of Worldviews: Imagining an Emancipatory Vision

One thing is clear that we are striving for alternatives. And no alternative is possible to visualize unless we look at the prevalent worldviews shaping the destiny of modern India. It is important to examine these worldviews, see their inner dynamics, go beyond and evolve possible alternatives. In fact, as one looks at contemporary India, one sees primarily three worldviews altering the reality around us. First, the ideal of liberalization is taking us to a new world of global culture, its technologized vision of the future. Liberalization, it is often thought, is creating a situation conducive to dramatic changes in our society: from tradition to modernity, from poverty to pleasures of consumerism. Second, there is an assertion of cultural narcissism manifesting itself in the ideology of *Hindutva*. It seeks to redefine secularism—one of the cherished ideals of progress. It is a force to reckon with—a force that is giving a new connotation to the nationalist project. Third, the rising subaltern voice, as it is manifesting itself in the political articulation by the Dalits and the lower castes, is challenging the established hegemony. It is, in fact, challenging a system in which privileges have always been monopolized by a tiny section of the elites.

The fact is that these three worldviews being articulated by divergent social forces convey three visions of the future not always compatible with one another. Because of these contrasting visions, the future, it seems, will be full of conflicts. A critical look at these changes and conflicts is likely to help us to evolve a new world-view we need to reconstruct the harmony we have lost.

I

Mythologization of Development

The economics of liberalization, a topic widely discussed, need not be repeated here. Instead, we will concentrate on the politico-ethical meaning of liberalization—what it means as a world view, how it affects one's priorities, relationships and life-projects. To begin with, it should be realized that liberalization, at least for those who desire it, means a new world—a world where one has finally overcome all odd ideological fixations like *swadeshi*, self-reliance and swaraj, a world where free market promises prosperity and affluence; a world where technology brings one nearer to the global culture. In other words, liberalization is seen as a truly modernist project with all its three major components: market, technology and globalization.

For the ruling elites, the acceptance of the mythology of liberalization becomes easier because these are not very good days for alternative social projects. Socialism is fast becoming a historical memory. Capitalism is fast getting an entry into what, till recently, was known as the 'socialist bloc'. This magical swing of the pendulum has undoubtedly given sufficient space to the proponents of free market to celebrate all around. Again, in India one is often asked to realize that there are limits to the Nehruvian project—its Fabian socialism, its mixed economy or the importance it attaches to the sovereignty of the nation and self-reliance. Instead, one is often reminded of sick public sectors. One is told that there is nothing public in public sectors; there is only dead weight of bureaucracy that denies initiative, cripples human agency, hampers growth.

There is also a belief that as the domain of technology is expanding fast and the international market network is universalizing itself, old ideas of self-reliance or sovereignty are no longer relevant. To survive is to compete. To compete is to accept the global market. This means liberalization which essentially implies the gradual withdrawal of the state from the market. The state need not interfere in the economic activities, for its only task, it is thought, is to create a situation conducive to the culture of free competition, a culture potent enough to transcend even national boundaries. This is what the IMF-World Bank-MNCs brand of development means. Rajni Kothari has expressed the growing 'disempowerment' of the state in the following fashion:

> The State in India, instead of occupying centre-stage in the social and economic arenas, is seen to be in retreat. This is obvious in the economic sphere from which it has been retreating over more than two decades now and, of course, most dramatically since 1991-92. But it is also true in the social sphere in matters such as providing opportunities to the minorities, the backward classes, tribal communities and women and children, encouraging people's initiatives and indigenous thinking in key areas such as education, environment, health and housing, and generally implementing the laws of the land for the betterment of the poorer and oppressed sections of society.[1]

A major socio-historical factor has to be understood in order to comprehend the phenomenon of liberalization. In fact, a significant change has taken place in the composition and character of the middle-class population in India. First, even numerically speaking, this class is a force to reckon with. The reason is that in postindependence India, because of industrialization and urbanization, there has been a significant growth of service sectors and modern professions leading to the proliferation of the new industrial-urban middle-class population. Second, the world view of this class, it appears, has altered dramatically.

A careful look at the history of the freedom struggle suggests that the middle-class that sought to accomplish the decolonization agenda was extremely sensitive to the question of national sovereignty, self-pride and cultural identity. It is true that none could deny the influence of the West—its education, and rational/liberal/scientific ideas—on the emerging middle-class. Yet, despite the overwhelming presence of the West and despite the asymmetrical power relations in colonialism, the middle-class retained its criticality; never did it forget to reassert the specificity of India's cultural uniqueness. Even a subaltern historian like Ranjit Guha accepts that, for instance, Bankim Chandra Chatterjee, who belonged to the middle-class, pleaded for a new historiography for India (Indian history must be written by Indians themselves in order to save it from the way the West appropriated and falsified it).[2] Likewise, this mission could be seen in the discourses of Rammohun, Vivekananda, Tilak, Gandhi, Aurobindo and Nehru. It was a class that created books like the *Geetharahasyam, The Hind Swaraj, The Foundations of Indian Culture* or *The Discovery of India.*

While narrating the contributions of the middle-class, particularly, the intelligentsia, A.R. Desai wrote:

> They were the pioneers, organizers and leaders of all political national movements. They brought ideas of nationalism and freedom to wider and wider sections of the Indian people, through educational and propaganda work which involved great self-sacrifice and suffering. They created rich provincial literatures and cultures, trying to impregnate them with the spirit of nationalism and democracy. They produced great scientists, poets, historians, sociologists, literateurs, philosophers and economists... .[3]

In fact, Desai saw a "broad middle-class basis" in the nationalist movement.

But things have changed in postindependence India. As the spirit of decolonization begins to fade away and many nationalist dreams collapse, one sees the new middle-class without the earlier mission. The demise of the Nehruvian era, it seems, is also an end to the link between the new middle-class and the memory of the freedom struggle. Now it is a class that allows itself to be seduced by consumerism, by the images the West emits through its new technologies of communication. It is a class that dislikes India, its poverty, its backwardness; it is a class that considers New York, London and Frankfurt as new places of worship. It is a class too "pragmatic" to be bothered about India's self-pride. It is a class that is likely to support the gospel of liberalization.

True, we ought to be careful about a grand generalization of this kind. Because the new middle-class is not a homogeneous group. For example, it is possible to see an extraordinarily sensitive section of the middle-class engaged in emancipatory activities like feminist or environmental movements or different grass roots activities. Yet, the point we wish to make is that, the context in which we locate the new middle-class has changed. It is a context in which the spirit of decolonization seems to have disappeared. It is a context in which there is growing disillusionment with the nationalist dreams. It is a context in which there are ever-expanding 'opportunities' because of globalization.

It is this release from the earlier 'fixations' that leads the new middle-class—once symbolized by Rajiv Gandhi—to imagine India of the twenty-first century: a project heavily dictated by the ethos of techno-economic liberalization and globalization.

The implications of liberalization are obvious. First, it is likely to mythologize development. Development tends to become primary; everything else—communitarian morality or social justice or self-reliance—becomes secondary. This leads to what is called 'catching up' syndrome. What the metropolitan West calls development ought to be attained or emulated at any cost. And this 'catching up' syndrome would perpetually retain the unequal relationship between the West and the non-West.

Second, liberalization is also a triumph of technology over politics. As technology becomes the most dominant evaluator of the quality of living (and this is what places the West at the top of the hierarchy of civilizations), all other non-technological questions related to cultural specificity or alternate forms of living become irrelevant. Kothari is right in arguing that this "technological paradigm has only strengthened the global structure of hegemony and aggrandisement."[4] As a result, in the age of liberalization you can no longer speak of the kind of society Gandhi or Mao visualized. Socialism or any other 'non-modern' form of living is equated with poverty or backwardness.

Third, even if liberalization promises economic affluence, its primary ethos remains elitist. It promotes consumerism. It encourages competitiveness at the cost of social justice and equality. It seeks to dissociate the individual from all sorts of cultural linkages. To put it simply, with more and more liberalization we would soon find ourselves in a society where there would be a wide cleavage between the consumptionist middle-class and the downtrodden, a society where all politico-moral questions related to justice, equality and sovereignty would be considered primarily as obstacles to development, its free market and its global culture.

II

Cultural Narcissism

Hindutva is another major force that has affected our politico-cultural life. What is striking is its paradoxical relationship with modernity. It is true that *Hindutva* as a force opposes one of the major components of modernity-universal secularism; it seeks to assert our 'cultural identity' sensitive to Hindu religious traditions. Yet, *Hindutva*, as it exists, cannot be imagined without modernist or political ambitions. For instance, it is deeply related to the politics of the nation-state. It seeks to capture political power; it wants to build up a strong nation-state based on the spirit of homogenized Hinduism.

This sort of political articulation of religion, it has to be realized, is not very new. It could be seen even in the discourses of the freedom struggle. Because if one looks at the history of colonial India, it is impossible not to see a close relationship between the emerging nationalism and the reinterpreted Hinduism.[5] India was often referred to as Mother Goddess, or compared with Kali, Durga and other Hindu goddesses. With his propagation of Ganesh Puja and Shivaji festival, Tilak aroused the imagination of the collective, and Gandhi often employed Hindu terms and symbols. Be it Vivekananda or Tilak, Gandhi or Aurobindo, there was a continual effort to reinterpret Hinduism, to tap its cultural resources in order to fight colonialism and the damage it did to our self-pride. Perhaps it was also felt that this reinterpreted Hinduism would provide linkages, bring an essentially pluralist society into a common nationalist front needed to cope with the challenge posed by an alien force.

For secular historians, this 'Hindu tinge' in the nationalist movement is a problem. True, Bipan Chandra agrees that nationalists like Tilak and Gandhi could by no means be equated with communalists. Yet, he insists that

> The Hindu tinge simultaneously generated unease and apprehension in the minds of the educated and politically conscious Muslims who were suspicious of a movement whose nationalist message was couched in religious terms,

> and who, therefore, saw the National Congress as representing a Hindu movement. It tended to repel them ideologically and made it difficult for them to join the Congress and the national movement.[6]

Therefore, he argues that efforts should have been made to separate the association of nationalism with Hindu religion in any way. Because, as Bipan Chandra argues,

> A multi-religion, multi-caste and multi-culture country like India could not afford to exalt, or claim to restore, any one religion, caste, culture or historical tradition; it could not afford to build the new by appealing to the past or by pretending to be restoring or reviving it.[7]

Yet, despite the visible presence of Hinduism in these nationalist ideals, it could not be equated with what is now known as *Hindutva*. The reason is that Hinduism as reflected in these nationalist ideals was critical and dialogical in spirit. It was critical of many ugly practices implicit in institutionalized Hinduism—the practice of untouchability or women's oppression. It was dialogical in the sense that it accommodated many alternate traditions emanating from the Western rationality, Christianity and Islam. Moreover, as the primary aim was to fight colonialism, it could not afford to see the other religious traditions like Islam as its primary enemy. It was Mahatma Gandhi who symbolized this critical and dialogical Hinduism. Not surprisingly, Gandhi who called himself a '*sanatani* Hindu' could assert with such confidence: "Hinduism is not an exclusive religion. In it there is room for the worship of all the prophets of the world."[8]

It should not, however, be forgotten that in the 1920s another brand of Hinduism began to emerge—the kind of Hinduism which can be seen in contemporary *Hindutva*. From V.D. Savarkar to M.S. Golwalkar—this Hinduism found its worldview that seeks to homogenize and militarize religion, a worldview that is absolutely unwilling to tolerate the autonomous identity of non-Hindus. Yet, the fact is that in colonial India, perhaps because of the overwhelming influence of the Gandhian struggle, this sort of aggressive Hinduism could never become a dominant force. The conflict, however, continued. Recall, for instance, Savarkar's relentless attack on Gandhi. For him, Gandhi "conspired to betray

Hindustan". Gandhi's "non-violent nonsense" did not have any appeal to Savarkar.[9] Savarkar often accused the Congress of being "anti-Hindu". For Golwalkar, Congressmen were traitors'. And in the freedom struggle the record of the RSS was not particularly encouraging. In fact, this militarized *Hindutva* with its communal politics was in conflict with the nationalist struggle for liberation—the struggle that Gandhi symbolized rather sharply. Perhaps this conflict manifested itself in the assassination of Gandhi by a Hindu fanatic heavily influenced by the Savarkar-Hedgewar-Golwalkar tradition.

Things are changing in postindependence India. In fact, the present form of *Hindutva* cannot be explained unless we relate it to some of the peculiarities of our times. To begin with, as the nationalist dream and subsequently the Nehruvian consensus collapses, India, as we are seeing, is passing through innumerable crisis points characterized by anarchy, chaos, violence and disintegration. Divergent ethnic/linguistic/regional protests have indeed posed a challenge to the centrality of the Indian state.

Likewise, the growing subaltern assertion and the emerging awareness on the part of the Dalits and the backward castes have undoubtedly weakened the old hegemonies. In other words, the entire project of nationalism—order, centralized nation-state, homogenization—is in crisis. To live in post-independence India is to feel the danger of disintegration. It seems that there is no meta discourse that can connect things; there is no united front that can represent divergent voices of caste, region, ethnicity and class. There is no grand "Gandhi-Nehru consensus". This has to be understood. In postindependence India the Gandhian experiment was already marginalized (although in contemporary intellectual traditions there is a renewed interest in Gandhi). It was the Nehruvian agenda of nation-building that, for quite some time, was the dominant ideology. It created a new dream: India—industrialized and secularized—fighting poverty, illiteracy and unemployment, and bringing about socio-economic equality. In a way, the Nehruvian consensus was based on the ideals of democracy, socialism and secularism. However, the grand dream did not materialize. It was this disillusionment that led to the gradual erosion of the Nehruvian consensus. Indeed, in this fragmented social reality Indian nationalism found itself in crisis. *Hindutva*, it can be said, is a reaction to this crisis. *Hindutva* is an attempt to reconstruct the lost consensus, to build up the cementing forces of nationalism. Essentially, it is trying to replace Nehruvian secularism and giving a new meaning to Indian nationalism. In contrast to Nehruvian secularism it speaks of a distinctive cultural identity to characterize Indian nationalism. This cultural identity, it is argued, can emerge out of what it regards as the deep-rooted Hindu civilization. As the proponents of *Hindutva* expect, it would unite different fragments, arouse a shared cultural-religious memory, create the collective symbols — the sacred texts, gods and goddesses, cultural heroes and heroines! For example, Savarkar articulated the agenda of united and homogenized Hinduism in his characteristic style:

> We Hindus, in spite of thousand and one differences within our fold, are bound by such religious, cultural, historical, racial, linguistic and other affinities in common as to stand out as a definitely homogeneous people as soon as we are placed in contrast with other non-Hindu people.[10]

There is another important factor beneath the growth of *Hindutva*. The subcontinent, it has to be accepted, has not been able to overcome the influence of pan-Islamization or Islamic fundamentalism. This has undoubtedly given a new connotation to *Hindutva* and it is now equally eager to discover its 'other'; all the prevalent evils—unemployment, poverty, destabilization, etc.—have to be explained in terms of the conspiracy launched by the 'other'!

This takes us to identify some of the salient features of *Hindutva* which can be identified as follows:

(a) *Hindutva* is political. The goal has been shifted from the spiritual domain to politics. Because the task is to create political unity and practise the politics of the nation-state. Recall, for instance, Savarkar's insistence on political unity. It was only through his "militarized Hinduism", he thought, India could regain its nationhood and remain united. It should not be forgotten that Savarkar was an advocate of "temporal *Hindutva*"; he separated *Hindutva* from religion and joined it to nationalism and science.

(b) It aims at emulating the traditions of semitic religions. Because it speaks of order and homogeneity. It speaks of a coherent, historically evolved Hinduism. But, as Professor Romila Thapar sees, unlike the semitic religions, "Hinduism cannot be described as a historically evolved religion with a founder or an ecclesiastical organization."[11] Instead, there are innumerable identities and communities in it. That is why, it can be said that in contemporary *Hindutva* there is an attempt to reinforce order and homogeneity on diverse, plural traditions.

(c) It is modernist in spirit, because nationalism is its goal. It aims at order and homogeneity. It was M.S. Golwalkar who articulated this modernist spirit rather sharply. For example, Golwalkar's agenda was to convince his countrymen that all the five components of a modern nation—geographical, racial, religious, cultural and linguistic—could be seen in Hindu India.[12] To begin with, according to Golwalkar, here is a country with a definite geographical unity, delimited by the sublime Himalayas on the North and the limitless ocean on the other three sides. Here is the ancient race—the Hindu race that professes the illustrious Hindu religion. Moreover, here is "a culture which, despite the degenerating contact with the debased `civilizations' of the Mussalmans and the Europeans for the last ten centuries, is still the noblest in the world."[13] And, finally, "there is but, one language, Sanskrit, of which these many `languages' are mere off-shoots". In other words, the goal, for Golwalkar, is to "re-rouse our national consciousness, and victory is in our grasp."[14]

(d) In fact, there are many other manifestations of this modernist spirit of *Hindutva*. For example, in our own times Hindu communalists with the clever use of modern technologies have succeeded in creating new signs and images. As a matter of fact, Sadhvi Rithambara has become the first mass leader in our society who has been created by a recorded cassette. With her hypnotising voice she takes one to the battlefield: 'once and for all' battle! Not solely that. With the twin images of Ram popularized through the posters and the stickers of the VHP—the image of *Ramlalla*, the child-god and the image of Ram as the masculine warrior god—Hindu fundamentalists propagate their message among both men and women.

(e) It is insensitive to diverse traditions as it seeks to annihilate differences. Recall the way Golwalkar defined India's nationhood.

. . . the foreign races in Hindustan must either adopt the Hindu culture and language, must learn to respect and hold in reverence Hindu religion, must entertain no idea but the glorification of the Hindu race and culture, i.e., of the Hindu nation and must lose their separate existence to merge in the Hindu race, or may stay in the country, wholly subordinated to the Hindu nation, claiming nothing, deserving no privileges, far less any preferential treatment—not even a citizen's rights.[15]

Perhaps the core doctrine of *Hindutva* can be summarized as follows:

(i) Hindus and Hindus alone constitute the Indian nation, since they are the original inhabitants and sole creators of its society and culture.
(ii) Hinduism is tolerant and hence superior to any faith.
(iii) The Hindu nation has been repeatedly conquered by aliens, particularly the Muslims.
(iv) Muslims, being irrepressibly and aggressively lustful by nature, rape Hindu women and force Hindu wombs into producing Muslim progeny; their legalized polygamy enables them to breed at a great pase, so that the existing Hindu demographic majority is fragile and vanishing and the reality is that Muslims will soon outnumber Hindus.

(f) Far from being self-critical, it constructs its 'other', its 'enemy' and it loses critical/dialogical spirit. It becomes aggressively violent. See the language of Sadhvi Rithambara, one of the militant proponents of contemporary *Hindutva*:

> The Hindu writes from the left to right, the Muslim from right to left. The Hindu prays the rising sun, the Muslim faces the setting sun when praying. If the Hindu eats with the right hand, the Muslim with the left. If the

Hindu calls India 'Mother', she becomes a witch for the Muslims. The Hindu worships the cow, the Muslim attains paradise by eating beef.[16]

(g) *Hindutva*, it has to be accepted, has got its appeal, particularly to a significant section of the upper caste Hindus. Apparently, it has got a 'cause': to construct a new India based on Hindu identity. Yet, it demands nothing: neither socialism nor diffusion of power. *Hindutva* has not an appeal to a class that is hostile to radical social transformation, a class that seeks to retain the status quo.[17] In fact, according to a group of contemporary scholars, this 'new form of religiosity' can be related to the anxieties of the middle-class: a class characterized by fragmentation and competition.[18] It is a class that needs an image of togetherness and it is *Hindutva* that seeks to fulfil this need without, however, challenging its basic material and economic interests. It can also be argued that *Hindutva* is designed to offer a counter thrust to the subaltern challenges to the Brahminical hegemony. Moreover, *Hindutva* has got an emotional appeal, particularly to a great section of the urban population experiencing the anonymity of modern living. It promises to give them back their culture and religion, it seeks to restore the lost community, it speaks of a stable identity, particularly at a time when identities are in flux. While analyzing the assertion of this "new Hindu identity", Sudhir Kakar makes an interesting observation. Kakar reflects on the social-psychological consequences of modernity—the way it leads to the separation of families and the loss of familiar neighbourhoods and ecological niches. This means that "one is in a state of permanent psychic mobilization and heightened nervous arousal."[19] It is in this context that the formation of a cultural or religious group serves a therapeutic function. As Kakar says, "the cultural group, which brings the 'primordiality' related to shared myths, memories, values and symbols to the fore, thus assumes a vital healing function.[20] In other words, as Kakar would suggest, *Hindutva* has got an emotional appeal to those for whom modernity is essentially an alienating experience. It is, however, a different question whether

Hindutva as an ideology is capable of challenging the pathologies of modernity and creating a humane world.

As a matter of fact, the consequences of *Hindutva* are likely to be disastrous. It breeds communalism, and in communalism, it has to be realized, there is nothing natural or spontaneous about community consciousness. Instead, it is engineered; it is manipulative; it is designed. In other words, the community in the name of which communal riots take place is largely an invented community seeking its invented 'other' to annihilate or destroy it.

Certainly, it can be argued that communal conflicts seek to distort real politico-economic conflicts. Unemployment, poverty, rootlessness, urban pollution—all these evils, it seems, create a situation conducive to violence. This violence manifests itself in communal riots. Because it is not difficult to see a huge section of the lumpen proletariat participating effectively in communal riots. See the irony of it. Communalism prevents one from seeing 'the real cause of one's politico-economic powerlessness; it creates a false enemy; it is, in other words, a kind of displacement. Communalism is, therefore, anti-revolutionary.[21]

Hindutva is posing a challenge to secular culture. It is true that secularism may have its discontents. Beneath it one can see what Professor Ashis Nandy would call the 'imperialism of categories';[22] it, may be elitist and, therefore, insensitive to ordinary people's faith, belief and practice. Yet, the alternative *Hindutva* is proposing is by no means liberating. There are two reasons. First, it does not create a situation conducive to the growth of religiosity/spirituality which spreads truly universal values like love, tolerance and solidarity. Instead, as religion is being mediated through the politics of power and manipulation, it divides, brutalizes and causes hatred. Second, in the name of criticizing secularism, it tends to oppose some of the egalitarian values of our times—acceptance of women as free and equal subjects, sensitivity to diversities and differences and relatively equal distribution of politico-economic power. In fact, with its cultural narcissism *Hindutva* often reinforces a closed, conservative, patriarchal ethos. There are all the tendencies in *Hindutva* that can make one suspect of its potentially fascist urge.

III

Dalit Assertion

It is impossible to remain indifferent to a new revolution taking place in Indian society. It is indeed a revolution because a caste-ridden society with its inequalities and hierarchies is transforming itself. The growing awareness among the oppressed castes, their political articulation, their faith that, in a mobile world it is possible to create a new future—everything, it seems, is posing a threat to the old hegemonies. It is indeed a challenge to the forward/upper caste domination in politics, economy and culture. This revolt aims at more and more diffusion of power and hence the democratization of the larger society. This is potentially an egalitarian project as its authors are those whom the Brahminical system has always sought to marginalize and silence. This revolt is indeed forcing us to rethink many of our cherished beliefs, not only the beliefs implicit in the Hindu caste society, but also many progressive beliefs about social transformation.

This revolt has got its own history. For example, one could smell this revolt in the Buddhist intervention, in the Bhakti movement and in the neo-Vedantic experimentations. Because, be it Gautama Buddha, Kabir or Chaitanya, Vivekananda or Dayanand—all sought to fight the tyranny of the caste system; they were eager to reinterpret Hinduism and emancipate it from many evil practices. Yet, it can always be argued that, broadly speaking, all these movements were initiated by caste Hindus. These movements, as a result, were 'reformist' in nature without a radical programme of socio-economic uplift. Against these "adaptive movements",[23] it is possible to see the assertion of a new language of dissent articulated by three great ideologues: Jotiba Phule, Ramaswami Naicker and B.R. Ambedkar.[24]

Jotiba Phule (1826-1890), a great revolutionary of the nineteenth century Maharashtra fought against Brahminism. He asserted that the low castes (whom he sometimes called Sudras and Ati-Sudras) were the original inhabitants of the country enslaved and exploited by the Aryans who had formulated a caste-ridden Hinduism (akin to inverting the traditional Aryan theory). He brought together the major peasant castes like the Kunbis, the Malis and the Dhangars along with the untouchable castes like the Mahars and the Mangs into a common united front against the Brahminical domination. The egalitarian ethos of the original peasant community fascinated him. Yet, Phule was equally eager to spread modern and scientific knowledge in contrast to the Brahminic and ritual-based *shastras*. It was this struggle against Brahminism that led him to evolve a new theistic religion called the *Sarvajanik Satya Dharma*. Phule attacked Hinduism at every point and even challenged its legitimacy. For him, it was not a legitimate religion, but a bag of tricks, a weapon of domination. In Phule's ideal family the father becomes a Buddhist, the mother a Christian, the daughter a Muslim and the son a *Satyadharmist*; in his alternate map there was no scope for a Hindu.

Another important event in the history of this struggle was the self-respect movement in Tamil Nadu led by E.V. Ramaswamy Naicker. Naicker (1879-1973) attacked the Vedic scriptures, the caste system and the very concept of God. For Naicker, he who propagates God is a scoundrel, he who worships God is a barbarian. He was against Hindi-Hindu nationalism, and he disliked the imposition of Hindi and stressed the theme of Dravidian/Tamil nationality. This indeed gave a momentum to the movement led by the non-Brahmins to challenge the Brahminical domination.

Likewise, B.R. Ambedkar (1891-1956), the Maharashtrian Mahar, fought relentlessly against caste domination. It was his firm conviction that the eradication of caste would remain impossible without the repudiation of Hinduism itself. With his fierce rationalism he opposed Hindu superstitions. Not solely that, he always thought of an alternative political front to the Congress which, according to him, was a unique platform of Brahminism and capitalism. It was this rebel and subaltern Ambedkar who, as history would recall, emerged through the 1927 *Mahad Satyagraha* in Maharashtra—a mass struggle of the Dalits to assert their human rights. He demanded separate electorate for the SCs. He formed the Independent Labour Party in 1937. He started the All India SC Federation in 1942. The Republican party he launched in 1957 or the historic mass conversion to Buddhism which he initiated in 1956—everything seems to suggest how he sought to create a culture in which the Dalits and the oppressed castes would overcome their silence, regain their human agency and create a just, rational and egalitarian society.

Ambedkar's politics, as M.S. Gore would argue, was a "protest ideology". For example :

> The burning of a copy of the *Manusmriti* at Mahad was one way of symbolically rejecting the rules that it specified and the doctrines of inequality at birth on which the caste system was based. As a method of communicating a message to an illiterate following, this had the same significance as the making of salt at Dandi by Gandhi. They both symbolized a rejection of the premise on which authority was based.[25]

Ambedkar evolved this 'protest ideology' because he thought that "inequality is the soul of Hinduism". Ambedkar quoted extensively from the *Manusmriti* and argued that Hinduism did not recognize equality or fraternity. Moreover, because of its innate hereditary principle, it was against utility; it dissociated intelligence from manual labour by denying the labourer access to knowledge. This critique does not, however, suggest that Ambedkar was inclined to Marxism. After all, the Marxists, for him, were a "bunch of Brahmin boys" not in a position to understand the meaning of "non-class contradictions". Instead, Ambedkar was fascinated by Buddhism. For him, Buddhism was superior to communism. In Buddhism he saw a moral principle based on the ideals of truth, love, individual freedom worth and equality. It should not be forgotten that Ambedkar described the triumph of Brahminism over Buddhism as counter-revolutionary.

In fact, Ambedkar's primary argument was that no united ancient India had ever existed. As a matter of fact, according to him, there were three India's preceding the Muslim period. These were :

1. 'Brahminism' describing the Aryan society of the Vedic period and in reality a barbarian phase.
2. 'Buddhism', with the Magadha-Mauryan empires embodying a 'Buddhist revolution', the rise of civilization and the assertion of basic forms of human equality.

3. 'Hinduism' or a 'Hindu counter-revolution' marked with Pushyamitra Sunga's rise to power in north India and associated with Manu, the triumph of caste, and the subordination of women and Sudras.[26]

With this demystification of the united ancient Hindu India (for example, Buddhist India, according to him, was invaded by Brahminic invaders), Ambedkar was challenging the nationalist school which, as he thought, was essentially a Hindu nationalist school. No wonder Ambedkar rejected even the 'left bloc' forming within the Congress during the 1930s. He accused Indian socialists of being unfaithful to their ideals due to their upper caste base. They were reluctant to give attention to caste, and no socialist movement in India, as he thought, could ignore this issue. Ambedkar was, however, eager to evolve a unique identity of the Dalits. That is why, as Gail Omvedt argued, "the conversion to Buddhism was seen, by Ambedkar and large numbers of those who took part, as a social rebirth, a gaining of a new identity, a way in which the *Dalits* were leading, not simply joining, a movement for the recreation of India."[27]

The point we are trying to argue is that the Phule-Naicker-Ambedkar tradition is not dead. In fact, with the increasing Dalit/backward caste awakening it is acquiring a new relevance. In postindependence India, politically speaking, it was the South that first witnessed a serious challenge to the Brahminical domination. For instance, the advent of the DMK in Tamil Nadu in 1967 saw the assertion of the backward non-Brahmins as a dominant group. And now this assertion is spreading all over the country and giving birth to new political equations. Two reasons can be put forward for this changing scenario.

(i) The 1970 saw the Green Revolution in several parts of the country. An important feature of the Green Revolution was the rise of the middle caste/class peasantry. It was indeed a process of empowerment that enhanced the status of the intermediate and backward castes like the Jats, Yadavs, Kurmis or Koeris in the North, Kunbis, Patels and Marathas in the West and Kammas, Reddis and Vokkaligas in the South. It is this enhanced economic power that is articulating itself in the new politics.[28]

(ii) Indian democracy, no matter how condemned by the radicals, is creating a situation conducive to drastic social transformation. As the lower and backward castes, because of the continual electoral participation, are becoming conscious of their rights, they are forming larger caste associations and groups having modern goals like political power, economic mobility and cultural and educational privileges. In fact, the numerical advantage (and this matters in democracy), the economic empowerment and the growing realization that politics is an effective tool for social mobility —all these factors, it seems, are creating a new space for the backward and oppressed castes to alter the established hegemonies.

True, the caste-factor in politics may not be appreciated by the 'doctrinaire modernists'. They fear that 'casteism in politics' may destroy modernity. But then, as Rajni Kothari argues:

> Politics is a competitive enterprise, its purpose is the acquisition of power for the realization of certain goals and its process is one of identifying and manipulating existing and emerging allegiances in order to mobilise and consolidate positions. The important thing is organization and articulation of support, and where politics is mass-based the point is to articulate support through the organisations in which the masses are to be found. It follows that where the caste structure provides one of the principal organisational clusters along which the bulk of the population is found to live, politics must strive to organize through such a structure.[29]

In fact, as Kothari would argue, the consequences of caste-politics interactions are just the reverse of what is usually stated. As Kothari says, "dialectical as it might sound, it is precisely because the operation of competitive politics has drawn out of its apolitical context and given it a new status that the 'caste-system' as hitherto known has got eroded and has begun to disintegrate."[30]

This changing event in India's socio-political life is significant. In a way, it seeks to fulfil one of the promises of modernity: the creation of a mobile, egalitarian and democratic society. As a result, it is challenging the very basis of the caste system: a system which cannot be imagined without the notion of purity and pollution, without rigid hierarchies and inequalities, without a fatalistic belief that birth is destiny.[31] Even M.N. Srinivas—who has taught us to see the possibility of mobility in the caste system (sanskritization)—is aware of its limits. Srinivas concedes: "Sanskritization does not always result in higher status for the sanskritized caste and this is clearly exemplified by the untouchables. However through the sanskritization of an untouchable group may be, it is unable to cross the barrier of untouchability."[32] Therefore, the mobility we are witnessing today —particularly, the mobility of the Mahars and the Chamars— cannot be explained by sanskritization. Because, as Yogendra Singh would say, there is an implicit paradox in the notion of sanskritization, for it "reinforces the normative system which is represented by caste stratification, but, it also, at least in principle, violates its basic tenet—the acceptance of the principle of hierarchy."[33] Perhaps this mobility is potentially radical; this is challenging the very basis of the caste system. Srinivas can also smell this conflict:

> As education spreads among the Harijans, it will be increasingly difficult for the caste Hindus to keep them in the condition in which they are today. There are also signs that the Harijans are organizing themselves to assert the rights which the Constitution gives them. As I said before, this will probably mean the occurrence of fighting between them and caste Hindus, and an immediate increase of tension, but the latter are bound to give way in the end. Let no one expect, however, that the process will be smooth, quick and non-violent. It would be against the nature of things to expect untouchability to disappear overnight.[34]

Perhaps with this conflict we are moving towards a democratic, achievement-oriented society where, instead of the monopolizat'on of power, its diffusion is likely to become more and more real.

The subaltern assertion, it seems, is powerful enough to enable Hinduism to look at itself and its evils. Because Hinduism as it exists, cannot be imagined without caste hierarchies inequalities, hence the growing attack on Hinduism by the new politics is perhaps more sharper and relevant than what one sees in reformist Hinduism. It is argued that reformist Hinduism was after all a project initiated by upper-caste Hindus. Therefore, despite all its best intentions, it could not totally comprehend the sufferings and miseries of the oppressed castes. But in this new project, it is argued, the oppressed themselves are the agents of history. The recovery of this historical agency, it is thought, would give more power, authenticity and legitimacy to the movement against caste-ridden Hinduism.

This assertion is giving a new meaning to the progressive agenda of social transformation. The progressives—particularly, the leftists—are more comfortable with "class analysis"; economic oppression, for them, is the primary oppression that determines all other oppressions. In this refusal to give legitimacy to caste questions Gail Omvedt sees the assertion of a "paternalistic enlightened leadership". "The Indian left and progressive elites", writes Omvedt, "allowed the maintenance of brahmanic assumptions of superiority and authority, the right of the elites to rule, and to assume the role of guardians."[35]

In fact, as it is argued, this new politics is speaking of the complexity of Indian reality; class analysis alone is not sufficient to explain this complexity, the multiplicity of oppression. For example, a Dalit is oppressed not solely because of his politico-economic powerlessness, but he is also oppressed because of his degrading ritual status. The experience of this humiliation is real and directly visible. And so long as it exists, it becomes exceedingly difficult for a poor Brahmin to identify himself with a poor Dalit. Therefore, it would not be wrong to say that in a caste-ridden society it makes sense to consider the Dalits and the backwards as real collectivities for political mobilization. Caste conflict exists in its own right and does not hide any other 'real' oppression.

The egalitarian character of this assertion notwithstanding, it is not free from contradictions. First, this politics often becomes exclusivist. As it is based on caste mobilization, it may not prove to be very sensitive to the other forms of oppression that transcend caste boundaries. The absence of 'non-caste politics' is something one must reflect on. Although this politics seeks to challenge the very basis of casteism, paradoxically, it enhances one's caste identity. Because of this contradiction the emerging politics is engaged in an ambivalent relationship with the modernist agenda. In fact, one's caste identity, far from withering away, tends to get intensified. It is used for secular pursuits: acquiring political power or finding adequate representation in government jobs. It is this new relationship that seeks to keep one's caste identity alive. That is why, it poses a threat to the modernist objective of a casteless society. It is, however, possible to argue that Indian modernity acquires a new meaning and historicizes itself.

Second, it often fails to distinguish the emancipatory tradition of Hinduism from its pathologies. It forgets that every Hindu is not necessarily obedient to the doctrines of the *Manusmriti*. It forgets that it is possible to remain a Hindu without being a casteist. It is not always necessary to feel ashamed of being a Hindu. But when the militant Dalit politics negates even the emancipatory tradition of Hinduism, it alienates many soft, tolerant or humane Hindus. They are called 'outsiders'. The assumption is that the Dalits or the backwards alone can think of and talk about the subaltern politics. This is also kind of appropriation and is no less dangerous.

Third, the very logic of caste (each caste tends to consider itself superior to its equals) may enter the domain of the new politics. If this happens, it is bound to destroy the unity of the oppressed castes. Not solely that. There is certainly a conflict of interest between the backward or intermediate castes (who have gained tremendously from the green revolution) and the *Dalits* who are largely landless peasants and workers.

Fourth, it is possible to see a cleavage between the leaders and the real subaltern masses. The fear is that the leaders can be co-opted by the system. And this might lead to the politics of manipulation. Far from trying to alter the conditions of the subaltern masses, the leaders can keep on playing with the same rhetoric. For instance, it is doubtful whether the leaders like Laloo Prasad Yadav, Mulayam Singh Yadav or Kanshi Ram can go beyond mere Mandalization and undertake any substantial land reform programme without which the condition of the Dalits cannot be altered.

These contradictions should not, however, deny the historic importance of the subaltern assertion.

IV

Emerging Conflicts

Conflict, it seems, is inevitable. Because these three trends—liberalization, *Hindutva* and Dalit assertion—are not necessarily compatible with one another. To begin with, one can speak of the conflict between the economic aspirations of the state and the political aspirations of the subaltern castes or masses. Liberalization demands the gradual withdrawal of the state from all sorts of welfare policies. But the political assertion of the Dalits and backwards would demand a more committed state dedicated to the oppressed castes and communities. Liberalization considers the rationale of the market as the most supreme rationale. But social justice or welfare is the primary agenda of the new politics. Liberalization seeks to "rescue" the individual from all collectivities. But the new politics is based on the memory of collective injustice. The conflict that is manifesting itself is the conflict between the two contrasting visions—market and state, technology and politics, efficiency and justice, individualism and collectivism. One can still recall the conflict centered on reservation. Reservation challenges the very fetish of `efficiency'; it demands a state committed to social justice. Those who oppose reservation, however, demand a more `neutral' state that asks the individual, irrespective of his/her socio-economic resources and cultural capital, to experience alone the cold logic of competition. Although, as it appears, the state has accepted the reality of reservation (with some amendments, of course), the kind of conflict we are talking about continues to exist.

Another important source of conflict lies in the fact that the emerging subaltern assertion is debunking the homogenized vision of a Hindu society implicit in the recent trend of *Hindutva*. In fact, this assertion is revealing how divisive/hierarchical/stratified the Hindu society is. As a result, it is felt, one's consent to *Hindutva*, in the ultimate analysis,would only help to hide the real contradictions and perpetuate the hegemony of the upper caste Hindus. Perhaps more than any 'secular'/'nationalist' force it is this subaltern assertion that has challenged and partly combated the growth of

Hindutva. Although the proponents of *Hindutva* are trying to co-opt the Dalits and the backwards, the fact is that this conflict is going to stay because it is a conflict between imagined unity and real oppression.

Culture is another realm in which this conflict is taking place. First, the individualistic ethos of liberalization is likely to be in conflict with the collectivistic ethos of caste politics. Second, the consumerism which has acquired added relevance because of 'globalization' is likely to create a situation in which more and more people would feel a wide cleavage between the desire intensified by the images and the actual resources to fulfil this desire. This would lead to perversion and violence in society. Third, as the fear of cultural invasion becomes widespread, the proponents of *Hindutva* would further justify their theory of cultural nationalism, With *swadeshi*, 'Hindu religious tradition' and our great 'cultural heritage', it is argued, all 'Western vices'—be it secularism or consumerism—can be fought and combated! The danger is that in the name of fighting cultural imperialism, the proponents of *Hindutva* may seek to promote an essentially patriarchal and conservative ethos, not particularly sensitive to human autonomy and women's freedom. In other words, as we would watch more and more Star TV/MTV, we would also see more and more Shankaracharyas asserting our 'cultural tradition'. Liberalization and fundamentalism would reinforce each other!

What is, however, important to note is that these three ideological currents—liberalization, *Hindutva* and Dalit assertion—need not be seen as discrete and discontinuous. In the actual realm of politics these ideologies, one may argue, overlap. For example, the proponents of *Hindutva*, despite the rhetoric of *swadeshi*, may not be hostile to economic liberalization. Or, to put it otherwise, the consumptionist new middle-class may feel equally comfortable with liberalization as well as *Hindutva*. Likewise, *Hindutva* may also create a space in order to accommodate the Dalit/backward caste voice. Moreover, the subaltern politics, despite its egalitarian ideals, may not be fundamentally different from the exploitative nature of what it otherwise condemns. In fact, in the absence of an emancipatory pedagogy, the subaltern energy is often released through misdirected channels: Mayawati and Kanshi Ram reducing the Dalit politics into an opportunistic game, Laloo and his disciples lumpenizing the backward caste assertion. These possibilities notwithstanding, the classification of the three types, we insist, is meaningful; it gives us the clarity we need to make sense of the societal conflict.

The conflict, as a matter of fact, is all around; violence is the order of the day. That is why, the question comes up. Is there any way one can come out of the crisis? Can a new vision be imagined to take India to the road to sanity?

V

Alternative Worldview

It is at this juncture that one begins to look at Gandhi. Gandhi was not just a person; he was a force, a movement, an idea. That is why, even today any debate on the nature of the future of India cannot remain indifferent to the Gandhian question. But one thing is certain. All the three trends in Indian politics we have talked about are not particularly sympathetic to Gandhi. For instance, any student of Gandhi's thought and life-practice can feel that the ethos of liberalization is essentially anti-Gandhian. Liberalization relies heavily on technology; it promotes the seductive image of the consumerist culture, and aggressive individualism is its objective. But Gandhi's *Hind Swaraj* reveals how his worldview was based on altogether different principles. Gandhi emphasized what he used to call 'soul force', not the power of technology. Not aggressive consumerism, but harmonic and peaceful existence based on true spirituality was Gandhi's ideal. Gandhi talked repeatedly about the evils of the satanic/modern/Western civilization. Likewise, the proponents of *Hindutva* would find nothing heroic in Gandhi, even if for purely strategic reasons they seek to appropriate him. The reason is that *Hindutva* is a kind of aggressive/militarized/patriarchal Hinduism and its anti-dialogical spirit is against plurality and alternative traditions. But in Gandhi one can see a kind of Hinduism based on dialogue, love, ahimsa, prayer and feminine qualities like perseverance, suffering and the art of dying.

In other words, Gandhi's soft Hinduism does not fit well into the map of hard *Hindutva*. Again, the emerging subaltern politics is unlikely to appreciate Gandhi. Broadly speaking, two reasons are put forward. First, it is argued that Gandhi's intervention was, after all, a kind of 'reformist Hinduism' based on 'integrationist principles'. That is why, despite all his concerns for the untouchables and Harijans, he could not go beyond the paradigm of Hinduism. But the champions of the Dalit politics tend to assert that to repudiate casteism is to repudiate Hinduism itself. Second, it is argued that in the Gandhian project upper caste Hindus were the agents of history and it was not a project initiated and practised by the oppressed castes. In other words, the Gandhian project was based on charity and dharma, not on revolutionary principles. To put it briefly, for the Dalits, Gandhi was not sufficiently radical and hence not fully relevant to the cause they seek to uphold.

The meaning of the above discussion is simple. Society is changing fast; old ideas are being increasingly questioned and challenged. There is no reason to remain fixated to old ideas. But, at the same time, it does not make much sense to celebrate everything 'new' without the slightest criticality. The kind of criticality we are talking about should be clear once we identify some of the components of the worldview we want to reconstruct.

Egalitarianism

Egalitarianism should be the principle of the new worldview. That is why, it would be sensitive to the emerging Dalit politics. Because no agenda of social reconstruction can remain indifferent to the reality of caste oppression in Indian society. And caste oppression cannot always be reduced into class terms. Caste struggle is real because of the very specificity of India's politico-cultural history. Any egalitarian project must support the struggles of the oppressed castes, their urge to fight the forward caste domination and hegemony. Yet, the new project cannot be equated with the kind of Dalit politics we are seeing these days. Because the Dalit politics tends to become exclusivist. We also witness a disturbing tendency. Here is a kind of politics that seeks power at any cost: politics without an emancipatory pedagogy.[36] Moreover, it should not be forgotten that there are many domains of oppression: not just caste, but also class, gender and ethnicity. Hence the new worldview ought to have a much broader horizon and perspective than the Dalit politics. It is in this context that one should look at, for instance, Gandhi. For the proponents of the militant Dalit politics, he was perhaps a villain. But then, we know that it is impossible to imagine him without his egalitarian spirit. True, it is possible to argue that he was sympathetic to the notion of *varnashrama*. We would, however, do injustice to him if we equate his ideal of *varnashrama* with the prevalent caste system. To quote Gandhi:

> The four divisions define a man's calling, they do not restrict or regulate social intercourse. The divisions define duties: they confer no privileges. It is, I hold, against the genius of Hinduism to arrogate, to oneself a higher status or assign to another a lower. All are born to serve God's creation.[37]

This is not to support Gandhi's *varnashrama*. The only point we wish to add is that it would be too reductionist an approach to regard Gandhi as a Hindu upper caste bourgeois leader. His subaltern heart manifested itself again and again in his relentless struggle against the practice of untouchability.

> Untouchability as at present practised is the greatest blot on Hinduism. It is (with apology to *Sanatanists*) against the *Shastras*. It is against the fundamental principles of humanity, it is against the dictates of reason that a man should, by mere reason of birth, be ever regarded as an untouchable, even unapproachable and unseeable.[38]

If the Dalit politics refuses to accept the egalitarian aspect of Gandhi, it denies itself. That is why, the new worldview we are proposing, despite its affinity with the causes the oppressed castes are fighting for, ought to be more open and accommodative in its pursuit for social justice and equality. The philosophy of egalitarianism is nobody's absolute monopoly.

Cultural sensitivity

The search for a radical and egalitarian ideal does not mean that the new worldview should be insensitive to our culture. Because a careful look at our history suggests that there were always alternative cultural currents against the hierarchical, oppressive Brahminical tradition. Be it the practice of Bhakti or the ultimate spiritual realization of the unity of all life or sensitivity to plurality and diversity—it is clear that the egalitarian spirit is not alien to our cultural tradition. For instance, Gandhi sought to tap these cultural resources in order to make his decolonization agenda truly effective.[39] It is this cultural sensitivity that should be an important part of the new worldview. And this is also one of the effective ways to resist the way Hindu fundamentalists seek to appropriate culture and thereby give a patriarchal conservative meaning to it.

Critical modernity

It is in this sense that critical modernization should be the essence of the new worldview. It is true that modern science and technology have contributed enormously to the process of emancipation of man from poverty, disease and many other natural disasters. It is also true that, because of science and technology, cross-cultural communication has become easier and, therefore, it has become possible for each culture to expand its horizon and stock of knowledge. To deny this emancipatory aspect of modernity is to deny the very spirit of human curiosity. Yet, our cherished modernity should be critical in spirit. Because it is difficult not to look at the discontents of modernity—alienation, disruption of the symbiotic relationship between the human species and the rest of nature, consumerism and death of local communities.

In our times critical theorists, postmodernists and eco-feminists have made us aware of the discontents of modernity. But what is striking is that even in our intellectual traditions one could see a critical attitude towards modernity.[40] Well, one can always argue that, for instance, the Gandhian agenda as reflected in his *Hind Swaraj* was excessively hostile to modernity. Yet, at the same time, it should not be forgotten that the project of modernity ought to be rescued from its Eurocentric and colonial ambitions. Critical modernization, as a result, can resist liberalization, the way it mythologizes technology and development and, therefore, denies many other important aspects of human existence: cultural sovereignty, social justice, equality and a principle of existence based not on the intensification of desires, but on a harmonic and symbiotic relationship with nature, environment and community.

State-society relationship

The new worldview, it is obvious, will demand a state committed to the welfare of people, particularly the subaltern sections of society. In other words, unlike what the proponents of liberalization want, the State, according to the new worldview, far from withdrawing itself, would intervene meaningfully in the economic sphere so that the fruits of development are distributed fairly evenly. But the desirability of a committed state does not mean that it should paralyze other agencies. There is nothing to celebrate if the state alone triumphs and other sources of power—innumerable people's committees decline. History has proved how even socialism can degenerate into state-terrorism. The committed state, it has to be realized, far from being authoritarian, ought to be engaged in a dialogic and meaningful relationship with the entire civil society. The goal is the empowerment of people and participation of innumerable local agencies in the developmental endeavour. Not bureaucratization, but decentralization of power is the objective. Neither an authoritarian state, nor a free market is visualized. A committed state organically linked with localized groups and people's committees is the aim of the new worldview. In a way, Rajni Kothari articulates this worldview succinctly when he says:

> The dominant tendency and mode of thought today is to place the State above the people, the security of the nation-State above people's security, the removal of real or imaginary threats to the State more important than persisting threats to the people and their survival. On the other hand to restore to the people their sovereignty is not to undermine the role of the State but to transform it . . . The role of the centralized State must decline. It will be very much there—some functions will have to be carried out by a centralized apparatus—but it is basically to operate in concert with other centres as well as other institutional spaces in civil society.[41]

Towards a shared platform

One of the problems of our times is that although divergent struggles are taking place, there is no meta theory or grand ideal that can connect these struggles. For instance, a major weakness of the Dalit politics, is its exclusivist character, its limited perspective. It seems that the Dalit politics has got not much to offer to those who too are struggling against domination (but not necessarily domination based on caste lines)—women struggling for their rights, workers struggling for better wages and service conditions, landless peasants revolting against big landlords. The point to remember is that these struggles, despite their relative autonomy, cannot be seen in isolation. The challenging task is to evolve a shared objective that can unite all these struggles: the vision of a casteless, egalitarian, participatory, non-patriarchal society.

It other words, the new worldview should not be exclusivist; it should have sufficient free space to accommodate multiple voices and then bring about a shared consensus. In this sense our proposed world view should be free from recent postmodern or even subaltern obsession—fear of unity or consensus or even any grand vision. It should also be recalled that it was this unitary vision that gave a new meaning to the Gandhian struggle in colonial India. Its strength was that, far from being exclusivist, it accommodated multiple voices; it was not limited to discrete or discontinuous pockets. It is, of course, true that this unifying struggle was not free from contradictions. Yet, the effectiveness of its search for a grand vision cannot be denied. It is this search that has to be explored and enriched further. That is the message of the new world view.

Primary of peace

The new worldview would celebrate peace. Because without peace and dialogic understanding a democratic, participatory or plural society cannot function. Everyone must cultivate the art of listening. Peace is impossible without faith—the faith that human beings can understand one another and resolve their conflicts.

One can, of course, argue that the new worldview would not be easily accepted. For the proponents of liberalization, it is too idealistic and utopian. For the ideologues of *Hindutva*, it is too soft to make sense. For the Dalit politics, it is too broad a vision. In other words, it can be said, there is no social base to sustain and nurture this worldview. But then, there are dissenters—the Gandhians, Marxists, environmentalists, spiritualists and feminists. Is it impossible for them to come together, initiate a dialogue and create a new social base for the kind of worldview we are proposing?

NOTES

1. Rajni Kothari, "Under Globalization: Will Nation-State Hold?" *Economic and Political Weekly* (July 1, 1995), p. 1595.
2. Ranjit Guha, *An Indian Historiography of India: A Nineteenth-Century Agenda and Its Implication* (Calcutta: K.P. Bagchi and Company, 1988), pp. 48-74.
3. A.R. Desai, *Social Background of Indian Nationalism* (Bombay: Popular Prakashan, 1982), p. 197.
4. Rajni Kothari, *op. cit.*, p. 1599.
5. See, for example, Bipan Chandra, *Communalism in Modern India* (New Delhi: Vani Educational Books, 1984), especially Ch. 5.
6. *Ibid.*, p. 144.
7. *Ibid.*, p. 152.
8. Quoted in V.V. Ramana Murti (ed.), *Gandhi: Essential Writings* (New Delhi: Gandhi Peace Foundation, 1970), p. 104.
9. See S.S. Savarkar and G.M. Joshi (ed.), *Historic Statements, V.D. Savarkar* (Bombay: Popular Prakashan, 1967).
10. Quoted in Jyoti Trehan, "Savarkarism" in Verinder Grover (ed.), *V.D. Savarkar* (New Delhi, Deep and Deep Publications, 1993), pp. 553-54.
11. Romila Thapar, "Communalism and the Historical Legacy: Some Facets" in K.N. Panikkar (ed.), *Communalism in India: History, Politics and Culture* (New Delhi: Manohar, 1991), p. 23.
12. See M.S. Golwalkar, *We or Our Nationhood Defined* (Nagpur: Bharat Publications, 1939).
13. *Ibid.*, p. 41.
14. *Ibid.*, p. 67.
15. *Ibid.*, pp. 47-48.
16. Quoted in Sudhir Kakar, *The Colours of Violence* (New Delhi: Viking, 1995), p. 213.
17. We say this because *Hindutva* as an ideology, it seems, is not eager to cope with the questions relating to economic inequality and

societal divisions. Its 'unifying' mission seeks to hide these contradictions—the contradictions that may lead to radical social transformation.

18. Tapan Basu, Pradip Datta, Sumit Sarkar, Tanika Sarkar, Sambuddha Sen, *Khaki Shorts and Saffron Flags* (New Delhi: Orient Longman, 1993).
19. Sudhir Kakar, *op. cit.*, p. 186.
20. *Ibid.*, p. 190.
21. For a sharp analysis of communal violence, see Asghar Ali Engineer, *Communalism and Communal Violence in India: An Analytical Approach to Hindu-Muslim Conflict* (Delhi: Ajanta Publications, 1989).
22. Ashis Nandy, "The Politics of Secularism and the Recovery of Religious Tolerance" in Veena Das (ed.), *Mirrors of Violence: Communities, Riots and Survivors in South Asia* (Delhi: Oxford University Press, 1990), pp. 69-93.
23. T.K. Oommen, "Sources of Deprivation and Styles of Protest: The Case of the Dalits", in his *Protest and Change: Studies in Social Movements* (New Delhi: Sage, 1990), pp. 254-71.
24. For a meaningful discussion on Phule, Naicker and Ambedkar, see Gail Omvedt, *Dalit Visions: The Anti-Caste Movement and the Construction of an Indian Identity* (New Delhi: Orient Longman, 1995).
25. M.S. Gore, *The Social Context of an Ideology: Ambedkar's Political and Social Thought* (New Delhi: Sage, 1993), p. 199.
26. Gail Omvedt, *Dalits and the Democratic Revolution: Dr Ambedkar and the Dalit Movement in Colonial India* (New Delhi: Sage Publication, 1994), p. 246.
27. *Ibid.*, p. 248.
28. Yogendra Singh, *Social Change in India: Crisis and Resilience* (New Delhi: Har-Anand Publishers, 1993), especially Ch. 2.
29. Rajni Kothari (ed.), *Caste in Indian Politics* (New Delhi: Orient Longman, 1986), p. 4
30. *Ibid.*, p. 20.
31. See, for instance, G.H. Ghurye, "Features of the Caste System" in Dipankar Gupta (ed.), *Social Stratification* (Delhi: Oxford University Press, 1991), pp. 35-48.
32. M.N. Srinivas, *Caste in Modern India and Other Essays* (Bombay: Asia Publishing House, 1962), p. 58.
33. Yogendra Singh, *Social Stratification and Change in India* (New Delhi: Manohar, 1980), p. 10.
34. M.N. Srinivas, *op. cit.*
35. Gail Omvedt, *Dalit Vision*, pp. 14-15.

36. No revolutionary struggle is possible without its emancipatory pedagogy. It is this pedagogy that restores one's agency, makes one critical, reflexive and dialogical. Moreover, it helps one to unlearn all that one has learned from the Establishment. For a brilliant analysis of emancipatory pedagogy, see Paulo Freire, *Pedagogy of the Oppressed* (Penguin Books, 1972).
37. Quoted in V.V. Ramana Murti (ed.), *Gandhi: Essential Writings*, p. 102.
38. *Ibid.*, pp. 355-56.
39. Bhikhu Parekh, *Colonialism, Tradition and Reform: An Analysis of Gandhi's Political Discourse* (New Delhi: Sage, 1989).
40. Fred Dallmayr, "Modernization and Postmodernization: Whither India", *Alternatives* (Vol. 17, No. 4), pp. 421-52.
41. Rajni Kothari, *State Against Democracy: In Search of Humane Governance* (New Delhi: Ajanta, 1988), pp. 70-71.

Conclusion

Spiritualizing Modernity

I am not particularly sure whether I can draw a set of final conclusions. The reason is simple. Here is a process of learning; it is not a finished product. Moreover, I do not have always clear answers to the questions I am raising. I live in a state of contradictions and ambiguities. For instance, I know that modernity has entered my body, mind and soul. I cannot escape it. Its science tends to define my cognitive map. Its technology shapes my everyday practice. Its reason arouses my individuality. Its empiricism makes me alert. In other words, I hear a call: 'The world is yours. Shape it. Transform it'. But then, at the same time, I know that modernity does not necessarily make me happy. I realize how its arrogance (arrogance of science and technology) causes violence—violence against nature and all that fails to cope with its logico-mathematical design: our awe and wonder, nostalgia and communitarian experiences of merger and surrender.

The idea of emancipation was closely linked with the agenda of modernity. Emancipation of man from the tyranny of tradition. But then, it is no longer possible to deny that modernity itself may prove to be a trap. Its mega structures, gigantic bureaucracy, and irresistible technology often deny man's authentic autonomy. Because the story of modernity is not simply the story of well-fed, well-clothed men; it is also the story of intense agony—loss of self and communication and relatedness. The fact is that even when Bacon and Descartes shape my mind, my heart cannot escape Gandhi and Ramakrishna. That is my ambiguity, my contradiction.

This is not to suggest that my book is just an 'objective' description of this ambiguity. Despite this ambiguity, I know that I am becoming more and more inclined to those who critique modernity. I am not a postmodernist. Because I do not share its relativism and moral indifference. I imagine the possibility of dialogic communication, the possibility of a spiritually regenerated world. I am not a traditionalist in the sense that tradition, for me, is a closed paradigm preventing me from learning from alternate possibilities. Yes, I know the dynamism and vitality of modernity. Yet, I am realizing that modernity is not free from its evils: the evils rooted in its fragmented worldview. I, therefore, learn from those who critique modernity and strive for an alternate way of relating to the world. For a careful reader, it is not difficult to get the following messages from my book:

(a) We need to evolve an intellectual climate that is critical, reflexive and open. This means that we ought to be alert and courageous enough not to get seduced by the West. Because it is important to isolate the emancipatory possibilities of modernity from its pathologies. It is equally important to tap our cultural resources in order to fight both Eurocentric modernity and orthodox traditionalism.

(b) Religiosity or spirituality as an experience of unboundedness, we should realize, is also emancipatory. It is this emancipatory urge that may help us to overcome the meaninglessness that the model of secular modernity often leads to. Moreover, it would help us to fight the appropriation of religion by the communalists.

(c) We should see the assertion of femininity as a new beginning. Not simply because it helps us to see the tyranny of some of our traditional practices. This assertion also helps us to realize that modernity, if not rescued from its militant Baconian project, may prove to be anti-women and hence anti-life. With femininity we are imagining a new world: harmonic, not divisive; holistic, not fragmented.

(d) We should see that modernity, particularly its Euro-American model, is not allowed to homogenize the world. Authentic emancipation is impossible in a world in which alternative cultures are not allowed to retain their differences. There are great possibilities in these differences—the possibilities that can rescue the world from consumerism, violence and aggressive technologization of the lifeworld.

(e) A closed/exclusivist mentality is not emancipatory, even if it tends to represent the voices of the marginalized and the downtrodden. What is needed is a dialogic spirit—something that unites diverse voices of sanity and arouses our spirituality, harmony, cultural sensitivity and egalitarian zeal.

All that I am suggesting is simple. Retain your criticality. Spiritualize your modernity. Fight traditionalism. But do not forget to see what is living in your tradition. And do not become exclusivist in your thinking and politics. Because with dialogue begins the real process of learning and emancipation. In fact, with this dialogic spirit that I have sought to cultivate in the process of writing this book, I realize that I am not alone in my endeavour. As I decide to conclude the book, I happen to rediscover Radhakamal Mukerjee—the great sociologist who once illuminated the University of Lucknow. I learn from his sharp comment on the 'destiny of civilization'.[1] I realize why he argued: "Oriental civilization through its intuitions and visions of metaphysics, art and mysticism, should supplement and correct what are now selling throughout the world as the 'clean' and unassailable universals of the scientific and mathematical genius of the West."[2] Because Mukerjee knew the pathology of the modern civilization—its 'bifurcation of nature': "One nature of the senses and emotions, appreciations and exaltations, and another nature of the mathematical axioms, theorems and equations."[3] He opposed this modernist/fragmented thinking and strove for "the profound oriental feeling of unity, continuity and interpenetration with cosmos."[4]

From Radhakamal Mukerjee I come back to my own time and realize that this search for a 'renovated symbolic system'—that unites body and spirit, intellect and intuition, facts and values, existence and transcendence—continues. For example, I see it in the language of Vandana Shiva, her celebration of the 'feminine principle'[5] Shiva sees the victory of modernity—or modern science as patriarchy's project—as the death of the feminine principle. Because modernity fragments, divides, separates and brutalizes. It leads to the domination over woman and nature. Shiva, therefore, pleads for the 'recovery of the feminine principle'. It transcends the 'dichotomized categories' of modernity. It is for unity, reciprocity, harmony and dialogicity. The 'feminine principle', argues Shiva, cannot be found in the Cartesian concept of nature. It can be seen in Indian cosmology because in it, as Shiva thinks, person and nature (*Purusha-Prakriti*) are a duality in unity. Shiva characterizes the 'feminine principle' in the following fashion:

> It is a recovery in nature, woman and man of creative forms of being and perceiving. In nature it implies seeing nature as a live organism. In women it implies seeing women as productive and active. Finally, in men the recovery of the feminine principle implies a relocation of action and activity to create life-enhancing, not life-reducing and life-threatening societies.[6]

From Mukerjee to Shiva—the message that I have learnt is that of harmony. Or, to put it philosophically, it is an urge to spiritualize modernity. Indeed, as I read Sri Aurobindo I realize why he reflected on the crisis of the 'age of reason' and thought of the advent of the 'spiritual age'. It is this dialogue with a saint that has enriched my sociology. I, therefore, wish to conclude this book by quoting from his profound writing.

"A spiritualized society would treat in its sociology the individual, from the saint to the criminal, not as units of a social problem to be passed through some skilfully devised machinery and either flattened into the social mould or crushed out of it, but as souls suffering and entangled in a net and to be rescued, souls growing and to be encouraged to grow, souls grown and from whom help and power can be drawn by the lesser spirits who are not yet adult. The aim of its economics would be not to create a huge engine of production, whether of the competitive or the co-operative kind, but to give to men—not only to some but to all men each in his highest possible measure—the joy of work according to their own nature and free leisure to grow inwardly, as well as a simply rich and beautiful life for all. In its politics it would not regard the nations within the scope of their own internal life as enormous State machines regulated and armoured with man living for the sake of the machine and worshipping it as his God and his larger self, content at the first call to kill others upon its altar and to bleed there himself so that the machine may remain intact and powerful and be made ever larger, more complex, more cumbrous, more mechanically efficient and entire.... It would regard the peoples as group-souls, the divinity concealed and to be self-discovered in its human collectivities, group-souls meant like the individual to grow according to their own nature and by that growth to help each other, to help the whole race in the one common work of humanity. And that work would be to find the divine self in the individual and the collectivity and to realise spiritually, mentally, vitally, materially its greatest, largest, richest and deepest possibilities in the inner life of all and their outer action and nature."[7]

NOTES

1. Radhakamal Mukerjee, *The Destiny of Civilization* (Bombay: Asia Publishing House, 1964).
2. *Ibid.*, p. 201.
3. *Ibid.*
4. *Ibid.*
5. Vandana Shiva, *Staying Alive: Women, Ecology and Survival in India* (New Delhi: Kali for Women, 1988), pp. 38-54.
6. *Ibid.*, p. 53.
7. Sri Aurobindo, *The Human Cycle* (Pondicherry: Sri Aurobindo Ashram, 1977), pp. 241-42.

Index